BINDING WORDS

D1566030

Topics in Historical Philosophy

General Editors David Kolb
                 John McCumber

Associate Editor Anthony J. Steinbock

BINDING WORDS

Conscience and Rhetoric in Hobbes, Hegel, and Heidegger

Karen S. Feldman

Northwestern University Press
Evanston, Illinois

Northwestern University Press
Evanston, Illinois 60208-4170

Printed in the United States of America

10 9 8 7 6 5 4 3 2 1

ISBN 0-8101-2280-4 (cloth)
ISBN 0-8101-2281-2 (paper)

Library of Congress Cataloging-in-Publication Data

Feldman, Karen S.
    Binding words : conscience and rhetoric in Hobbes, Hegel, and Heidegger /
Karen S. Feldman.
        p. cm. — (Topics in historical philosophy)
    Includes bibliographical references and index.
        ISBN 0-8101-2280-4 (cloth : alk. paper) — ISBN 0-8101-2281-2 (pbk. : alk.
paper)
        1. Conscience. 2. Hobbes, Thomas, 1588–1679. Leviathan. 3. Hegel, Georg
Wilhelm Friedrich, 1770–1831. Phänomenologie des Geistes. 4. Heidegger,
Martin, 1889–1976. Sein und Zeit. I. Title. II. Northwestern University topics
in historical philosophy
BJ1471.F45 2006
170—dc22

                                                                2005027949

For Niklaus

Contents

Acknowledgments

I would like to express my appreciation to Peg Birmingham, Will McNeill, and Michael Naas for their generous feedback and encouragement during this book's early stages; to Stephen Houlgate for his assistance with the initial formulation of my goals; and to Beth Ash and Paul Davies for preparing me for this work.

An extended stay in Germany brought me into contact with many people whose insights were essential for refining the scope and argument of this book. I thank Anselm Haverkamp for providing me excellent support, colleagues, and institutional identity at the *Graduiertenkolleg* "Representation, Rhetoric and Knowledge" at the European University at Viadrina; and Christoph Menke for incorporating me into the Department of Philosophy at the University of Potsdam and including me in valuable colloquia. I am indebted to Vanessa Offen and Julia Teller for help and friendship in the face of unexpected difficulties; to the devotees of the former laptop section of the *Staatsbibliothek zu Berlin* for their quiet companionship; and to my interlocutors Georg Bertram, Stefan Blank, Marcus Coelen, Andrea Kern, Matthias Muehling, Juliane Rebentisch, and Ruth Sonderegger.

This book has profited from my time at the University of California, Berkeley. I thank Judith Butler for helping to bring me to Berkeley and for excellent advice along the way; Michael Mascuch, chair of the Department of Rhetoric; and Anton Kaes, chair of the Department of German. Ellen Cox and James Martel have been my most steadfast and scrupulous readers and provided invaluable commentary. I am also fortunate to have had the intellectual and personal camaraderie of Aaron Belkin, Julia Davis, Graham Harman, Niklaus Largier, Helen Lennon, and Deirdre Levine; and of colleagues and friends at Stanford University who have generously invited my participation in many rewarding colloquia and events, above all Hans Ulrich Gumbrecht, Robert Harrison, Joshua Landy, and R. Lanier Anderson.

I am indebted to Eric Smoodin for much practical advice; to Gerhard Richter and Michael Naas for their fine suggestions on the manuscript; to John McCumber for his support and assistance; and to Susan

Betz, Rachel Delaney, and Anne Gendler at Northwestern University Press, and also to Lori Meek Schuldt for careful copyediting. Primal thanks belong to Marjorie Cowen, Scott Cowen, Margo Feldman, and Aaron Feldman, all my parents.

I gratefully acknowledge the German-American Fulbright Commission for the Fulbright Scholarship under the auspices of which the bulk of this book was written; the Herzog August Bibliothek Wolfenbüttel for hosting me for a portion of my grant period; the German Research Foundation (DFG) for a postdoctoral fellowship; and the German Academic Exchange Service (DAAD) for a preparatory summer program.

A shorter version of chapter 1 appeared in "Conscience and the Concealments of Metaphor in Hobbes's *Leviathan*," *Philosophy and Rhetoric* 34:1 (2001). Portions of chapter 2 and of the conclusion appeared in "The Binding Word: Conscience and the Rhetoric of Agency in Hegel's *Phenomology of Spirit*," *Qui Parle* 14:2 (Spring 2004), and also in "Die Endlichkeit des Performativen: Das Gewissen in Hegels Phänomenologie des Geistes," in *Diesseits des Subjektprinzips: Körper-Sprache-Praxis*," edited by Thomas Bedorf and Stefan A. B. Blank (Magdeburg: Edition Humboldt, 2002), 55–67. Portions of chapter 3 appeared in "On the Performative Difficulty of *Being and Time*," *Philosophy Today* 44:4 (2000) and in "Heidegger and the Hypostasis of the Performative," *Angelaki* 9:3 (2004).

BINDING WORDS

Introduction: On Metaphor, Conscience, and Bindingness

Both our philosophical and everyday conceptions of conscience come to us by way of a tradition of wildly incompatible figures and images. They include figures of activities, such as seeing, hearing, telling, judging, biting, strangling, gnawing, punishing, and torturing; spatial and architectural figures, as of the heart, a courtroom, an inner hell, and a church building; and heterogeneous images of conscience as spark, worm, natural light, inscription, and feeling. But can conscience be described in terms that are unambiguously literal and direct? What is conscience, in literal terms? None of the aforementioned figures offers us unmediated, nonfigurative epistemological access to what conscience truly might be. Even such apparently direct and familiar representations of conscience as a voice, a faculty, or an internalized set of norms are no less a matter of figures than Victor Hugo's image of conscience as an ineluctable gazing eye or Herman Melville's comparison of the heaving tides of the sea to the conscience of a remorseful soul.[1] The very incompatibility of the diverse figures listed previously—which mix qualities of corporeality and spirituality, spatiality and agency, organism and event—poses certain epistemological problems, for even if any one of these figures were in fact a literal description of conscience rather than a figurative representation, on what basis would we recognize the appropriate criterion for distinguishing the literal from the figurative term? The apparent lack of such a criterion renders an epistemological dependence on figures indistinguishable from the bottomlessly metaphoric character of any terminology by means of which conscience can be described. This bottomless figurativeness betokens conscience's catachrestic character, where catachresis is the trope or necessary metaphor that fills in where no proper term is to be had. With catachresis, there need not be anything "underneath" figurativeness; indeed, there may be no literal foundation or remnant to be excavated.[2] In light of this understanding of catachresis, it would be impossible to restore literalness to a rightful and secure position. These references to catachresis and my claim for the fundamentally catachrestic character of any description of conscience are not offered here, however, as spoiling tactics that would level all further discussion to a flat claim that all language is metaphor. The effort in the following pages is rather to show that in fact neither of these two moves is a tenable last resort and thus to disrupt the fantasy of a last resort or leveling claim with regard to the literal-figurative distinction and to do so in light of the positing and performing elements of figures and texts.

If conscience is in fact represented only and everywhere in terms of figures, then can it be certain that conscience exists at all? Does figuration, in other words, offer us any guarantee that what is thereby figured is anything more than a fiction? While figures may be epistemologically necessary to represent conscience—that is, insofar as we know conscience only by way of figures—these figures do not secure for us the ontological status of conscience. Are sheer figures and sheer metaphors *binding* on existence? Do they in fact have any genuine effect, any actual impact, on existence itself? The ontological status of that which is represented by means of tropes—that is, its actuality or existence—would seem, logically, to be unaffected by the figurative representations that govern the epistemology of conscience. However, the epistemological and the ontological are not so easy to keep separate from one another. A metaphor is generally assumed to illuminate how, or what, something is, but metaphors assert at the same time, in an implicit or weak fashion, *that* that something is, at least on some level of existence. On the other hand, where we have *only* metaphors to describe an entity, and no proper terms, then the ontological status of that entity would seem to be fragile and questionable, for the entity appears to be only tenuously anchored in determinacy and in existence. Insofar as conscience appears to be given form solely via metaphors and catachreses, the binding power of these figures, and indeed of figuration in general, upon conscience's existence is in question.[3]

And if conscience is in each case figured, how can we certify that it is binding upon human beings? How can conscience be claimed to exist concretely, to impose itself upon us and oblige us? How could we even verify the existence of such a binding force? The notion of "binding" is key here, because it is what makes conscience more than just one arbitrary example of the nexus of figure, positing, and ontology. For with conscience is at stake the binding character, force, or act of what is, in principle and *as* principle, most binding. The question of how to formulate references to such binding—including an ungoverned element of oscillation between the nominal, adjectival, and verbal valences of the word "binding"—takes on particular significance when what is at issue is the existence of a faculty, sense, or internalization that is taken to be responsible for how ethics, ideals, duties, and faculties are conceived as binding upon a self and its acts. And yet the very existence of such a process or quality of binding itself can be called into question, for the same reasons that allow us to question how figures may be binding upon existence, because "binding" is of course also a figure. It is a figure that covers over at least as much as it reveals with respect to that to which it is supposed to refer; for what *is* a bond in the context to which we refer here? Is it a necessity, a connection, an obligation, or something else? The formulations "binding force" and "binding power" are likewise problematic because they proleptically explain "binding" in terms of force and power instead of leaving entirely open precisely how binding happens, what its mechanisms might be, and where its agency might lie. For this reason I resort in this book to the nominalization "bindingness" where I wish to abstract from a particular instance of binding to the general quality or activity that it might be taken to exemplify, and also where I wish to foreground both the uncertainty surrounding the agency and mechanisms of binding as well as the question of whether or how such binding takes place at all.[4]

For just as we depend on a bottomlessly figurative understanding of conscience, the suggestion that conscience binds us is also built upon an epistemological lacuna. In other words, "binding" is epistemologically significant as a term for how we understand our relationship to our word, to contract, to a future, and to others to be a necessary and obligating relationship; and yet it is always possible that something binding may be contravened. Something binding is in one sense absolute, but it can also be abrogated, ignored, broken, and otherwise treated as a nonentity or as a dispensable fiction. The question of how catachresis may be binding upon existence is not precisely the same question as that of the relationship between an act and a binding duty, ideal, or faculty. Nonetheless, the figuration of each kind of bindingness takes on different forms, as we shall see, in different philosophical accounts of binding language and the bonds of conscience.[5]

The investigations of the figurative representations of conscience and its bindingness are taken as the starting point in each of the following chapters for considering whether the texts in which these accounts of conscience are located can *themselves* be viewed as binding. What are the implications of each text for the actual world and for concrete existence— how do these texts impose themselves upon us and oblige us? Can a text be considered to be binding, and how might such binding compare to the way that conscience is represented as binding within that text? Bindingness is thus at stake in this book at two levels. First, there is an investigation of how, *within* each of the texts considered, conscience is described as binding upon us. Second, I consider performative textual binding, that is, with regard to how the text in which conscience is described may itself be seen as binding upon the reader and upon the world, insofar as the works examined operate beyond the constative level of description and argument, producing effects that cannot be contained within the realm of the constative.

Kant and the Crossroads of Conscience

Is our epistemological access to conscience and to its binding character dependent on catachreses because we cannot literally see or hear these phenomena, and thus we are compelled to borrow terms from the realms of the visible and otherwise sensible? If a lack of direct perception is the main obstacle to describing conscience and how conscience is binding in sheerly literal terms, then the relationship between the oppositions sensible/insensible and literal/metaphoric would be that described by Martin Heidegger in his lecture course *The Principle of Reason* (1955–56). Heidegger there claims that the distinction between metaphoric and literal language belongs to a presumed division between sensible and insensible realms, a division which Heidegger calls into question by pointing out that it is not our senses that sense (nor our ears that hear and our eyes that see), but rather it is *we* ourselves who sense, see, and hear *through* our senses, through our organs of eyes and ears. Heidegger suggests that sensory perception and its faculties are not clearly distinguishable from thinking and interpretation; the organic seeing and hearing of the eyes and ears cannot account for how we see or hear a particular perception *as* something—for example, how we see a particular object *as* a statue of Apollo or hear a series of sounds *as* a fugue. Hence the processes of sensory perception and "taking-as," or interpretation, are intrinsically interwoven.[6] The distinctions sensible/nonsensible and literal/metaphoric are products rather than givens; they are made, not natural. The *presumed* naturalness of these distinctions covers over the continuous operation of thinking interpretation, or taking-as, that underlies and even creates the distinctions between the two realms. The same act or operation of thinking and interpretation underlies the distinction sensible/insensible and literal/metaphoric. It is, in effect, the condition of those distinctions, and yet remains unthematized when we make those distinctions. The presumption—which Heidegger takes as the essence of metaphysics—that the sensible can be delimited in a stable fashion from the insensible, and its corollary, namely, that literal meaning can be reliably demarcated with respect to figurative meaning, are not simply eradicated by Heidegger; rather these distinctions are shown to be posited, to be a product of a thinking, of a hermeneutical moment.[7]

Heidegger's discussion of metaphor unsettles the idea that our reliance upon figures to represent conscience rests upon a mere perceptual difficulty, namely, that we cannot *see* conscience with our eyes. But are there other reasons for the difficulty in representing conscience and how it is binding? For Immanuel Kant the problem of how moral law is binding upon us constitutes a crossroads in philosophy between theoretical and practical reason. Figuration is not at all his focus—Kant employs with no apparent worry the figures of voice, judge, and court to describe conscience. But his *Critique of Practical Reason* (1788) indicates a profoundly metaphysical, rather than perceptual, problem with portraying moral law as binding upon practical reason, that is, as binding upon the determination of the will. In his preface and introduction to the *Critique of Practical Reason*, Kant insists on indirectness with regard to the pure practical reason that would be the locus of such bindingness. While the question of how morals are binding is, according to Kant, ultimately a question of the existence of *pure practical* reason (i.e., the determination of the will apart from all empirical grounds), his inquiry must focus instead on *practical* reason (the determination of the will, including on the basis of empirical grounds); for if even the mere existence of pure practical reason were to be decided or assumed, the need for a critique of it would be thereby negated. There is no need and even no possibility to critique pure practical reason, for whatever this faculty might be, as a form of freedom to which empirical concerns are irrelevant, it must contain its own standard for delimiting its own use.[8] Kant's *Critique of Practical Reason* must therefore evade a too-hasty assertion of the existence of pure practical reason; it must steer clear of the pure practical reason that is its ultimate interest and focus instead, according to Kant, on mere practical reason.

The indirectness that Kant demands in addressing the binding force of morals upon practical reason hints at a question regarding the binding force of inquiries and beginnings. For Kant, even to inquire into the *nature* of a pure practical reason would indirectly imply *that* pure practical reason exists—and thus the *Critique of Practical Reason* is written *not* as an inquiry into the nature of pure practical reason but as an inquiry into practical reason that may eventually discover that such practical reason may be pure. Kant's requirement that we *not* begin with the question, "What is pure practical reason?"—because such a question, in presuming the existence of pure practical reason, would abrogate the need for critique—suggests that for Kant, even inquiries, texts, and critiques have a strange force that must be taken into account in formulating the proper starting point. An inquiry into the *nature* of pure practical reason would in effect bind us to the assumption or even an implicit claim that there *exists* a pure practical reason, at which point the critique would have to cease, because such a faculty—freedom itself—bears no critique. In order to avoid binding itself, even indirectly or implicitly, to the assertion that there is a pure practical reason, the *Critique of Practical Reason* must consider the *possible* conjunction of purity, practicality, and reason on the one hand while delaying an assertion of the *actuality* of pure practical reason on the other hand. This conjunction of purity, practicality, and reason is, moreover, the location of a conscience that binds us as free and rational creatures. Kant demands a delicate and careful approach to this binding force, which requires that we hold off from even implying that pure practical reason exists, where pure practical reason is precisely what renders morals binding upon us. From the perspective of Western philosophy following Kant, then, conscience is by no means just one example of the figurativeness or catachrestic character of all language and terminology. Rather, conscience is one term for the crossroads that is bindingness—the connection of theoretical and practical reason, of possibility and actuality, as well as duty and act. Conscience may be one name for the question of how these bonds are constituted or of whether they exist at all.

Rhetoric, Binding, and Performativity

My focus is on how conscience is posited by means of diverse rhetorical gestures and figures, and also on whether mere language can be understood as binding on the existence of that which is posited. Both of these questions concern the performative aspects of rhetoric, namely, whether and how figures are not only representative of that which they represent but also in some binding fashion *represent into existence* that which they represent. It would be, however, reductive to pose the question as: "Do figurative descriptions of conscience in each case represent it, or do they create it?" For the divide between representing and creating turns out to be an unstable one within the rhetoric of each of the texts I will examine. The term "rhetoric" here does not refer only to persuasive speech, a set of figures, or a study of elocutionary technique. Rather, the following readings attempt to show where rhetoric enables and even verges on performativity in various figurations of conscience; where rhetoric involves the inscenation, the active unfolding, and the spilling over of a text's saying into its doing; and where precisely the bonds between saying and doing are at stake. The propinquity of rhetoric and performativity is in fact inherent to the notion of rhetoric itself insofar as rhetoric is conceived in terms of action, deed, effects, and their production. It is thus to be shown in the following chapters where, in the figuration of conscience, performativity operates and binding occurs, or fails to do so, via rhetoric, thereby subverting a concept of rhetoric as simply persuasive language and tropes. I will examine the intertwining of the epistemology of conscience (its representations by means of rhetorical figures) with the ontology of conscience (the question of its existence) in three catachrestic representations of conscience that are central in shaping our contemporary suspicions and hopes for the role that conscience might play in our lives, namely, those that appear in Hobbes's *Leviathan,* Hegel's *Phenomenology of Spirit,* and Heidegger's *Being and Time.* I make no claims for a direct lineage among these authors but instead attend to the distinct ways in which each portrays the relationships among figuration, bindingness, and conscience.

It is not only the rhetorical gestures of the accounts of conscience *within* each text that are at stake, however. The three representations of conscience that I discuss are significant, I will show, precisely insofar as in each case the *text* wherein the representation of conscience appears is itself implicated in the self-creation of conscience. In each case conscience is not only *represented* but also *produced* in some fashion in and by the text. Hence I will also consider how the very texts in which those figures for conscience appear may be binding upon us and our world; in other words, I will raise the question of the bindingness of texts—whether and how a text can be binding upon its readers. In this context, I will also examine the rhetoric of performing agency and how it pertains to texts—whether we can consider text as performers, performances, or even as performatives.[9]

My understanding of rhetoric and figuration in terms of performativity and the question of bindingness reflects the ramified heritage in the late twentieth and early twenty-first centuries of J. L. Austin's famous *How to Do Things with Words.*[10] In Austin's lectures, originally delivered at Harvard University in 1955, performative utterances are defined in contrast to constative utterances; whereas constative utterances are statements that may be true or false, an utterance is performative when "the issuing of an utterance is the performance of an action, and specifically the performance of the action declared in the utterance."[11] Marrying, christening, and promising are classic examples of performative statements; each creates a bond of some sort between human beings. While Austin was certainly not the first to think of utterance in terms of action rather than simple constatation, the significance of Austin's introduction of the distinction between performative and constative for the philosophy of language, with its emphasis on truth-value and a correspondence theory of truth, are not to be underestimated. Nonetheless, in the course of *How to Do Things with Words,* Austin came to either supplement or replace— depending on how one reads the text's transition in Lecture Eight—the constative/performative distinction with the locution/illocution/perlocution schema. "Illocution" and "perlocution" can be seen as facets of performativity insofar as they refer to supposedly different elements of what an utterance does—illocution being the doing performed *in* the utterance (such as warning, hinting, and advising), and perlocution being the result accomplished *by* the utterance (such as persuasion, the production of fright, or the selection of a particular course of action by another person).

Austin's shift from performativity to illocution/perlocution has significant implications. Whereas the performative/constative schema distinguishes two different types of utterance, the locution/illocution/perlocution schema refers to elements that may belong to every utterance. That is, the dualistic terminology related to performative/constative differentiates between types of utterances and specifies certain utterances as doings and others as mere sayings. Locutionary, illocutionary, and potentially perlocutionary aspects, however, belong to *every* utterance. If illocution and perlocution are taken to be mere differentiations within performativity or types of performativity, then every utterance is performative because every act of utterance is a doing of some kind and has effects, certainly at least the most minimal effect of producing an utterance.

The reception and expansion of the triad locution/illocution/perlocution—notably in the work of John Searle—has shifted the emphasis in subsequent philosophy of language toward the vocabulary and elaboration of locution, illocution, and perlocution rather than to an elucidation of the concept of performativity as the performance specifically of an act referred to in an utterance.[12] The term "performativity" has nonetheless acquired new life insofar as it has been taken up in other disciplines including literary criticism, rhetoric, anthropology, ethnography, sociology, cultural studies, gender studies, and theater studies. The performativity originally associated with Austin is taken to apply to diverse realms and media, including nonverbal action, art, and fiction. This lability of the term "performative" derives in part from the insight that, according to a certain interpretation of performativity as "doing," *every* utterance is performative and thus performativity theory offers an opportunity to examine in any linguistic context the interplay between doing and saying. What is more, as Judith Butler writes about gender performativity, the term "'performative' itself carries the double-meaning of 'dramatic' and 'non-referential.'"[13]

The range of uses of the term "performativity" could be said to dilute the specificity of the Austinian insight regarding the explicit performative, the performative that does precisely what it says. The simultaneous broadening and dilution of the term "performativity" is apparent especially where the term "performativity" lends itself to apparent synonymy with performance, that is, where "performativity" is used to mean "having the quality of a performance." In this usage the term "performativity" appears to refer to a presumed essence of performance—some quality that performances have that is more specific and condensed than performance itself and that nonetheless makes performance performance. This performative quality, or essence of performance, consists in doing, accomplishment, action, presentation, and representation. It is this active quality, conceived as an essence of performance, that is referred to and hypostatized in the term "performativity" taken in the broad sense. The nominal and hypostatic term "performativity" delimits and apparently holds under control the sheer doing, presentation, and accomplishment to which it refers. On the other hand, precisely the hypostatized quality of performance is at the same time revivified in the term "performativity"—which retains, more than the term "performance," the resonances with doing, executing, accomplishing, and acting. Hence the term "performativity" simultaneously hypostatizes the active quality of performance, making it into an essence, and revivifies performance by evoking its processual and active character.

The resulting slippage between the terms "performativity" and "performance," wherein sheer doing, accomplishment, execution, and action are evoked in both their hypostatic and dynamic character, opens up new ontological territory. Doing, accomplishing, executing, and performing are actions that result in acts; they are events that can be seen in terms of products. And yet in its nominal form the term "performativity" hypostatizes precisely the active and eventlike quality that it is supposed to evoke. The revivifying slippage between the terms "performance" and "performativity" unsettles the hypostasis of performance as an event and product and lets it be seen in turn as an agent or subject, or at the very least as an acting that functions grammatically much like an agent. In the slippage between "performance" and "performativity," the "I" of the classical Austinian performative is apparently lost, but it is recuperated in subtle ways. In the terminological conflation of performance and performativity, the loss of overt centrality of the "I," which is so prominent in Austin's explicit performatives, allows performance to be seen as something subjectlike in itself. It is also a way that performance can seem to become, itself, performative. The performance need not say "I," but it does becomes subjectlike, and what it produces as a fact is itself, its own content. A performance is indeed what comes into existence by being performed, hence one can say that performance performs itself; it is an "I-less" performative that in being uttered or acted effects the content of its action. The hypostatic notion of performance is thus partly unsettled insofar as performance is seen as activity; performance becomes the "I" whose effect or product is nothing other than the content of the performance. In this regard performance taken as performative preserves the "I-ness" that characterizes the explicit performative, that is, the strict definition of performative provided by Austin in the first seven lectures. The performance becomes agent without becoming "I," without becoming subject. The re-infusion of performativity into performance revivifies performance, displacing performance from its hypostatic pigeonhole.

The term "performativity" is thus attractive and powerful with regard to interdisciplinary and extraphilosophical work related to questions of performance. The substantive element of the term "performance" is unsettled by the vocabulary of performativity, such that the character of performance as activity on the one hand and as thing or product on the other hand are simultaneously evoked. What is more, the confluence of performativity as activity and performance as product produces a field of hypostatic play, where construction, effecting, doing, and making are not broken down into simple categories of agent, actor, substrate, product, and effect. In another slippage in the synonymy between performativity and performance, performance is taken to be performative, that is, the character of performance is articulated not as mere representation but rather as constructive, transformative, and powerful, as performing-into-being with resonances of the Austinian "doing" associated with Austin's description of performative utterances. The term "performance" may be hypostatic, for it refers to a thing, but it is also deployed as denoting an agent as well as an event and a product, unsettling the hypostasis of performance in ways that affect our notion of agent, subject, event, and product. Thus, for example, in the context of theatrical performance, Josette Féral writes, "Performance does not aim at a meaning, but rather *makes* meaning insofar as it works right in those extremely blurred junctures out of which the subject eventually emerges."[14] Performance is in this conception not representational but rather productive of its meaning, for it constructs or posits the subject of the performance in the performance itself.[15] The subject that emerges out of the performance is a catachrestic one, for there is no previously established proper name for it. The emergence of that subject, moreover, is a manifestation of how performance may prove to be binding upon existence. In the case of conscience, it is the emergence of a subject for whom the question and possibility of bindingness is definitive.

Augustinian Conscience and the Metaphorics of Space and Agency

Let us turn briefly to a fifth-century text that could be seen as a forebear of the modern understandings of selfhood, conscience, and bindingness that will be discussed in the following chapters. Augustine's *Confessions* provide a rich example of the connections between the catachrestic characterization of conscience and the questions of bindingness to which I have referred—concerning how figures may be binding on the existence of the conscience figured; how obligations may be binding upon conscience; and how the text in which the figuration of conscience takes place may itself turn out to be binding upon its reader.

The *Confessions* offer both a treasury of mixed metaphorics of conscience and a model of how hypostatic metaphorics of witnessing and spatial interiority cover over entirely dynamic figures for the act of binding—a binding that is inseparable from the confessing that the text itself performs—and for bindingness conceived more abstractly. Bad conscience in particular evokes a rich metaphorics; it is associated throughout Augustine's works with wounds, stings, prickles, noise, and confusion. It is described as captive, wild, and attacking. As an agency it accuses, castigates, stimulates, disturbs, bites, presses, smolders, tortures, and strangles; this is a wormy conscience that eats you away. Bad conscience as an autoaffective, punishing agent, whose tortures may take place simply in punishing language, is illustrated vividly in book 8 of the *Confessions:* "What said I not within myself? With what scourging of condemning sentences lashed I not my own soul?"[16] Bad conscience is specifically connected with memory and a temporality of the past. It acts as a witness in recalling past events, and the torturing that it performs occurs in its mere recollection of faithlessness and removal from God. It is precisely such a recollection of the past that is inscenated in Augustine's *Confessions,* as with the incident of young Augustine's robbing the pear tree and more generally in the recollection of his repeated failures to embrace God's truth as he has promised to do. In this regard the *Confessions* themselves perform the function of bad conscience as an agent-witness whose testimony regarding the past produces suffering in the present.

Centuries later, as I will show in my first chapter, Hobbes will claim that the privacy, inwardness, and concealment of conscience threaten the integrity and truthfulness of its testimony as a witness. But for Augustine, conscience is the most reliable witness because conscience is by definition *conscientia coram Deo,* conscience before God. We are never concealed from God, not primarily because God has all-powerful vision but because God's own being is infused in us, in our conscience. Conscience is not solely a witnessing agent but also refers to an interior space, a space or a place within (*intus*), the seat of God in ourselves. The figures of conscience as interiorized do not capture the active element of conscience, especially with regard to the activity of what is known as good conscience. Good conscience is not just a passive, vessel-like space in us that God occupies but is instead the *active* loving that relates and binds us to God.

Whereas bad conscience exists through memory and with respect to the past, good conscience is oriented toward hope and the future (although the so-called future at issue is outside temporality, for it is a future with eternal God); it is oriented toward the kingdom of God, which is not itself temporal. With regard to the difference in temporalities between good and bad conscience, good conscience is not good because it *recalls* good works performed, in the way that bad conscience tortures us in the recollection of past failures and our remove from God. Good conscience's goodness instead derives from the very goodness of God, the goodness that makes us love God. Hence a good conscience is one that is clean of sin, one that does not have to suffer from the recollection of faithlessness or wrongdoing; it loves God, and this loving is itself the opening of a future with God. As loving, this conscience is closely connected with the heart, the organ of love. The heart is not, in this model, primarily an interior space, but an *organ*, a *working* place.[17] Although Augustine frequently uses in the *Confessions* such phrases as "in my heart" or "in the heart," the *Confessions* themselves also testify that the heart is not merely a place—it is active and productive. It is Augustine's heart that should tell God of the robbery of the pear tree: "Let my heart tell thee."[18] The heart speaks; it in fact makes confession; it makes the *Confessions* that we read, the *Confessions* which are themselves nothing other than the account of Augustine's conscience. Making confession is in this respect not primarily tied to memory and the past but to a present bond of love between a human being and God, a bond which is itself forged in the *Confessions*.

The bond between a human being and God is not literally to be understood in spatial terms, as pertaining to the simple presence of God inside human beings, although Augustine does write that the heart is the seat of God in the human soul and employs metaphors of house, den, and cellar. In the spatial characterization, the heart is the place of one's proper being. It is, as Augustine says, "wherever or whatever I am [*ubi ego sum quicumque sum*]."[19] Nevertheless, when Augustine considers the "in" directly, the "insideness" that seems to guarantee conscience's existence before God and which makes conscience such a good witness turns into a question. The problem with portraying God as interiorized is most obvious in *Confessions* 1:2, where Augustine wonders, "When I invoke [God] I call him into myself, and what place is there in me fit for my God to come into me by?"[20] God is not *outside* Augustine in need of some way in. He is already *inside* him; thus writes Augustine: "Since therefore I also am, how do I entreat thee to come into me, who could not be, unless thou wert first in me? . . . I should not be at all, unless thou wert in me."[21] These lines at first confirm the model of interiority and God's presence in human beings. But Augustine adds to this statement in such a way that the model of interiority is no longer sufficient. For Augustine continues, "or rather I should not be, unless I were in thee." The idea that God is *in* Augustine is turned on its head. God is not *in* Augustine, but rather Augustine is *in* God. What looks like an interiority of the "I" turns out to be the inherence of the "I" in God. With respect to God, we are not creatures with interiors—not just because he can see into us, into the "abyss of human conscience,"[22] but because God's *presence* "in" us nullifies the difference between interiority and surface, inner and outer. Insideness therefore breaks down as a model of the relationship between God and human being, for Augustine says just as certainly that he is *out of* [*ex*] God and also *through* [*per*] God at least as much as he is *in* God. Augustine writes, "I should not be, unless I were in thee, out of whom, through whom *and* in whom all things are." The preposition "in" therefore fails here to convey any proper relationship. "In" is in fact a thoroughly inadequate description of the relationship between Augustine and God. If God is not in me, but I am *in* God, *out* of God, *and* through God, then our relationship is not a matter of human interiority. It is therefore also not the case that I am what I truly am "inside" myself. Interiority is not at issue as much as the activity of binding oneself to God, as the activity of a conscience that is not a bad conscience or a witness alone, but a conscience—here nearly indistinguishable from the heart—whose inscription is the *Confessions*.

The *Confessions* can themselves thus be read in terms both of good conscience and bad conscience. They are the witness of Augustine's own past failures with respect to God, and insofar as in recounting these failures he tortures himself, the *Confessions* are his suffering in recollection. They are in these respects his bad conscience before God. But the *Confessions* further are themselves, as the *act* of confessing, also Augustine's binding and bond to God. They do not merely recount through recollection the good conscience of good works and faith in the past; rather, they are as confessions also Augustine's hope for the eternal future with God. Hence conscience is not only a theme in the *Confessions;* rather, the text of the *Confessions* is itself a *work* of conscience, an ongoing operation binding Augustine to God. Confession is an act that is performed out of a bond and that itself is a form of binding. The text of the *Confessions* is thus on the one hand a constatation and representation of a narrative content and on the other hand a productive, active binding of Augustine—and, indirectly, of the reader—to the God who is addressed therein.

I have suggested that the figures for conscience in Augustine do not represent conscience in terms only of agent (witness, judge, tormenter) or place (*intus,* seat of God, heart), but rather that conscience is also represented as an *activity* of loving that binds us to God. What is more, these representations of conscience as binding Augustine to God appear in a text that itself should bind Augustine and even his readers to God. This binding occurs in the very unfolding and performance of his confessing in the text. It occurs in the text insofar as the text actively binds Augustine and the reader to God. Hence it is as a text that confesses, that performs confession, that the *Confessions* straddle a border between textual constatation and performance.

The following chapters will examine in greater detail three central instances in modern philosophy of intersection between the bindingness of conscience and the bindingness of the text in which the account of conscience is situated. The question of exemplarity and of the way in which examples represent, posit, and construct that which they should exemplify are also themes that necessarily resurface throughout the book, most explicitly in the first chapter, on Hobbes's *Leviathan*. There, I scrutinize Hobbes's suggestion regarding the capacity of metaphor (and, implicitly in his account, of catachresis) to performatively posit what it represents. Hobbes describes the origins of private conscience in the context of condemning metaphor. Hobbes uses conscience as his example for the dangers of metaphor, but in fact private conscience proves to be a source of danger to language, knowledge, and the stability of the commonwealth in its own right. The story of conscience in Hobbes is a warning as to the dangers of privatized knowledge and the dangers of figurative language. It is also a warning regarding the performative dangers deriving from the ungovernable connectibility of names, precisely given how metaphor may prove binding upon truth and hence existence, that is, by means of the copula "is" that binds subjects, predicates, and in principle the order of names, which is truth itself. The discussion of the word "conscience" in *Leviathan* can be seen as a turning point of suspicion in the history of early modern philosophy regarding both metaphor and the role of conscience as a foundation for ethics.[23]

The second chapter concentrates on Hegel's description of conscience's failures and contradictions in the sphere of morality in the *Phenomenology of Spirit*. Specifically, I explain the contradictions of conscience in the *Phenomenology* in terms of the tension between what I characterize as the performative successes and rhetorical failures of conscience's declarations. Hegel's chapter on conscience—a critique of the Kantian conscience that enjoys an immediate relationship to duty—narrates the manifold failures that conscience suffers because it is unable to establish itself as immediately bound and determined by the duty of which it is immediately certain. Conscience's declaration of its certainty of its duty *should* bind conscience immediately to its act of duty—an act which, having its own existence, is in fact not unconditionally bound to the conscience that performs it. The declaration, however, that should reflect the immediacy of the bond between conscience and its duty itself takes on the labile character of an act and thus turns out to be an inadequate bond. Action, the duty that requires it, and the agency that performs it cannot be held together successfully by means of a simple declaration.

The problems that beset Hegelian conscience are exemplary both to Spirit and to the readers of the *Phenomenology* with regard to demonstrating, as Hobbes foresaw in a different way, the problematic character of private conscience as a binding principle of shared morality. What is more, the difficulty conscience displays in establishing its words as binding is illustrative of the difficulty of determining whether Hegel's own text can be considered binding; for indeed the *Phenomenology* claims for itself a certain binding force on the existence of the Spirit whose unfolding it narrates. Thus in light of Hegel's discussion in the preface to the *Phenomenology* of the lifeless concept and its becoming, I consider how the *Phenomenology of Spirit* is supposed to be binding upon the actual unfolding of Spirit's existence. I focus especially on the "is" by which the *Phenomenology*'s speculative sentences do not merely connect a subject and predicate but instead should *unfold* the progress of Spirit and in that respect should represent *into existence* Spirit's successive forms.

The third chapter turns to Heidegger's *Being and Time* in order to consider the bonds and constraints of its rhetoric on the question of being. The analytic's reliance on figuration and catachresis, given the inherent inexactitude and inappropriateness of all terms for the investigation into being, provides the starting point for an understanding of *Being and Time* as a rhetorical text. Moreover, I show that Heidegger's writing style performs what it describes in the analysis of the unhandy tool, namely, insofar as the words of the investigation are themselves conspicuous, obtrusive, and obstinate in their very unhelpfulness and inaccessibility to understanding. Heidegger's discussions of *theoria* and of the access to the question of being are also investigated as crossroads of figuration and performativity. The question of how the call of conscience is binding upon Dasein, as described in Heidegger's chapters of *Being and Time* on the call of conscience, suggests that the account of conscience occupies a peculiar performative role with regard to *Being and Time* as a whole.

I conclude the book with a discussion of the relation between figuration and textual performance, focusing on the difficult question of the location of doing—that is, the location of agency—for it is agency and the responsibility of agency that risk elision in the approximation of rhetoric to performativity.

It is not my goal in the following pages to discover or found a new

principle for conscience, nor to point to a crisis in contemporary conscience, nor even to emphasize the value of conscience for a just or ethical society. There is in this respect no normative claim in this book with
regard to conscience and how it is or should be binding. I also do not attempt to offer a history of the concept of conscience, and thus I do not
deal with many sources relevant to such a history, including the formidable work of Foucault concerning the discourses and institutions of the
modern period that helped shape the practices surrounding conscience—its examination, its control, its discipline, and so on. My focus is
on the agency of figures and texts and on how that agency appears in the
context of these landmark works across the span of modern philosophy. I
investigate the figures and rhetoric of conscience in Hobbes, Hegel, and
Heidegger and then show how, in distinct ways, the question of bindingness not only turns out to matter *within* any of these single investigations
of conscience but also pertains to how binding is performed at the level
of the text with respect to that which these texts could be said to enact, to
effect, or to accomplish.

Hobbes's *Leviathan:* Conscience and the Concealments of Metaphor

In the course of condemning metaphor and figurative language in *Leviathan,* Hobbes offers the example of the word "conscience" to illustrate the dangers of metaphor. According to Hobbes, "conscience" was originally the name for public, shared knowledge, but Hobbes narrates a history in which a metaphoric characterization of conscience as private, individual knowledge came to supplant the earlier meaning. Hobbes suggests that this metaphoric shift in effect instituted a new sphere of private knowledge, a sphere threatening to the security of the commonwealth and the binding principle of public authority upon which it is based. Insofar as the production of private conscience is said to have been accomplished by a metaphor, trope and rhetoric are implicated by Hobbes in the performative production of private, individualized knowledge and its political implications. Of course, the vocabulary of performative production is anachronistic to seventeenth-century England. Nonetheless the explanations in *Leviathan* of how private conscience came into being and of how metaphor corrupts the order of names indicate that metaphor's danger derives from what we might characterize as a range of performative effects, effects not only upon the *representation* of the public/private distinction but also upon the actual *existence* of the public and private realms. Error and deception first became possible in the public sphere, according to Hobbes, when knowledge was disengaged from the guarantee of witnesses. Hence Hobbes's arguments in *Leviathan* in favor of the preservation of proper meaning and against metaphor and figurative language correspond to an anxiety regarding both the absence of the binding power of witnesses on the validity of knowledge and the incipient power of privacy in a commonwealth based on obedience to sovereign authority.

Performativity and what I have called "bindingness" are at issue in Hobbes's *Leviathan* in several respects apart from the question of conscience.[1] They are, most famously, involved in his treatment of the binding character of promises, of declarations, and of words in general—in particular with respect to the pledge of loyalty to the sovereign upon which the commonwealth is based and also with respect to the declarations of law by the sovereign.[2] In addition Hobbes's own text has been characterized in terms of performativity. Samuel Mintz, for instance, argues that in his construction of the Leviathan metaphor Hobbes imitates God's performative.[3] Tracy Strong suggests that *Leviathan* can be read not only as a text about politics but also as a political *act*, namely, as the grounding or inauguration of a scripture that serves for politics in the same way that holy scripture serves for religion.[4] In this reading, sovereignty is said to be established by the text, by means of the representation that the text carries out or performs. Hobbes's description in *Leviathan* of the metaphoric positing of private conscience is thus one among many points where the text demonstrates a concern for the binding force of language and texts upon politics.

While in comparison with religion and sovereignty conscience is not a topic of terribly heated debate in Hobbes research,[5] nevertheless conscience in *Leviathan*, which Hobbes uses to illustrate the dangers of metaphor, is no incidental example with regard to Hobbes's concerns. I will show in this chapter that although Hobbes's discussion of conscience and metaphor is not a lengthy one, conscience may be seen to be *the* most dangerous metaphor for both Hobbes's nominalism and his political philosophy as a whole, for it is precisely the metaphoric shift in our understanding of conscience that, in Hobbes's account, corrupts knowledge into opinion, making error and deception possible. The metaphoric redefinition of conscience instantiates both the danger that metaphor poses to Hobbes's nominalist model of truth as the order of names and the danger that privacy poses to the stability of the commonwealth. The details of Hobbes's story of the corruption of knowledge and truth by metaphor, however, indicate that they are constitutively vulnerable to the corruption that Hobbes attributes to punctual instances of metaphor.

Hobbes's Condemnations of Metaphor

The seductive ornamentality of rhetorical language, its inconstancy and ambiguity, its capacity to incite the passions and to deceive—these elements are central to Hobbes's well-known concerns regarding what he calls "abuses" of speech, the safeguarding of truth and the security of the commonwealth. In *Leviathan* Hobbes repeatedly censures metaphor as deceptive; he considers tropes and figurative language to be abuses of speech, and he excludes metaphors from the proper language of "demonstration, counsel and all rigorous search of truth. . . . [Metaphors] openly profess deceit; to admit them into counsel, or reasoning, were manifest folly" (59).[6] Metaphor poses a threat to the stability of the commonwealth in part because it is a device of eloquence, which by Hobbes's definition appeals to the passions:

> Neither endeavour [speakers in an assembly] so much to fit their speech to the nature of the things they speak of, as to the passions of their minds to whom they speak; whence it happens, that opinions are delivered not by right reason, but by a certain violence of mind. Nor is this fault in the *man*, but in the nature itself of *eloquence*, whose end, as all the masters of rhetoric teach us, is not truth (except by chance), but victory; and whose property is not to inform, but to allure.[7]

In this passage, eloquence is the instrument of passion, violence of mind, and victory rather than of appropriateness, reason, and truth. Eloquence seduces and allures, it does not inform. Thus Hobbes argues that a counselor should avoid "all metaphorical speeches, tending to the stirring up of passion" (246). Likewise Hobbes writes with respect to the effects of eloquence in governmental assemblies:

> In an assembly of many, there cannot choose but be some whose interests are contrary to that of the public; and these their interests make passionate, and passion eloquent, and eloquence draws others into the same advice. For the passions of men, which asunder are moderate, as the heat of one brand; in an assembly are like many brands, that inflame one another, especially when they blow one another with orations, to the setting of the Commonwealth on fire, under pretense of counselling it. (248)

With respect to assemblies and thus to political matters, the contagion of passion—itself described eloquently in this passage—is the danger of eloquence, for metaphor and eloquence are both inspired by passion and inspiring of passion. As containing the potential to inflame people's passions against the good of the commonwealth, the rule of the passions and eloquence—and hence metaphor, their vehicle—clearly threatens the commonwealth and the pledge to the sovereign, which should instead be safeguarded by reason, truth, and appropriate language.

Hobbes's condemnation of metaphor and other devices of eloquence may appear to be incongruous with his own eloquent and rhetorical style in *Leviathan*. Victoria Kahn argues, however, for the performance-like character of *Leviathan*, demonstrating that *Leviathan* rhetorically and strategically inscenates the rejection of figures and rhetoric:

The *Leviathan* acts out a *rhetoric* of logical invention in two ways. First of all, it presents us with a logical argument that, Hobbes tells us, is in itself persuasive, and thus aims to be a substitute for and to foreclose all further rhetorical debate. But once rhetorical debate has been logically foreclosed, the structure and techniques of rhetorical debate are reintroduced in what Hobbes hopes to have mapped out as the realm of logic.[8]

Kahn's reading is a subtle elaboration of the rhetorical and logical sophistication of Hobbes's rejection of rhetoric. It offers an answer to accusations of simple performative contradiction on the part of Hobbes when he condemns metaphor and eloquence within a highly rhetorical text.[9] In a similar vein James Martel argues that Hobbes's highly rhetorical style in *Leviathan* belongs to the strategy of the text, insofar as the text's rhetorical flourishes highlight the problematic nature of the authority behind the very text that appears explicitly to condemn such flourish.[10]

Hobbes does not, however, univocally condemn eloquence—quite the contrary. For instance, he writes that "reason, and eloquence, though not perhaps in the natural sciences, yet, in the moral, may stand very well together. For wheresoever there is place for adorning and preferring of error, there is much more place for adorning and preferring of truth, if they have it to adorn" (702).[11] What is more, Hobbes's condemnations in *Leviathan* are inconsistent with his less negative assessment of metaphor in other texts. For instance, whereas in *Leviathan* Hobbes's explication of the importance of using words in their proper sense is combined with an invective against metaphor, in *De Corpore* the discussion of metaphor is less vehement:

> Names are usually distinguished into *univocal* and *equivocal*. . . . *[E]quivocal* [are] those which mean sometimes one thing and sometimes another. . . . Also every *metaphor* is by profession *equivocal*. But this distinction belongs not so much to names, as to those that use names, for some use them properly and accurately for the finding out of truth; others draw them from their proper sense, for ornament or deceit.[12]

In this context, the use of metaphors for purposes other than the finding out of truth is condemned, but the equivocality of metaphor itself is not. Hobbes offers a positive evaluation of the capacity to make the comparisons essential to metaphor and of the freshness and novelty of new expressions in his "Answer to Sir William Davenant."[13] Here what seems to worry Hobbes more than the use of metaphor and eloquence to inflame the passions is the possibility that those passions may attach to errors of thought and provoke insurgency. Hobbes divides eloquence into two parts, one part of which is devoted to clarity and elegance and thus to logic, the presentation of truth. The other part of eloquence serves the passions:

> Now eloquence is twofold. The one is an elegant and clear expression of the conceptions of the mind; and riseth partly from the contemplation of the things themselves, partly from an understanding of words taken in their own proper and definite signification. The other is a commotion of the passions of the mind, such as are *hope, fear, anger, pity;* and derives from a metaphorical use of words fitted to the passions.[14]

Metaphor is here associated with the part of eloquence that persuades by means of stirring the passions and thus with the part of eloquence that is dangerous to the commonwealth.[15] But the passage also shows that Hobbes is not simply an enemy of eloquence, for eloquence also includes the clear and explicative character of speech that derives from proper use. Thus despite Hobbes's specific invectives against eloquence, his condemnation of eloquence is by no means equivocal. Rather, it pertains only to the commotion of passions.[16]

In contrast to what I have shown thus far, even Hobbes's condemnation of eloquence is not univocal. As Ross Rudolph notes, emotions are for Hobbes not primary obstacles to the proper use of reason.[17] In this vein Hobbes writes, "The desires, and other passions of man, are in themselves no sin. No more are the actions, that proceed from those passions, till they know a law that forbids them" (114).[18] The problem with metaphor's appeal to the passions is not the passions in themselves. It is rather the ease with which the passions can be manipulated by eloquence: "But that [eloquent speakers] can turn their auditors out of fools into madmen; that they can make things to them who are ill-affected, seem worse, to them who are well-affected, seem evil; that they can enlarge their hopes, lessen their dangers beyond reason."[19] The passions cannot be condemned in themselves, according to Hobbes, because it is the passions that lead to the establishment of the commonwealth and the rise of human beings above the state of nature—specifically "fear of death; desire of such things as are necessary to commodious living; and a hope by their industry to obtain them" (116). To this extent, the passions are the condition of the formation of the commonwealth. The passions are also what people have in common, although the objects of passion differ in different people. The sameness of the passions in human beings is also what allows people to read each others' hearts and to have their own hearts read. Thus passion is the condition of the readability and legibility that form the condition of fulfilling Hobbes's exhortation in the introduction to *Leviathan* to read oneself.[20] Insofar as they are the key to the heart and thus to a metaphorically instituted interior space of legibility, the passions are also connected to the constellation of trope and conscience.

The Abuses of Speech

We have seen that metaphors are dangerous to the commonwealth insofar as they are able to stir people's passions in such a way as to distort their judgment and provoke them to actions contrary to the good of the commonwealth and hence contrary to their own good. Hobbes also implicates metaphor directly and indirectly in a variety of "abuses" of speech. Such corruption of language is not trivial but instead represents a thoroughly political danger, for language is, according to Hobbes, the condition of the existence of society, of the commonwealth, and hence of peace:

> The most noble and profitable invention of all other, was that of SPEECH, consisting of *names* or *appellations,* and their connexion, whereby men register their thoughts; recall them when they are past; and also declare them one to another for mutual utility and conversation; without which, there had been amongst men, neither Commonwealth, nor society, nor contract, nor peace. (18)

Without speech, here defined as names and what connects them, Hobbes claims that there would be no possibility of remembering thoughts nor of communicating them to other people. Without speech, there exists therefore no possibility for the establishment of and subordination to a sovereign authority, and hence no possibility to leave the state of nature. Speech and language are central to the goal of securing a stable commonwealth, in part because the commonwealth and its sovereignty are based on a *declaration* of a transfer of rights to a sovereign.[21] Hobbes's concern with proper signification and his condemnation of the devices that threaten to corrupt it reflect a concern for the binding power of that declaration.[22]

Within Hobbes's nominalist model of language, metaphors exacerbate the dangers of inconstancy and insignificance in the signification of words, and these corruptions of proper signification endanger the stability of the commonwealth—all this fully apart from the problem of metaphor's influence upon the passions.[23] What Hobbes calls "insignificance" refers to a name that signifies no thing, an "empty name"; Hobbes associates it with the use of metaphor in the context of abstraction.[24] In partic-

ular Hobbes worries about "the vain philosophy of Aristotle" that turns
ways of speaking into ontological categories which are not sheerly intellectual. He links the danger of abstraction directly to the possibility of dis-
obedience and thereby to potential political upheaval:

> But to what purpose, may some man say, is such subtlety in a work of this
> nature, where I pretend to nothing but what is necessary to the doctrine
> of government and obedience? It is to this purpose, that men may no
> longer suffer themselves to be abused, by them, that by this doctrine of
> *separated essences*, built on the vain philosophy of Aristotle, would fright
> them from obeying the laws of their country, with empty names; as men
> fright birds from the corn with an empty doublet, a hat, and a crooked
> stick. (674)

The insignificant words created by abstraction are, in Hobbes's view, tools
by which philosophers and students produce insignificant doctrine that
could attenuate the obedience of the members of the commonwealth.
The insignificant names and abstractions built upon metaphors are thus
linked to the potential for insurgency, the highest danger to the commonwealth. Hobbes associates the inconstancy of words with self-
deception; inconstancy permits confusion and an incorrect registration
of concepts, undercutting the foremost proper use of speech, namely, "to
serve for *marks* or *notes* of remembrance" (20) for oneself.[25] The inconstancy of words endangers this function, for it enables "men [to] register
their thoughts wrong, by the inconstancy of the signification of their
words; by which they register for their conception, that which they never
conceived, and so deceive themselves" (20). Inconstancy allows people to
falsely believe that they have conceived things that they have not in fact
conceived; it is for this reason implicated in a mechanism of self-
deception.

    Metaphor, in contrast to inconstancy, is seen as instrumental in the
abuse of speech that consists in the deception of others, that is, when one
"use[s] words metaphorically; that is, in other sense than that they are ordained for; and thereby deceive[s] others" (20). Whereas Hobbes associates inconstancy with self-deception and the registration of thought to
oneself, metaphor is an abuse of speech that corresponds to the use of
speech for making knowledge public and sharing it with others.[26] Metaphor, as the misapplication of a name, is implicated in falsity and deception because for Hobbes truth is itself nothing other than the usage of
words according to their proper meaning. Deception results from metaphor because, as Hobbes notes, "truth consisteth in the right ordering of
names in our affirmations" (23), and thus "a man that seeketh precise

truth had need to remember what every name he uses stands for, and to place it accordingly" (23). The proper use of names according to their standard meaning, therefore, is itself truth. Indeed truth exists only *as* this right ordering of names and so belongs to the order of language rather than to things themselves: "*True* and *false* are attributes of speech, not of things. And where speech is not, there is neither *truth* nor *falsehood*" (23). As the use of a word other than in its ordained sense, metaphor deceives and errs, for truth *is* nothing other than the "right ordering of names" (23).

The Dangers of Conscience

Hobbes condemns conscience in *Leviathan* as a source of principles for human decision and action in a commonwealth. As he sees it, the problem with conscience as a principle of action is that it renders each individual the inventor of his own rules and judge of his own actions. Individual conscience is incommensurable with the public authority that both defines a commonwealth and is binding upon it:

> Another doctrine repugnant to civil society, is, that *whatsoever a man does against his conscience, is sin;* and it dependeth on the presumption of making himself judge of good and evil. For a man's conscience, and his judgment is the same thing, and as the judgment, so also the conscience may be erroneous. Therefore, though he that is subject to no civil law, sinneth in all he does against his conscience, because he has no other rule to follow but his own reason; yet it is not so with him that lives in a Commonwealth; because the law is the public conscience, by which he hath already undertaken to be guided. Otherwise in such diversity, as there is of private consciences, which are but private opinions, the Commonwealth must needs be distracted, and no man dare to obey the sovereign power, further than it shall seem good in his own eyes. (311)

In Hobbes's account, conscience not only is inferior to civil law as a principle guiding action but is in general at odds with civil society and the good of the commonwealth. The fact that conscience is private—that it is in effect an "own reason"—renders it problematic for the commonwealth for several reasons. It may be erroneous and is subject to no outside source of correction. Likewise, because it is private, conscience does not possess any binding power outside the individual, private sphere. People may be bound by their own individual consciences, but insofar as consciences differ, standards of action differ, and this difference in standards leads to the undermining and distraction of the commonwealth. In addition the conflicts in private standards produce conflicting actions that disturb the peace of the commonwealth. The rule of private conscience is thus associated with primitive life and with the state of nature. The institution of civil law is an invaluable and ultimately essential improvement over individual conscience for the stability of the commonwealth, for it provides a public standard for guiding actions, enforced by the sovereign power.[27] It is a form of public conscience, binding and objective for all.

The divergences and conflicts produced by private judgment and opinion are threatening to the stability of the commonwealth, for they break with what Hobbes describes as the public character of knowledge, reason, and law. Hence Hobbes criticizes the notion "that men shall judge of what is lawful and unlawful, not by the law itself, but by their own consciences; that is to say, by their own private judgments" (330).[28] The association of privacy with reason when Hobbes writes of each man following his "own reason" is particularly problematic, for reason implies universality and veracity and should not produce conflicting judgments. Thus private opinion, private reason, and private conscience may not be the source of rules in a commonwealth. In fact precisely because private principles of action are threatening to the commonwealth, the function of the commonwealth is in part to establish public rules and what Hobbes calls "public reason."[29] Hobbes thus writes with respect to miracles that "we are not every one, to make our own private reason, or conscience, but the public reason, that is, the reason of God's supreme lieutenant, judge" (436). Likewise Hobbes considers seditious and a sign of disease of the commonwealth the notion "that every private man is judge of good and evil actions" (310). Privacy is dangerous to the principles of the commonwealth, for it mitigates the subject's submission to the will of the sovereign. The concept of private conscience makes such danger possible, for privacy is thereby granted an entire sphere that can be seen as an actual counterpart to the public sphere and hence to public reason and judgment.

How is this privacy characterized in figurative terms? The private realm of opinions that conscience both inaugurates and exemplifies is represented in *Leviathan* by means of interiority. Hobbes's text, as well as contemporary rhetorics of conscience, employ a phraseology surrounding conscience that utilizes spatial models of interiority or insideness, as indicated by the association of conscience with the preposition "in."[30] Thus the "pretence of covenant with God, is so evident a lie, even *in* the pretenders' own consciences, that it is not only an act of an unjust, but also of a vile, and unmanly disposition" (161); and "as much as *in* his own conscience he shall judge necessary" (323); and "there is scarce a Commonwealth in the world, whose beginnings can *in* conscience be justified" (706).[31] It could be argued that the phrase "in conscience" and the use of the preposition "in" with "conscience" are mere conventions and do not tell us anything about the actual dimensions of conscience or the true character of privacy. It is my claim, however, that precisely the catachrestic character of the description of conscience—that is, that there is no proper, literal portrayal of conscience—indicates that there is no other, *more* accurate model to which to appeal. In other words, there is no underlying *true* form of conscience that interiority can be said reliably to stand in for or represent. In the absence of a proper model of conscience, the interiority ascribed to conscience by means of the verbal conventions of the association of "in" and "conscience" is taken literally; the catachresis of interiority is taken as properly characterizing the unrepresentable privacy of conscience. Conscience's unrepresentability is thereby covered over by the figure of interiority that purports to represent it.

The privacy that is represented by a rhetoric of interiority is not only *described* by means of that figuration, however. It is also, as I will show in the next section, claimed by Hobbes to be *produced* or "represented into being" by means of that figuration. The privatization of conscience portrayed in *Leviathan* conforms to what Judith Butler describes in *The Psychic Life of Power: Theories in Subjection* as a process of internalization—which is not the importation of something into an already existing interior but instead the very production of the opposition interior/exterior: "This process of internalization *fabricates the distinction between interior and exterior life.*"[32] In the case of Hobbesian conscience, privacy itself is fabricated; it is not simply a previously existing datum and not a pregiven sphere of consciousness.

The Invention of Private Opinion

The theme of conscience in *Leviathan* arises in the context of definitions of words that are seemingly much more central to Hobbes's philosophy and to his conception of language, namely, "science" and "opinion." Whereas Hobbes equates science with "conditional knowledge, or knowledge of the consequence of words," opinion is defined as a conclusion where the discourse is not grounded in definitions, or where the definitions are wrongly joined. Following these clarifications, Hobbes adds the following explanation of the meaning of the word "conscience":

> When two, or more men, know of one and the same fact, they are said
> to be CONSCIOUS of it one to another; which is as much as to know it
> together. And because such are fittest witnesses of the facts of one
> another, or of a third; it was, and ever will be reputed a very evil act,
> for any man to speak against his *conscience:* or to corrupt, or force
> another to do so. (53)

This account of the word "conscience" places its origins in the adjective
"conscious," defined by Hobbes as sharing knowledge. "To be conscious"—to know with someone—is by this definition to know in a public
or shared way. Co-consciousness among a group of people is thereby
equated with knowing, where witnesses serve to maintain the publicity or
potential publicity of knowledge and hence of the truth of that which is
known. For this reason Hobbes emphasizes the connoted relation between knowledge and witnesses in the word "conscious." Similarly, the
word "conscience," according to Hobbes, originally referred to how
knowledge was witnessed by and thus monitored in its accuracy by the
presence of others similarly "conscious." Thus in Hobbes's tropological account, the "ordained" meaning of the noun "conscience" was closer to the
root meaning "knowing with others." The truth of specific facts was originally safeguarded by the shared witnessing that goes on in community
life, and the hypostatized conscience is therefore considered inviolate.
The inviolability of such knowledge and its factual character derived from
the fact that it belonged to a group of witnesses and hence to a public
sphere.[33] Knowledge as a whole was associated with witnesses and with the
verifiability they offer. This public knowledge of fact was reliable, and this
reliability and incorruptibility remain attached to the concept of conscience.

   According to Hobbes, the word "conscience" came to be applied
metaphorically to the knowledge of secret, individual private facts and
thoughts: "Afterwards, men made use of the same word metaphorically,
for the knowledge of their own secret facts, and secret thoughts; and
therefore it is rhetorically said, that the conscience is a thousand witnesses" (53). The metaphoric borrowing whereby the word "conscience"
is supposed to have come to refer to the knowledge of "secret facts, and
secret thoughts" is not an undistinguished example in Hobbes's discussion. With the metaphoric use of conscience, private thoughts come to be
seen as things that can be known and thus as having some claim to truth
by the mere fact that they are known by the person whose thoughts they
are. Thus according to Hobbes's account, knowledge is itself more
broadly defined through the metaphoric use of the word "conscience" to
also refer to such private thoughts. Knowledge came by this metaphor to

include something that is constituted in isolation, and the publicity of thought and knowledge thereby gave way to secrecy and privacy. Hobbes's story of conscience suggests that the metaphoric use of the word "conscience" as meaning "knowledge with oneself" ultimately itself *redefined* truth and knowledge as privately constituted and in principle therewith *invented* the sphere of private reason and own judgment.

The problem with conscience's newer meaning is that the word maintains the connotation of witnessing and the inviolability that goes along with the conception of knowledge that is shared and confirmed by witnesses. In the metaphoric use of the word "conscience," however, witnessing is not presumed to entail external witnesses in the form of other people but refers instead to the possibility of *self*-witnessing. Hobbes's reference to the metaphor of conscience as "a thousand witnesses" confirms the problem of figuration in general with regard to the conditions for preserving truth and constancy of words. That is, insofar as it rhetorically *can be said* that conscience *is* a thousand witnesses, conscience *seems* to provide the same guarantee of the validity of its knowledge as had the public sharing of knowledge that had been known as "conscious," because witnesses are invoked. But, as Hobbes indicates, once knowledge and truth are taken into the private sphere, they are defined in the absence of external witnesses. In such concealment, private opinion comes to substitute for private knowledge. The "thousand witnesses" inside oneself, alluded to in the metaphoric use of the word "conscience," fail to live up to the guarantee that public scrutiny provided in preserving conscience as a source of knowledge instead of opinion. Thus the fact that it *can* rhetorically and metaphorically be said that conscience is a thousand witnesses clearly shows that rhetoric allows and indeed abets the corruption of not only the knowledge that is known by conscience (which is anyway only private opinion in masquerade) but also the nature of knowledge as a whole.

With the metaphoric use of the word "conscience" to mean private judgment, private reason, and private thought, knowledge is taken out of the sphere of vigilant, genuine witnesses and rendered corruptible. Moreover, corruption is precisely what followed the metaphoric extension of conscience to refer to private knowledge; for according to Hobbes, in a further step, people capitalized on the connotations of integrity and knowledge associated with the original understanding of "conscience":

> And last of all, men, vehemently in love with their own new opinions, though never so absurd, and obstinately bent to maintain them, gave those their opinions also that reverenced name of conscience, as if they would have it seem unlawful, to change or speak against them; and so

pretend to know they are true, when they know at most, but that they think so. (53)

According to this train of thought, after the rhetorical shift wherein "conscience" came to refer to private *knowledge*, out of self-love and vanity people also bestowed the name "conscience" on private *opinions*.[34] Private opinion is thereby elevated to the status of knowledge and granted a measure of respect and even sanctity, for the name "conscience" retains the association with the inviolability of shared knowledge.

What is also remarkable is that Hobbes's account suggests not only that private opinion was given the name "conscience" by means of this metaphoric borrowing but also that opinion itself *arose* from this borrowing. As the preceding quotation indicates, following the metaphoric use of conscience to refer to witnessing one's own knowledge, men were in love with their "new" opinions. That is, Hobbes characterizes as *new* the opinions of the men who metaphorically used the term "conscience" to name their private facts and thoughts. This suggests that the sphere of opinion *itself* was new, that is, that private opinion *arose* in the crucial tropological moment described in Hobbes's account. It is as if the metaphoric extension of the word "conscience" *invented* the possibility of private opinion, to which the obstinacy of individuals in love with their own newfound privacy clung. The inviolability associated with public knowledge is thereby transferred to a *newly instituted* realm of individual opinion, and this transfer takes place within the privacy of a metaphorically fabricated sphere of individual conscience.

The Concealments of Rhetoric and the Dangers of Paradiastole

Although I have focused on the dangers that Hobbes ascribes to metaphor, Quentin Skinner claims that for Hobbes the more dangerous figure is "paradiastole," or more simply, rhetorical redescription—namely, the figure of speech where one phenomenon is differently named in order to attach different valuations to it. Skinner argues that this figure operates in Hobbes as a spoiler to any notion of moral science and is therefore Hobbes's primary object of concern when it comes to figurative language.[35] In Skinner's analysis, paradiastole makes moral science untenable insofar as paradiastolic formulations can express and evoke inappropriate passions with regard to that which is being described. I borrow from Skinner's important analysis in order to argue that it is in one respect too narrow: Hobbes's account of conscience suggests that it is above all the *concealment* of the figurative character of figures that makes *both* metaphor and paradiastole worrisome for Hobbes. It is not just that one figure is more dangerous than another but rather that the *concealments* surrounding figures make each of them dangerous to the order of names and ultimately to the political stability of the commonwealth.

Skinner explains the figure of paradiastole within the history of rhetoric in ancient Rome, the Renaissance, and early modern England. Although terms and definitions vary somewhat, Skinner notes that in each case, this figure evokes worry concerning the application of names of virtues or vices in such a way as to make those qualities and acts to which the names are applied appear less or more acceptable than they might, and should, otherwise appear. Skinner cites Quintilian's encapsulation of this rhetorical figure: "whenever you call yourself wise rather than cunning, or courageous rather than overconfident, or careful rather than parsimonious."[36] According to Skinner, Hobbes is more pessimistic in *Leviathan* than in *The Elements of Law* or in *De Cive* with respect to the possibility of overcoming the threats of paradiastole and hence about the possibility of genuine moral argument and agreement on how to apply evaluative terms.[37] Skinner's explanation of the problem of rhetorical redescription in Hobbes emphasizes Hobbes's pessimism regarding our ability to "see" particular actions for what they truly are, given the "tinctures" of our passions.[38] Paradiastole is dangerous in this context because it in no way signals that it is rhetorical, nor for that matter that it is a *re*-description.

Hobbes's story of the metaphoric corruption of the word "conscience," however, shows that it is not just a figure operating on its own that is dangerous; rather, it is the lack of public signaling of its figurative character that is dangerous in the case of both paradiastole and metaphor. In contrast to the case of paradiastole, in which different words and valuations attach to the same object, person, or act, in Hobbes's story of conscience the word and the valuations attached to conscience remain the same, while that to which the word and its valuations refer changes—that is, from a public witnessing that guarantees knowledge to a private self-witnessing that elevates private opinion. The word "conscience" in Hobbes's account comes to be applied to private knowledge, but this "private knowledge" is in fact private judgment in disguise, and it is further supplanted by private opinion. The word "conscience" and its connotations of knowledge and witnessing grant the sanctity of shared, witnessed knowledge and fact to private knowledge but also to subjective judgment and even mere opinion. Thus the very name "conscience," based on its origin in knowledge and publicity, seems to remove what goes by that name from the realm of debate and suspicion. Hobbes's tale of the privatization of conscience offers a case in which the constancy of the name also carries with it a particular valuation, even while the phenomenon that goes by that name is altered.

The reason for Hobbes's resistance to paradiastole is, according to Skinner, that rhetorical redescription allows for the shift in attachment of valuations, especially of moral valuations, to particular cases to which they are not suited. In effect, the true nature of the act being described and the proper moral valuation that is its due are concealed by the rhetorical redescription. As with conscience's metaphorization, rhetorical redescription entails a double concealment, where the fact *that* a shift in meaning is concealed is *itself* also concealed. In both paradiastole and metaphor, an explicit characterization of figure *as* figure is lacking. There is no indication that a renaming has taken place. It appears that it is the absence of the trace of renaming, the absence of a signal of the figurative usage, that renders these figures particularly dangerous.

Hobbes's story of conscience indicates that the privatization of knowledge opens truth itself to redefinition and corruption. The trouble with metaphor, as Hobbes's story of conscience suggests, is that when there is no mark of metaphor *as* metaphor, the concealment effected by metaphor's privatization offers no safeguard against the possible corruption of the language and hence of the truth in that properly ordered language. In particular, metaphor—as opposed to simile, for example—sets forth an order of names in an assertion without necessarily making public the fact that these names are employed figuratively. Metaphor does not announce its gesture of renaming. The same is true of paradiastole—it does not mark itself as a redescription, and thus it conceals its strategic force. If the metaphoric extension of "conscience" from a knowing with others to a knowing interior to oneself were instead marked *as* metaphor, then the redefinition of conscience as private opinion would have to settle accounts with the original meaning. The extension of meaning, when concealed *as* such an extension, leaves meaning open to corruption. Metaphor bears no sign of the "as" or "like" that would point to original conditions, such as original meaning or the private will of a metaphor maker; metaphor conceals its provenance, its intention, and even the fact that it is metaphor. These concealments also, then, conceal the possibility of the corruption of truth, defined by Hobbes as the proper order of names, by the language of the metaphor.

Hobbes's example of conscience is therefore no mere example of the dangers of metaphor, it is also an exemplum, a moral anecdote, for it contains a particular moral not only about knowledge but about metaphor itself.[39] To put it briefly, the peculiar danger of metaphor is that it has no "con-science"; it removes the guarantee of truth that comes with public knowledge. On Hobbes's account, true "con-science" and metaphor are opposed, for metaphor is in multiple ways, as will be detailed subsequently, a matter of concealment. While the metaphoric extension of the word "conscience" proves dangerous, however, in rendering the knowledge that was public corruptible, it is also inventive, powerful, and performative. The metaphor that allows "conscience" to mean "private knowledge" *produces* that very sphere of private knowledge. Thus as concealed and concealing, not just conscience but metaphor itself produces a danger to what Hobbes considers a necessarily public, shared truth in the proper ordering of names. The power of metaphor in Hobbes's own account thus exceeds the danger he ascribes to the corruptibility of knowledge into private opinion.

The Conditions for Law

In order to draw out several ways in which concealment and the dangers of privacy are paramount for Hobbes, it is helpful to consider Hobbes's requirements for full publicity of civil law, corresponding to various possibilities of concealment in legislation. This topic may seem remote from the question of the internalization of conscience, but in fact there are significant comparisons to be made in terms of concealment, the binding authority of language, and the publicity of knowledge. For instance, just as Hobbes worries about the nonunivocality of terms introduced by metaphor into the order of truth, he also worries about the chaos that nonunivocal language poses to law: "The written laws, if they be short, are easily misinterpreted, from the diverse significations of a word, or two: if long, they be more obscure by the diverse significations of many words" (262). The fact that words have multiple significations means that the process of correct interpretation and judgment is a perilous one. Metaphor is thus one element of inconstancy that threatens the univocity and authority of law: "For the significations of almost all words, are either in themselves, or in the metaphorical use of them, ambiguous; and may be drawn in argument, to make many senses; but there is only one sense of the law" (267).

When Hobbes discusses civil law, he is concerned to elucidate what makes such law binding upon members of a commonwealth. According to *Leviathan*, the binding character of law derives from the complete explicitness and publicity of the conditions under which the law is expressed. Hobbes's treatment of the applicability of laws to individuals suggests that the understanding of law *as* law is what makes it binding; this corresponds to Hobbes's worry that the *lack* of understanding of metaphor *as* metaphor renders it dangerous.[40] Hobbes's discussion of civil law centers on the fact that laws apply only to those who are able to know them: "The command of the Commonwealth, is law only to those, that have the means to take notice of it. Over natural fools, children, or madmen, there is no law" (257). Only those people capable of knowing the law are subject to it, and this requires knowing it *as* law. An explicit understanding of law *as* law makes law binding, for otherwise a person has no access to what law is and therefore cannot know it as an obligation. The communication of law *as* law thus requires detailed treatment by Hobbes, for it entails both the communication of whatever the law proscribes or permits and the communication of the binding force of that law upon all who understand it as law. In other words, the bindingness of law must be explicit in every law. The institution of civil law (as opposed to laws of nature) requires complete publicity of the conditions of legislation.

For these reasons, Hobbes's first requirement of civil law is that it be rendered explicit through signs to those to whom it applies: "The law of nature excepted, it belongeth to the essence of all other laws, to be made known, to every man that shall be obliged to obey them, either by word, or writing, or some other act" (259).[41] Civil law must be made known, that is, it must be shared with those who are to obey it. Words, writing, and acts are all public means of sharing; they draw upon signs, that is, ways of communicating with others, rather than upon the private marks by which, as we have seen, thought registers itself to itself. Hobbes also requires that the provenance of the law, that is, the *source* of its authority as law, must be made public: "Nor is it enough the law be written, and published; but also that there be manifest signs, that it proceedeth from the will of the sovereign" (259). Law is binding only when the fact or proof of its authority is rendered coexplicit with its particular stipulations. Publicizing the fact of a law's authority is what renders it understandable not just as a law stipulating something but *as* law and thereby as binding. Moreover, because words have "diverse significations" (262), Hobbes recognizes that the laws themselves may be ambiguous, as I have indicated. What must also be made explicit and public in a law in order to render it fully binding, therefore, is the *intention* behind the law, that is, its original, private meaning according to its legislator:

> The legislator known; and the laws, either by writing, or by the light of nature, sufficiently published; there wanteth yet another very material circumstance to make them obligatory. For it is not the letter, but the intendment, or meaning; that is to say, the authentic interpretation of

the law (which is the sense of the legislator,) in which the nature of the
law consisteth. (261–62)

Along with publicizing the law itself, the intention of the law must be
made public. Such privately determined meaning of the law, as constituted by the legislator, preserves the law *as* the law it is, and thus this privately determined meaning must be made public in order that the law be
known as the law that it is by those who are able to know it.

Publicity is thus the first and final mark of the law's determination
as law. An act that contravenes a law is more criminal, in fact, when it violates not just the word of the law but its publicity and all its conditions.
Hobbes writes:

> Where the law is publicly, and with assiduity, before all the people read,
> and interpreted; a fact done against it, is a greater crime, than where
> men are left without such instruction, to enquire of it with difficulty,
> uncertainty, and interruption of their callings, and be informed by pri-
> vate men. (291)[42]

Made public in all its aspects and conditions, law assumes its full force.
Law must be known *as* law to make it binding. The "as" encompasses the
public, explicit, and linguistic aspects of the law. First, the stipulation
must itself occur in public signs, such as words, writing, or act. Second, the
source of the law's authority, which constitutes the stipulations *as* law,
must be communicated along with the law. Finally, the proper interpretation of the law, *as* the law that it is, must accompany the law. The private
meaning or intention of the legislator is precisely what must be made public, in order to continually determine the law *as* what it is. The multiple
and yet interrelated conditions of the "as" here illuminate the explicit understandings that Hobbes believes are necessary for the constitution
of law.

How does the making public of law in its various aspects relate to the
question of the dangers of metaphor and figurative language? The conditions of civil law in effect prescribe a remedy for the corruption of public meaning: make public all the conditions of a signification in order to
render it binding. The source of the authority of the language that stipu-
lates the law and the authorized interpretation of that language, rendered
coexplicit with the word of the law, together mark it *as* law. If we compare
the danger of metaphor as privatizing to the requirements Hobbes sets
forth as what makes law binding, we can relate to metaphor's lack of public "con-science" his call for publicity and openness with respect to the linguistic acts of legislation.[43] The requirements for civil law suggest that only

publicizing the conditions and intentions of a significant assertion guarantees the preservation of the assertion in its proper meaning. The private sphere of conscience invented by metaphor, as well as the potential privacy of meaning in metaphor, therefore contravene in multifarious ways the publicity that renders law binding.

The Corruptions of Metaphor

Near the end of *Leviathan,* in a chapter on "Darknesse from Vain Philosophy," Hobbes turns from a discussion of individual names to the relations between names as expressed by other words—specifically by the various conjugations of the verb "to be." The forms of "to be," according to Hobbes, indicate necessary relations between names:

> [Other words] serve to show the consequence, or repugnance of one
> name to another; as when one saith *a man is a body,* he intendeth that the
> name of *body* is necessarily consequent to the name of *man;* as being but
> several names of the same thing, *man;* which Consequence is signified by
> coupling them together with the word *is.* . . . For the placing of two
> names in order may serve to signify their consequence . . . as well as the
> words *is,* or *be,* or *are,* and the like. (673)

The verb "to be" expresses a *necessary* connection between names, establishing that they belong together. In a similar way, according to Hobbes, the mere juxtaposition of two words may signify a necessary connection between them. In this respect, Hobbes suggests that the word "is" is not even necessary in language, for Hobbes is unsure whether all languages have a word that corresponds to it, and indeed he suggests that the order of consequence would seem to adequately substitute for it.[44] The connections between names are, however, along with names themselves, a central ingredient of the definition of speech, as Hobbes's definition of speech makes clear: "Speech consist[s] of *names* or *appellations* and their connection" (18).

The conjugations of "to be" express necessary relation, for they portray one word as a consequence of another. The conjugations of "to be" thereby participate in the constitution of truth, as they are the words that order names rightly:

> [W]hen we say, *a man is a living body,* we mean not that the *man* is one
> thing, the *living body* another, and the *is,* or *being* a third: but that the

> *man,* and the *living body,* is the same thing; because the consequence, *if he be a man, he is a living body,* is a true consequence, signified by that word *is.* (674)

"Is" is an expression of the necessary connection of names, according to Hobbes. The word "is" does not express a third "thing" apart from "man" and "living body." Instead "is" communicates the truth of the connection of those two names. It makes public the belonging together of the two names which it both separates and connects in the predicative assertion. The "is" thus brings into public not only the names it connects but also the truth of their belonging together, which renders each a consequence of the other. The "is" is a sign of truth, for in it the proper ordering of names is established in light of their identity. *Philosophia Prima* is, for Hobbes, nothing other than the "right limiting of the significations of such appellations, or names, as are of all others the most universal; which limitations serve to avoid ambiguity and equivocation in reasoning, and are commonly called definitions" (671). The "is" is therefore central to truth and to philosophy.

What does metaphor have to do with this discussion of the connection of names by the word "is"? Metaphor, as that which uses the "is" to connect two names that are *not* unconditionally connected, constitutes untruth in Hobbes's nominalist understanding of truth. Unlike simile, as we have seen, metaphor does not publicize or announce itself as a figure; metaphor makes use of the "is" and other words for being but does *not* make explicit that it is not using the "is" with regard to an unconditional connection. Conscience, once again, illustrates Hobbes's point: once metaphor allows one to override the necessary connection of "conscience" to communal knowledge and instead to connect conscience to privacy—by means of such a metaphoric statement as "conscience *is* a thousand witnesses"—the withdrawal of conscience *and* of the connection between "conscience" and "witnesses" from the community of knowers allows a further, concealed redefinition of conscience, that is, as private opinion, now rendered inviolable as conscience. In other words, metaphor has no "con-science"; the "is" of which it makes use suggests that the names it connects belong together necessarily. Because it keeps the fact of its metaphoric character private, the use of "is" to connect names that do not necessarily belong together corrupts the truth-maintaining function of the "is."

Hence the danger of metaphor is not simply that truth is obscured by the metaphoric use of *names.* Rather, the usage of the "is" in a metaphoric assertion, and therefore outside ordained meaning, constitutes a concealed destabilization of the "is" and hence of truth as a whole. "Which insignificancy of language . . . hath a quality, not only to hide the truth, but also to make men think they have it, and desist from further search" (686). Insignificant, inconstant, and metaphoric language pose a *double* danger to knowledge—they obscure the truth *and*, with the help of the "is," the fact that truth is obscured. Proper usage, as constituted by the pre-given order of names, is not only the public expression *of* truth; it *is* truth itself for Hobbes. Improper usage results in inconstant, insignificant language that poses as truth. Thus improper usage not only abuses the names it articulates, it hides the fact that their use is in fact abuse. If proper usage is truth, improper usage is untruth, for it allows names to be connected unjustifiably. Proper usage maintains the public standards of meaning; improper usage begins with a private, individual usage that—if taken on by a public at large without express acknowledgment of its impropriety—corrupts truth as the proper order of names.

Because metaphor departs from the established order of names and makes use of the "is" improperly, its usage opens up a lawless realm of ambiguity and inconstancy, where there is no guarantee as to what sort of meaning will result on the part of the one who hears or reads the metaphor. The interpretation of the meaning of a metaphor by others, in other words, is also private. Hobbes explains that mental discourse draws upon a private train of associations to which others are subject when they hear it:

> When a man thinketh on any thing whatsoever, his next thought after, is not altogether so casual as it seems to be. Not every thought to every thought succeeds indifferently. . . . [W]e have no transition from one imagination to another, whereof we never had the like before in our senses. (11)

Rhetorical devices, including metaphor, persuade people precisely because they draw upon a reserve of private associations, which follow one from another involuntarily.[45] One is not free from one's own train of thought, for the succession of thought is constrained by experience, according to Hobbes. Previously established, private patterns of thought thus determine on an individual basis the train of associations deriving from any word. Moreover, this train of thought is not subject to public scrutiny because it passes rapidly. The succession of thought cannot be interrupted at will, for "thought is quick" (13).

There are two sides to this danger of involuntary association. First, the fact that use of a word apart from its ordained meaning evokes a train of thought may be manipulated in order to intentionally pervert truth, as illustrated in the story of the metaphorization of conscience, where the inviolability of public knowledge is transferred to conscience as private opinion. Second, the fact that a train of thought is conditioned, according to Hobbes, by individual sense experience means that the use of a word outside its proper meaning could call up an unintended train of associations.[46] In the latter case, meaning and therefore shared knowledge are up for grabs, for the succession of thought is involuntary and immediate. Thought is not free, for it is governed either by some desire or by the involuntary association of thought itself. Proper usage of words—especially of the "is"—makes use of the train of thought so as to preserve truth as the right order of names and, presumably, a related right order of associations. Metaphor, on the one hand, leaves thought free of that order and thus free for untruth, and, on the other hand, subjects thought to a private and individual train of thought, which may involuntarily corrupt the truth of the right order of names itself. Again, therefore, we see that figurative language and the abuse of the "is" makes possible a turn to an individual, isolated realm of thinking where corruption of truth is possible.

Metaphor is thus dangerous to truth because it connects names with "is," and this connection portrays these names as necessary consequences of each other. That is, metaphor abuses the "is" that does not name any thing, that is not a "third thing" apart from subject and predicate but rather expresses necessary connection. Metaphor thereby orders names improperly and evokes involuntary associations. But once that disordering of names has taken place, truth is up for grabs, not only because the names have been abused and are thereafter open to private corruption but also because the "is" has been abused. Hence metaphor is not only an abuse of the names that make up speech, it is also an abuse of the "is" that orders those names and thereby constitutes the crucial ingredient of truth defined as the order of names. When "is" is employed in this way—as a signifier of contingent, rather than necessary, connection—truth is opened to corruption. Truth is even more open to corruption by the abuse of "is" than by the abuse of particular names, for not only particular names are put in danger but also and more important the system of relations of identity and necessary consequence. When conscience undergoes the redefinition whereby it "is" an internal witness as opposed to a public knowledge, not only conscience but "is" suffers a debasement. When the "is" has been abused, not one name but the condition of truth as a whole is endangered.

It may seem an unlikely place to confirm this account of the corruptibility of the "is," but Hobbes's discussion of transubstantiation in *Leviathan* demonstrates a strange corruptibility of the "is," as a connection that belongs both to proper ordering and to figuration. Hobbes argues in *Leviathan* that the doctrine of transubstantiation, which takes the sentence "This is my body" literally, commits an abuse of language, whereby representation is mistaken for predication. Thus "the words, *This is my body*, are equivalent to these, *this signifies,* or *represents my body;* and it is an ordinary figure of speech: but to take it literally, is an abuse" (611–12). In this interpretation of liturgy and the phenomenon of transubstantiation, the word "is" does not literally stand for a necessary relation of truth. "Is" does not mean "is," in this exceptional instance. Rather, the word "is" is itself a figure for representation and signification. Representation is here itself figuratively represented by "is." The figurative use of "is" fills in for representation, and thus it would be abuse to take this "is" literally, insofar as the "is" in its literal use implies necessary connection rather than the contingency of representation and figure that Hobbes ascribes to the liturgy.[47]

Metaphor and figures of speech are thus not only dangerous to truth inasmuch as they abuse the names that are the elements of language; they also abuse the connection between these names. Yet at the end of the chapter on speech, Hobbes mitigates his own accusations against metaphor and figurative language. Hobbes suggests, contrary to what we have seen earlier, that metaphors do in fact mark themselves as departures from proper language, announcing themselves as questionable and therefore offsetting their own deceptiveness. Hobbes notes that the right ordering of names is subject to inconstancy by virtue of the fact that the passions and individual, private interest may influence our choice of names. In a passage that serves as an example of Hobbes's worries about both paradiastole and metaphor, Hobbes concludes,

> For one man calleth *wisdom,* what another calleth *fear;* and one *cruelty,* what another *justice.* . . . And therefore such names can never be true grounds of any ratiocination. No more can metaphors, and tropes of speech; but these are less dangerous, because they profess their inconstancy; which the other do not. (29)

The inconstancy of names that "bear a tincture of our different passions" (28) makes such names unreliable sources of reason and knowledge, for there is no standard to guarantee that these names have been ordered rightly. Hence, as indicated earlier, Skinner uses these same lines as support for his claims about paradiastole, for Hobbes here relegates metaphors and tropes to the category of unreliable names, on account of their inconstancy, that is, as names used outside the realm of proper usage. Yet Hobbes notes here that because such tropes *profess* that inconstancy, that is, make public the fact that they extend beyond the proper usage of names, they are for this reason *less* dangerous.[48]

In other words, Hobbes is claiming that insofar as figurative language signs itself as departing from the right order of names, it mitigates its own corruptive influence. As the discussion of the conditions of law indicates, publicizing the status of law along with law itself makes it valid and binding; here, copublicizing the fact of a metaphor's metaphoric character makes the usage acceptable. Although this passage partially exonerates metaphor and tropes, it also supports Skinner's argument regarding Hobbes's anxiety about the rhetorical figure of paradiastole, that is, the rhetorical redescription whereby different valuations and passions are evoked by means of the use of a different name. For in the case of applying the name of a virtue to a specific act or a specific moment of human life, the word "is" connects the virtue as if by necessary juxtaposition to that act or moment. Thus the inconstancy of names that does not *profess* its own inconstancy, whether in metaphor or paradiastole, is the danger at issue. The concealment of figuration and of the contingent character of its connection of names, more than figuration itself, is the danger.

Although Hobbes's account of conscience censures metaphor and the privatization of knowledge, the end of the chapter on speech nonetheless redeems metaphor somewhat, insofar as metaphor is said to "profess" its own "inconstancy"—that is, to make public the fact of its departure from proper meaning. While the story of conscience may appear utterly inconsistent with the rehabilitation of metaphor (one claiming metaphor is private and therefore dangerous, the other claiming that as publicly proclaiming its inconstancy, metaphor is not so dangerous), it is important to note that the same moral applies in either case: *privatization* is a danger, for only public knowledge of names as naming what they name— preferably in a context that copublicizes the source of their authority and intended interpretation—keeps them from corrupting truth as a right order of names. When figurative language at least announces itself as figurative, the fact of its improper usage and the endangerment of truth is publicized. The impropriety and the potential disruption of truth is thereby made available to public scrutiny, and conscience is restored to its vigilance.

Leviathan and Metaphor

Hobbes appears to commit a glaring inconsistency: How are we to read his central reference to the "leviathan," if not as a metaphor?[49] How else, except metaphorically, could we understand the connection of the commonwealth to the sea monster that in the book of Isaiah is said to earn the wrath and punishment of God (Isa. 27:1); to a creature in Psalms whose multiple heads are said to have been crushed and fed to desert creatures (Ps. 74:10–15); or to the proud, terrifying, and impervious monster in the book of Job (Job 41:1-34)? Only the very last verses of the latter reference, wherein the biblical Leviathan is described as unique, fearless, and prideful, are cited by Hobbes in his first chapter of the section "Of Commonwealth."[50] But in the introduction to *Leviathan,* where the figure of the Leviathan is introduced, it is not with reference to such characterological aspects of the biblical Leviathan, but instead as a segue to a discussion of the "body" of the "artificial man" that for Hobbes is the commonwealth: "For by art is created that great LEVIATHAN called a COMMON-WEALTH . . . which is but an artificial man" (ix). Could there be a literal understanding of body at work here, even where Hobbes compares aspects of the commonwealth to blood, nerves, muscles, and other components of an organismic body? How should we understand Hobbes's resort to figuration in his connection of the body of an artificial man to a commonwealth?

To point out a resemblance between the commonwealth and a living body does not require metaphor or other tropes. Similes and analogies would suffice, for example, when Hobbes suggests that "public ministers resembleth the nerves, and tendons that move the several limbs of a body natural" (227). Here the declarations of resemblance provide explicit comparisons rather than tropological ones. No necessary consequence— necessary consequence, as we have seen, being one of the dangers of inexplicit figures of comparison—is suggested.[51] Such explicitly comparative formulations as simile and analogy do not violate the understanding of the words "is" and "are"; instead they have a "con-science" in that they publicly mark their figurative character with "like," "as," or some other word apart from "is." They publicize the fact *that* they make a comparison, and so they do not pose the same dangers of private trains of thought as do metaphor and rhetorical redescription. Is Hobbes thereby acquitted of having contravened his own explicit condemnation of metaphor, if he makes only a simile or analogy between a body and a commonwealth? Indeed, *Leviathan* is rife with such analogies, for instance, describing thoughts as scouts for desire (61) and money as the blood of the commonwealth (238–39). On the other hand, Hobbes "abuses" the words "is" and "are" frequently—according to the definitions of the abuse of language that we have examined, as when he writes that "sovereignty is the soul of the Commonwealth" (208) or that "the two arms of a Commonwealth are *force and justice*" (256).

It is difficult to read literally Hobbes's commonwealth "body," and yet what option is there, except to decide between *either* a literal *or* a metaphoric reading? The question of how to read the invocation of the body— and with it, the figure of the Leviathan and hence the book *Leviathan*— hangs on this dichotomy between proper and improper use, between literal and figurative. As we have seen, there is within the book a story of conscience's transformation that is said to take place by means of a figure, and yet that transformation by means of a figure determines the actuality of the literal. The figuration-into-existence of private conscience within *Leviathan* allegorizes the art of figuration *as* an art of positing and of production, such that what is figured *becomes* a literal, worldly entity. Likewise it is by *art,* as we have seen, that the commonwealth or artificial man is created. The art that creates the artificial man is not mere *artifice,* not simply "unnatural." Human beings are capable of figurations, positings, and performatives; the natural world and the natural body are posited in language, and indeed a commonwealth body is constituted out of pacts and covenants.[52] Both a natural body and the artificial body of the commonwealth, the latter depending upon a right ordering of names, are *rendered* bodies by the artifice of a linguistic truth—that is, by a truth that is defined solely as the order of names.

Hobbes's references to the "reading" of hearts reflects the confounding of the corporeal and the linguistic even in the introduction to *Leviathan:* "The characters of man's heart, blotted and confounded as they are with dissembling, lying, counterfeiting, and erroneous doctrines, are legible only to him that searcheth hearts" (xi–xii). Hobbes figures the heart in terms of written language, or "characters." And yet these written characters have been blotted and confounded with the *acts* of dissembling, lying, counterfeiting, and so forth. How *could* the human being be legible, in this account, when corporeal body, material letters, and acts of deception converge in the "heart"? The human being would be legible only to those who could negotiate the multiple dimensions of body and language that converge *in this very figure* of confounded characters of the heart. The convergence of figures and bodiliness in the example of the legibility of the heart suggests that the body of the commonwealth is not "artificial" as *opposed* to the "natural" body. Artifice and the inconstancy of language belong together in human beings, for even to posit a "natural" heart is to elide the resonances with which Hobbes himself associates the legible heart. Thus the body, writing, speech, and act are here connected from the beginning of *Leviathan,* where *reading*—reading oneself, reading hearts, reading others—is taken as the goal of *Leviathan* as a whole, in which Hobbes declares that he will "set down my own reading." The book, the Leviathan figure, the commonwealth, the body, writing, speaking, and acting are brought together in Hobbes's introduction in such ways as to render *illegible* the distinction between figuration and literal description.

The Corruptibility of Being

Hobbes's story of conscience presumes a prior order of truth and a system of usage in which words were used only in their proper senses. His story of conscience tells of a fall from literal meaning into figurative meaning and portrays it as one and the same as the fall from public to private constitution of meaning. Metaphor, according to Hobbes's account, was the mechanism of the corruption of meaning and knowledge, for metaphor abuses the order of names and allows private opinion to supplant public knowledge in a concealed way. The exemplary story of conscience does not explain the following, however: Precisely what *opens* the way to metaphor? How could figurative language insinuate itself into a perfectly ordered, nonmetaphoric system of names? There must already exist a point of instability in the ordering of names if metaphor can insinuate itself there at all. Moreover, metaphor seems to be able to insinuate itself *anywhere* in the order of names—this is one reason that Hobbes finds it so very dangerous. It is not just individual names themselves that are vulnerable to metaphor; the *order* of names is vulnerable to metaphor, for that order is determined by the links created by the verb "to be." Given the corruptibility of the entire order of names, the "original" site of abuse could just as well be the word "is" as the name "conscience"—as in the adage Hobbes cites so critically, "conscience is a thousand witnesses." Are the witnesses here invoked metaphorically and thus improperly, or is the word "is" the location of impropriety? What would be the criterion for making this decision? The order of names is corrupted by the infinite utility of "is," by the sheer principle of connection that enjoys an indifference to that which it connects.[53] Aristotle, condemned repeatedly in Hobbes's text, confirms the condition of the downfall from literal to figurative; he articulates the instability of the "is" that holds together a proper order of names in claiming: "*To de on legetai men pollaxos*," "The term 'being' is used in many senses," or "Being is said in many ways."[54]

Hobbes blames metaphor for the inconstancy of language, as concealing both a proper order of names and its own abuse of that order. Yet the condemnation of metaphor as the source of the inconstancy of language conceals the fact of the *constitutive* inconstancy of language. Metaphor is thus not extrinsic to the order of names. Stories of corrupted

proper meanings require metaphor to conceal this constitutive inconstancy. Where truth is an order of names, completely public "con-science"
is always impossible, for both names and the "is" as the sign of truth conceal their intrinsic corruptibility.

What We May Say

Even the opening paragraphs of *Leviathan* demonstrate the corruptibility
of language by the extended use of names and the labile character of the
"is." The introduction to *Leviathan* is in part a consideration of art, likeness, imitation, and making, in which Hobbes uses the "is" to associate the
various elements of the body with machines, for example, "for what is the
heart, but a *spring*" (ix), and various elements of the commonwealth to a
body, for example, "the *sovereignty* is an artificial *soul*" (ix). These uses of
"is," however, are made within an explicit context of artificiality; that is,
Hobbes first talks about the "art of man" in making an artificial animal as
an imitation of nature as God's art of making of the world. Hence
Hobbes's use of the "is" for the purposes of comparison is not necessarily
what he would deem a corrupt use of names, for he makes explicit the
conditions of comparison in which he uses the "is."

Hobbes makes these comparisons by means of the "is," however, in
the context of questions that are apparently rhetorical. But the first of
these questions in particular can be read not as a merely rhetorical question but as instead as asking precisely the central question of how representation and figuration can be binding upon existence. Hobbes asks,
"Why may we not say, that all *automata* (engines that move themselves by
springs and wheels as doth a watch) have an artificial life?" (ix).[55] While
the question of life and Hobbes's mechanistic philosophy thereof is an
important one,[56] for the considerations of how a figure or even a text may
be binding, it is more significant that the question "Why may we not
say . . . ?" is *the* question that lies behind the suspicions of figures, of
proper language, and of the nature of truth. For as Hobbes well shows, we
in fact *may* say that automata have an artificial life. And we *may* also say
that "conscience is a thousand witnesses," and we *may* also call private
opinion by the name "knowledge" or "conscience." We *may* also thereby
both conceal a state of affairs and represent into existence a state of affairs
through the use of words. The possibility of saying these things is nothing
other than the possibility of connecting words in various ways and of
thereby performatively creating a bond between them. The possibility of
using words wrongly, of abusing words, is an inherent possibility of words,

including the connecting "is"—that for Hobbes should be a binding sign of truth.

The art of the human being is such that one *may* say that the heart *is* a spring, that the public ministers of a commonwealth *are* its nerves, and also that conscience *is* a thousand witnesses. What we may say, or write, as Hobbes well knows, may be dangerous, in that it performs a certain ordering of names, an order that might contravene the order of truth that should be binding but turns out to be unstable. The art of the human being is such that we may imitate God, says Hobbes in his introduction; but even the *imitation* of God may also accomplish a binding—hence human beings can also constitute a Leviathan, by means of the pacts and covenants that resemble the fiat by means of which God pronounced humankind into being. What Hobbes calls "the art of man" requires the performative capacity of words, the bindingness of language on the world, a bindingness within which human beings live and by means of which they represent into existence that which they are and that which they depict.[57] This is also the world of promises and concealments; however, both promises and concealments depend upon the very essential possibility that one *may* say and thus *may* represent into existence. Hobbes's own rhetorical flourish does not undercut his condemnation of figuration; rather, it confirms the performative element of positing and the lability of the "is" that connects names in an inherently corruptible fashion.

2

Hegel's *Phenomenology of Spirit:* The Performative Successes and Rhetorical Failures of Conscience

In the previous chapter I examined how, in Hobbes's seventeenth-century account of conscience, metaphor and figurative language function performatively. For Hobbes, the metaphoric usage of the word "conscience" to refer to a solitary knowing instead of a shared knowing invents the sphere of private conscience and private opinion; likewise figurative usage destabilizes the order of names that constitutes truth. Both instances thus demonstrate the ways figures may prove binding upon existence and truth. But what if we consider the relationship between performativity and rhetoric in a larger sense, namely, when the latter is understood not only in terms of metaphor and trope but also as the effectual character of discourse? In this chapter I will argue that Hegel's analysis of conscience in the *Phenomenology of Spirit* (1807) depicts the quintessentially unstable relationship between saying and doing; Hegelian conscience fails not performatively but instead rhetorically, and thus his account of conscience illuminates the unforeseeable rhetorical repercussions of performative saying. In its illustrations of the inadvertent effectivity of speech acts, the chapter on conscience in the *Phenomenology* also reveals the unaccountable effectivity of our own speech acts, for we are subject to the same kinds of performative misfires as is conscience. What is more, the account of the misfires of conscience's speech acts could be read as well as instructing us with regard to the rhetorical potential for misfires, or simple failures, of the *Phenomenology of Spirit* itself, if we consider the *Phenomenology* as a speech act.

The emphasis here on effectivity does not mean that the effectivity of rhetoric is dissociable from figuration in Hegel's chapter on conscience. Indeed, Hegel illustrates the inadequacies, contradictions, and one-sidedness of self-certain conscience by means of a series of figures. The voice of conscience, the moral genius, the community of consciences, the beautiful soul, the hypocrite, the confessor, and the judge each embody a doomed and contradictory form of conscience. Within the *Phenomenology*'s narrative, conscience's own declaration inadvertently disrupts conscience's attempts to become entirely actual—insofar as conscience says too much, too little, or something that subverts the binding character for which it strives. Thus we will consider in this chapter how conscience performatively *succeeds* in actualizing itself by means of a declaration; but what it thereby, and unwittingly, makes actual are the contradictions and one-sidedness that are intrinsic to it. Conscience *fails* for this reason to be the unproblematic, immediately self-certain moral consciousness that it should be. For one, the inadvertent actualization of its contradictions by means of its declaration of its duty frustrates conscience's attempt to convince other consciousnesses of its moral character. Yet without this recognition of others, conscience cannot truly be all that it is supposed to be. In addition, while the declaration of conscience succeeds in performatively actualizing conscience as objective and universal, this actualization in fact produces contradictions for conscience. The declaration fails to unify conscience with its binding duty, and hence it fails to make conscience entirely commensurable with its act and with the duty of which it is certain.

The rhetorical failures of conscience's performative declaration land conscience in a constellation of contradictions between declaration and bindingness that propel Spirit forward. Insofar as the *Phenomenology* is an account of Spirit and its unfolding, we will see in the following pages to what degree excessive, unwitting discursive effects produce certain moments of failure *within* the text of the *Phenomenology* in the case of conscience. But Hegel's chapter on conscience is also significant as regards what constitutes "binding" not only for conscience in the *Phenomenology* but also for us who read it. These moments of failure on the part of conscience owing to excessive, unwitting discursive effects and results are also constitutive of *our* experience; for we are ourselves Spirit, in Hegel's understanding. Hegel's account of the complicated bond between saying and acting, and the unforeseeable rhetorical repercussions of performative saying, thus constitute an issue not only for the conscience described in the text but also for *us* when we attempt to establish such a bond. For we who read the *Phenomenology* are also, at the same time, as forms of Spirit, the topic of that text. What is true for Spirit should be at various levels true for us. The difficulties that befall conscience as it attempts to establish its word as binding, which should in turn guarantee that such duty is binding upon conscience, dramatize the imperfection of our own attempts at guaranteeing to others the morality of our individual convictions and our certainty of our duty. The text of the *Phenomenology* is thus peculiarly binding upon us, its readers; for it is, as I will show toward the end of this chapter, not only an abstract analysis of the unfolding of a theorized Spirit but also an analysis of that which we ourselves are. Conscience in Hegel's *Phenomenology* allegorizes the susceptibility of performatives to actualizing the unexpected—to accomplishing more than, less than, or something other than what was foreseen. In its illustrations of the inadvertent rhetorical effects of binding performative declaration, the chapter on conscience in the *Phenomenology* stages the vulnerability of our own speech acts to excessive and unpredictable effects. Hence the intrinsic risk of discrepancies between what we mean to say, what we actually do say, and what we accomplish in saying it is illustrated by Hegel's chapter on conscience in the *Phenomenology of Spirit*.

The formulation here of the tension between performativity and rhetoric is in certain respects narrower than in the previous chapter. It is more strictly indebted on the one hand to Austin and the definition of a performative as an utterance that does not state something true or false but instead performs what it says; and on the other hand to an understanding of rhetoric as a matter of effectivity—as how effects and meanings follow from particular formulations rather than from intentions and speaking subjects. Hence Judith Butler writes, "as a rhetorical agency, the Hegelian subject always knows more than it thinks it knows, and by reading itself rhetorically, i.e., reading the meanings it unwittingly *enacts* against those it explicitly *intends,* it recovers ever greater dimensions of its own identity."[1] This characterization of a rhetorical agency and of rhetorical reading invokes disruptive enactments or productions of meanings that do not fit the Austinian model of the performative. In this regard the term "rhetorical" refers not to specific elements of figurative language but rather to a dimension of enactment, performance, and production. Rhetoric is thus marked here by the inherent effectivity by means of which a result is achieved through language, despite the intentions of the agency to which those results are ultimately attributed.

Conscience's Dilemma

Let us begin by focusing on the frustrations that beset conscience in the *Phenomenology*. Conscience attempts to establish, for itself and for others, that it and its deeds are bound by duty in an unmediated fashion, and thus that it *is* moral conscience. This attempt takes the form of a declaration by conscience of its self-certainty:

> The content of the language of conscience is the *self that knows itself as essential being*. This alone is what it declares, and this declaration is the true actuality of the act, and the validating of the action. . . . This assur-

ance thus affirms that consciousness is convinced that its conviction is
the essence of the matter. (396/479)

The declaration is supposed to guarantee conscience's actualization and
recognition by others, for it should once and for all establish the unmediated bond between conscience and its certainty of its duty. In other
words, the declaration of conscience is on the one hand supposed to *reveal* to others that conscience is immediately bound by duty and on the
other hand thereby to *accomplish,* with the recognition of all, the final unfolding of conscience in which it truly attains such immediacy. The declaration is thus not intended by conscience as a constative statement of its
certainty. It is rather, to use a vocabulary that is obviously anachronistic
with respect to Hegel, conscience's attempt at a performative actualization of itself. Nonetheless, with its declaration conscience lands itself in a
set of predicaments with respect to what it has actually said about itself,
namely, that it has said more than, less than, or something otherwise antithetical to what is required to accomplish its own actualization and
recognition by other moral consciousnesses. In its declaration conscience
inadvertently shows itself to be one-sided in ways, as I will indicate subsequently, that thwart its actualization and throw into question the bonds of
certainty and immediacy that are supposed to guarantee the moral character of conscience and its duty.

It is in the sections on culture and morality, before the appearance
of conscience, that saying, as well as what saying accomplishes, first comes
to be at issue for the consciousness that is the subject of the *Phenomenology*.[2] The particular relationship between saying and doing one's *duty,*
however, and the kinds of recognition that result from doing one's duty,
are first investigated in Hegel's account of conscience. Hence in the dialectic of conscience, classic problems of rhetoric, persuasion, and deception arise with respect to duty, dissemblance, and their relationship to
conscience's private convictions. Here Hegel is close to Hobbes (although, of course, removed from him by 250 years and a somewhat different philosophical tradition) insofar as a kind of nominalism and its corruption are at stake—that is, insofar as the *name* of duty is supposed to
provide some guarantee of the morality of that duty, but is shown, as a
mere name, to be untrustworthy. In contrast to Hobbes, however, performative declaration is more explicitly at issue in the *Phenomology* than it was
in *Leviathan*—first, as the resolution of the problem of conscience's dissemblance and displacement; and second, with respect to the problem of
the incommensurability of conscience and its acts. In addition, the power
of discursive performance is also more concretely at issue in the *Phenomenology*'s depiction of hypocrisy, which conceals conscience's evil by means

of a declaration. Finally, a performing-saying is a necessity for conscience and the resolution of its contradictions, inasmuch as a reconciliatory yes is what brings acting conscience and judging conscience together and thus accomplishes the transition from the standpoint of morality to the standpoint of religion.

The conscience depicted in Hegel's *Phenomenology* is a distinctly Kantian conscience, for it is defined by an unmediated relationship to its duty, a bond of individual certainty. As is the case with sense-certainty at the very opening of the *Phenomenology* and again throughout at various stages of Spirit's unfolding, certainty initially appears to be an unmediated bond but turns out to be shot through with various forms of mediation. In an implicit criticism of Kant, whose *Critique of Practical Reason* had been published nineteen years earlier, the form of Spirit that is conscience is shown to be inadequate to the immediacy that it claims for itself. The apparent immediacy of the Kantian conscience is revealed by Hegel to contain the elements of its own undoing. In keeping with the propulsion of Spirit's unfolding by progressive contradictions, the failures of language in the dialectic of conscience to make conscience actual turn out to be the direct result of the *successes* of the performative declaration of conscience. In other words, insofar as conscience's performative declaration *succeeds,* conscience is drawn into contradiction and *failure* with regard to what it has in fact said and what it is supposed to be.[3] Thus the multiple insufficiencies and miscarriages of conscience derive not from the *inadequacy* of its performative declaration but from the *successes* of its performative declaration, which produce rhetorical failures, that is, failures in having unwittingly said more, less, or something other than what it meant to say.

I focus here on the account of conscience in the *Phenomenology* rather than the chapter on "Good Conscience" in the *Philosophy of Right* because the former offers more to the question of the bindingness of words in several respects. First, Hegel does not emphasize the declarations and language of conscience in the *Philosophy of Right* but instead focuses on conscience's self-certainty.[4] Second, the place of language in the text of the *Phenomenology* as a whole, as a hinge or mechanism of reflexivity, is far more significant than in the *Philosophy of Right.* While the *Philosophy of Right* unfolds the concept of right, in the *Phenomenology* consciousness unfolds in reflecting on itself. Hence the place of language in the text of the *Phenomenology* demands more attention. For example, whereas hypocrisy is *explained* in the *Philosophy of Right,* it is *discovered* in the *Phenomenology of Spirit;* hypocrisy is one of the forms that consciousness takes and is compelled to overcome in the progression of consciousness and of the text itself.

Hegelian *Gewissen* versus Hobbesian *Conscientia*

The shortcomings that Hobbes's and Hegel's accounts exhibit with respect to conscience as a foundation for morality reflect the etymological and tropological associations of the respective words for "conscience" in English and German. As the previous chapter has shown, Hobbes's account of conscience depends upon a purportedly more original meaning of the word that refers to shared knowledge, that is, "con-science." For Hobbes, the use of the word "conscience" to refer to—and moreover to produce by interiorization—a private sphere is the residue of a corruption by which public "con-science" and knowledge in general have been privatized and interiorized. The privatization and mediation of Hobbesian conscience by metaphor turns out to prove conscience's weakness as a foundation for morality. Hegel's account of conscience, in contrast, depends upon the etymological associations of the German word *Gewissen*. The "con-" of "conscience" is obviously not present in the German *Gewissen;* the German word emphasizes certainty rather than sharedness or a public knowledge. Conscience is literally *gewiß*, it is a form of certainty, a certainty of its own conviction. The dialectic of conscience in the *Phenomenology* unfolds as the necessary undoing of the *Gewißheit* of *Gewissen*. Thus it is conscience's certainty—and specifically the immediate and individual character of Hegelian certainty—that makes conscience dependent upon impulse and inclination, subjective, even evil, and thus disjoins conscience from the universal duty which it claims as binding upon itself.

In distinction from Hobbesian conscience, Hegelian conscience does not engage in rhetorical redescription out of vanity and self-interested duplicity, for the self-certain Hegelian conscience is incapable of feigning knowledge. This conscience is instead defined by the immediacy of its knowledge, an immediacy of utter and genuine certainty. It is precisely the immediacy that characterizes Hegelian conscience that draws it into contradiction and dissemblance. The dissemblance that conscience enacts in Hegel's text, in contrast to the dissemblance at stake in Hobbes's account, is a logical consequence of the essence of this form of Spirit rather than a calculated deception of others. Thus the function of declaration also differs in Hobbesian and Hegelian conscience. Whereas for Hobbes the declaration of individual conscience tends toward a self-serving dissemblance in which opinion is substituted for knowledge, conscience's declaration in the *Phenomenology* attempts to actualize conscience's genuine conviction. Thus the language of Hegelian conscience is not deceptive, for it is unable to produce a *false* actualization of its genuine conviction. Its function is simply to actualize immediate conviction, in a declaration of assurance: "Its intention, through being its own intention, is what is right; all that is required is that it should know this, and should state its conviction that its knowing and willing are right" (397/480). In other words, the truth of conscience, its self-certain conviction of its binding duty, is not opposed to falsehood or deception, because this conviction is too immediate to admit of any subversion.

> Therefore, whoever *says* he acts in such and such a way from conscience, speaks the truth, for his conscience is the self that knows and wills. But it is essential that he should *say* so, for this self must be at the same time the universal self. (397/480, first emphasis added)

In language the self of Hegelian conscience is actual, and it is all that needs to be made actual for the universality of duty to be established. The declaration thus allows for a performative translation between conviction and assurance, between individual and universal, such that the difference between them is itself *aufgehoben* (sublated).[5] Hence "what is valid for that self-consciousness is not the *action* as an *existence,* but the *conviction* that it is a duty, and this is made actual in language" (396/479). Although there is in Hegelian conscience an aspect of interiority, in that conscience withdraws "into" itself and away from worldly matters into pure duty, nevertheless this withdrawal always takes place within the environs of a community. Because it takes itself as immediately bound to a duty that is universal, conscience in Hegel requires the recognition of other consciences.[6]

Despite these comparisons, the two accounts of conscience are incongruous on several levels. Hobbes purports to offer a story of the use and abuse of the word "conscience" and of the effects of that abuse on knowledge and the order of names. Hegel's conscience, in contrast, is a form of Spirit; it is not a determinate historical, etymological, or even psychological moment. Moreover, whereas Hobbes's account is of conscience's corruption from an earlier, genuine public "con-science," Hegel gives an account of what conscience *is,* in its essence and its contradictions.[7] Thus Hegel's account of conscience unfolds what conscience necessarily *is,* rather than, with Hobbes, considering conscience as a metaphorically constituted name for ethical subjectivity. Finally, Hobbes's story of conscience is the story of the fall of conscience from shared knowledge to private knowledge to private opinion. In Hegel, conscience also suffers falls, namely, falls into contradictions—although for Hegel conscience's fall ultimately propels it from the immediate self-certainty of itself as duty, through the contradictions of the act of conscience, through the voice of conscience, the moral genius, the community of consciences, the beautiful soul, hypocrisy, confession, and judge, into absolute Spirit.

The Emergence of Conscience in the *Phenomenology of Spirit*

Conscience initially appears in the *Phenomenology* as a resolution to the antinomy of the moral worldview, wherein duty—which is an absolute and the truth of morality—is seen not to exist *in* the very consciousness that is supposed to be moral. The moral consciousness that precedes conscience finds its truth and reality in pure and binding duty, but it is itself separate from that duty. This disjunction between moral consciousness and the duty that makes it moral shows that the moral consciousness is in contradiction with itself, and thus moral consciousness "flees from this with abhorrence back into itself" (383/463–64). This moral consciousness that has fled back into itself becomes "pure conscience." The section on conscience that follows stages the unfolding of a decidedly Kantian conscience as the successor to the moral consciousness that has fled the disparity between duty and itself, a conscience that retrieves its morality out of contradiction by "retreating into itself" (383/464). The moral consciousness becomes conscience when it is "returned into itself [*in sich zurückgekehrt*]" (385/466), by bringing duty, its truth, from a position beyond consciousness back into itself. Conscience, in retreat from the dividedness that characterized moral consciousness and its duty, achieves morality as a state of immediacy, a state of "purity" that admits of no negation, no otherness, and no disparity between it and the binding duty that is its truth.[8] Since the object of conscience's knowledge is nothing outside of itself, there is no divide nor difference between conscience's knowing and what it knows, "the separation of the in-itself and the self has been done away with" (385/466).[9] Conscience is thus sheer self-certainty, the complete immediacy of self-assurance.[10]

Conscience is different from its predecessor, the moral consciousness, in that the pure duty that is conscience's truth is located within itself and hence is not unattainable for it. Because duty is duty *to act,* however, conscience must also consist of *action,* that is, the performance of its duty. The failed moral consciousness, in contrast, could not act, because the pure duty in which it finds its truth is so removed from actuality that it "consists in the empty abstraction of pure thought" (386/468). Conscience does not have the problem that moral consciousness has of bringing its duty from a beyond into actuality, for outcomes and intentions are not here in opposition and are not even at issue; conscience acts immediately, just as it knows its conviction immediately, and thus conscience simply "knows and does what is concretely right" (386/467). Through action, moreover, the duty of which conscience is certain should be actualized and gain the recognition of others.[11] The deed of conscience translates the essence of duty into its existence, it brings individual conviction into "something that has standing and existence" (388/470, translation modified). The act is the translation of conscience's conviction into an actual universality, and the recognition by others of this objectivity is also a recognition of conscience's universality. To put it another way, action is the being-for-others of the in-itself that binding duty is for conscience.

Thus conscience must perform its duty, it must act, in order truly to be conscience—both because duty demands action and because action permits others to confirm the universality of conscience's duty. Action, however, is also an in-itself and is for that reason separable from the conscience—the being-for-self—whose act it is. Indeed action is alien to conscience's being-for-self, because the reality to which conscience relates is an "actuality in itself" (389/472, translation modified). Thus action, which conscience's duty demands, also comes to reveal the discrepancy and contradiction within conscience, between the purity of its duty and the actualization of that duty. Hegel contrasts this possibility of conscience attaining recognition from other consciences to moral consciousness, whose truth exists only in pure thought alone and that therefore "does not act, or actualize anything at all" (388/470). The duty in which the moral consciousness that precedes conscience finds its truth remains pure and universal, for moral consciousness does not taint it with actualization, determinacy, and individuality. But precisely because moral consciousness does not act, it has no possibility for winning the recognition of others of its moral character. Its duty never achieves actualization and therefore remains an abstract universal.

The discrepancy between the in-itself character of action and the for-itself character of conscience is the direct source of the following contradiction: while conscience is the certainty of itself as pure duty, the reality and content of that duty exist "only in a *specific* actuality" (386/468, translation modified). The universality of the duty performed in the action turns out, therefore, to be in contradiction with the particularity associated with the action, and conscience falls apart into moments of contradiction between knowing pure duty and acting in a necessarily determinate (and hence impure) manner. In other words, conscience is certain of its pure duty, but actual duties and acts of duty are specific and are therefore not each entirely or solely the essence of pure duty. This contradiction recapitulates the dilemma of moral consciousness, which could not actualize its duty because of the remove of universality from the actuality and particularity of action. The specificity of individual duties is not commensurate with the purity of duty that conscience knows, for each action is an in-itself, which upon entering actuality and taking on being becomes a part of circumstance and has manifold results, conditions, and connections (389/472). This actuality is, moreover, a plurality, and hence evokes a plurality of duties. Conscience cannot relate immediately to such plurality and specificity, however, for it is the knowledge of *universal* duty, and it is the unity of self and duty. Conscience is for these reasons the "pure negativity" (387/469) of the difference between moral consciousness and its object.

This contradiction between the purity and immediacy of conscience's relation to duty and the multiplicity and actuality of determinate action further reveals the split between knowing and acting conscience, and it demonstrates that conscience cannot perform the duty that it is bound to perform. The rest of Hegel's chapter plays out the manifold aspects and movements of precisely this split. In one moment, conscience knows pure duty, that is, the knowing conscience knows a pure duty whose content is simply its own certainty and thus is not determinate. In its other moment, conscience must act and must give its action a content, a content that is necessarily in discrepancy with the purity of duty. Thus the problem of conscience's action—and, as I will show, its language—is a rhetorical one, in that the dutiful action is simultaneously and essentially the enactment of that which it does not intend, namely, the evocation of conscience's discrepancy with its duty: "What conscience thus expresses as duty in its action, it simultaneously denies. . . . Action is at the same time flight from action."[12] The very act that should embody conscience's duty denies that duty, such that specific action itself is incompatible with the universal duty that conscience must perform in order to be conscience.

Conscience, Evil, and the Name of Duty

The discrepancy between the universality of duty and the immediacy that characterizes conscience's certainty of itself forces conscience into the contradiction that conscience can equally well be evil or good, for any determinate content can occupy the place of duty as long as it is immediate.[13] Any determinate and individual content of duty that is derived from such pure immediacy can therefore come only from the natural elements of consciousness, from "impulses and inclinations" (390/473) with immediate determinations. Conscience thus falls into contradiction with itself inasmuch as it is supposed to be determined by duty rather than sheer impulse. Furthermore, conscience is shown to be open to any content and therefore to caprice, but more importantly to evil, where evil is defined as a disparity between the contingency and naturalness of inclination and the demands of pure duty.[14] Evil is a matter not primarily of malice or antigodliness but instead of putting one's own law above universal law, and thus an evil consciousness is determined by desires, nature, arbitrariness, and contingency, all of which are the antithesis of the universality to which conscience lays claim.[15]

Thus the *Philosophy of Right* emphasizes conscience's evil as its embrace of the "arbitrariness of its own particularity" (*PR* 167/261). Hegel explains that because conscience may make its particular will as universal duty into the content of its act, evil is a constitutive possibility for it. "The abstraction of self-certainty is always a part of *evil . . . only* the human being is good—but only insofar as he can also be evil. Good and evil are inseparable" (*PR* 167/261). Hegel adds that the declaration that one follows one's *own* conscience, as if conscience were a matter of individuality and not of universal duty, reveals the one who makes the declaration to be evil, insofar as evil *is* nothing other than taking an individual principle—subject to contingency and arbitrariness—as the principle of action, adhering to it instead of to the universal. This is a higher form of wrong, for wrong is defined as the simple difference from the universal. Hegel offers the maxim: "Therefore, when anyone says that he is acting according to his *own* law and conscience against others, he is saying, in fact, that he is wronging them" (402/486). The *Philosophy of Right* makes clearer how wrong is simply a difference from the universal: "If the particular will *for itself* is *different* from the universal, its attitude and volition are characterized by arbitrariness and contingency, and it enters into opposition to that which is right *in itself;* this is *wrong*" (*PR* 113/169). Evil is to self-consciousness what wrong is to consciousness; where consciousness may have a will that happens to be contrary to the universal and is for this reason wrong, self-consciousness instead takes as its principle a law that is contrary to the universal. In evil self-consciousness, the principle of the will exists for consciousness. The wrong will of simple consciousness, on the other hand, is the will (without principle and law, which are matters for self-consciousness) that is contrary to the universal.

The vulnerability of conscience to evil derives in part from a problem of naming, for what something is named or called by others is irrelevant to conscience, which finds its truth in its own conviction. Hence Hegel writes:

> Since morality lies in the consciousness of having fulfilled one's duty, this will not be lacking when the action is *called* cowardice any more than when it is *called* courage. The abstraction *called* duty, being capable of any content is also capable of cowardice. (391–92/474)

Hegel's assertion indicates that conscience is not bound by names but rather by its conviction, and thus it is bound by a particular rather than the universal. Hence conscience is open to evil, for conscience takes a principle for itself, but only its conviction serves to validate that principle. The contradiction into which conscience falls at this stage is a problem of rhetoric, insofar as the *name* of duty conflicts with the particularity that may instead be the content thereof. Hegelian conscience here appears to recapitulate the predicament that Skinner describes of rhetorical redescription: "What others call violence and wrongdoing, is the fulfilment of the individual's duty to maintain his independence . . . what they call cowardice, is the duty of supporting life. . . . but what they call courage violates both duties" (391/474). Insofar as duty is an abstraction, the name "duty" derives not from the content of a particular act but from the consciousness of having done duty. Hence while the acting conscience may call its action duty, holding fast to the one element of abstract duty, other consciences may perceive the acting conscience as violating another element of abstract duty, and thus as evil.

While this conflict of names may look like a recapitulation of the dilemma of rhetorical redescription, in that one and the same act is evaluated differently and thereby differently named, the dilemma of conscience here instead illustrates the rhetorical *condition* for the figure of rhetorical redescription, namely, the incommensurability between concrete acts and abstract values. That is, whereas rhetorical redescription is a figure of eloquence by which a concrete act is characterized by attributes that carry a particular moral value, the conflict of naming in the previously described instance derives from the diverse elements of abstract duty to which the acting conscience and other consciences may be holding in their perception of the act. Conscience in Hegel is defined by its immediate relationship to duty, and thus it does not allow for the calculated manipulation that Skinner points to in Hobbes's worries over rhetorical language; nevertheless, the incommensurability between the naming of moral values and the acts to which these names are applied is the condition of rhetorical redescription and of what Hegel describes as conscience's evil.

Dissemblance and the Problem of Recognition

From the disjunction between any specific action and the conviction that is the measure of what is called duty issues not only conscience's evil but also what Hegel calls conscience's dissemblance or displacement (*Verstel-*

lung), as well as the attempted overcoming of that displacement by a performative declaration, for it is the intervention of conscience's declaration that resolves the contradiction that *Verstellung* brings to conscience and its recognition. Nevertheless, as we will see, the problem of conscience's freedom from its specific acts comes to be reproduced with respect to conscience's freedom from its speech acts, that is, from the declarations of its duty and of its own being as that of conscience.

Verstellung involves the problem of how conscience enters into concrete existence through an action and thereby comes to exist for others. Conscience's existence for others, indeed its acknowledgment by other similar consciousnesses, is not incidental but rather is required for conscience's genuine existence. The problem with conscience's entry into existence for others and the possibility of dissemblance arises, as we have seen, from the "in-itself" character of its act. That is, conscience is itself sheer conviction of its duty, and yet in its action consciousness also "gives being to a specific content [*setzt eine Bestimmtheit als seiend*]" (394/477). In ontological terms, the fulfillment of binding duty in a particular action gives the action particular *being*, an actual, concrete existence, different from the universal and hence different from the conscience that performs the act. Thus, as Hegel points out, conscience is ultimately free from any specific acts that it performs. In fact, both acting conscience and acknowledging conscience are "free" from this action, for the act has its *own* being; it even *is* its own being. In other words, the problem of conscience acting is that conscience and certainty are not themselves action.[16] Once conscience's action takes on being and specificity, it is free from the conviction and the universality that defined it as an act bound by duty. The acknowledging consciousness can therefore no longer be certain about the acting consciousness; the self-certainty that they both share has become actual in an act that is now foreign to both of them. The recognition that the act was supposed to attain, and that was supposed to confirm the universality of conscience, instead brings uncertainty and nonrecognition by others.

The incommensurability between conscience and its action produces a contradiction concerning place or presence, that is, concerning the impossibility of conscience to be present *in* the very act by which conscience has nevertheless to attain the recognition of other consciences. "What, therefore, it [acting conscience] places before them it also 'displaces' [*verstellt*] again, or rather has straightway 'displaced' or dissembled" (394/477). Conscience performs its action as a measure of binding duty, but the performance itself is the occasion of the action taking on both specificity and freedom from the conscience that performs it and other consciences. Thus conscience "is not present [*ist da heraus*] at that point where others imagine it actually to be" (394/477). Conscience's knowing is *outside* the act, which means that the act cannot be acknowledged by others, since what must be acknowledged is conscience's *knowing* as its universality. The recognition that confers universality on the act is therefore not given insofar as an act is incommensurable with the universality of binding duty and does not have the self of conscience *in* it. Hence this foreignness of the act to both acting conscience and other consciences is conceivable as a difference of *place,* and is supported by the possibility of translating *Verstellung* as "displacement." Although Hegel's wording lends less support to the following approach, this difference between conscience and its act is also understandable in temporal terms, that is, in terms of the possibility of conscience *remaining with* or *in* its act. Conscience's freedom from its acts would then have to be considered in terms of a difference in temporality, the difference between the temporality of the punctual action and of the conscience that outlives it. Conscience cannot be *in* its acts, not primarily because there is no space *in* an action—for conscience is no more spatial in character than action is—but rather because conscience and action are simply incommensurable. They are utterly unlike one another and thus cannot *be* one another, and cannot be *in* one another either. The problem of *location* and interiority is therefore here seen as another form of the problem of identity and existence, the problem of the presence of conscience, when its *presence in* action is necessarily a displacement and dissemblance.

The Rhetorical Failures of Conscience's Performative Declaration

The declaration of conscience should resolve the problem of conscience being in its action—and hence the problems of dissemblance and evil—and thereby bring conscience recognition by other self-consciousnesses. Indeed in this account of conscience and its declaration, action is not alone what mediates between consciousnesses, but action *declared to be duty* is the "middle term [*Mitte*]" (396/479). Language is intrinsic to the unfolding of conscience, for it performatively transforms mere action into duty.[17] What conscience declares is nothing other than Spirit's certainty of itself and of its own truth. Moreover, this declaration is in itself the actualization of the act of duty in the eyes of other consciences; there is no other source of validity for conscience's deed. The declaration of conscience is therefore the performative transformation of conscience's act into objective duty; the declaration is no mere supplement to the action of conscience but is instead what makes the action into an action of conscience, an action done by the self-consciousness of duty and validated as such. Hegel's account also shows, however, that the performative declaration of conscience, by its very success, draws conscience into deeper contradictions. The declaration of conscience turns out performatively to render conscience in different moments both too subjective and too objective, too particular as well as too universal, and thus intensifies the alienation of conscience from its act and from the recognition it was supposed to achieve. In this regard, the performance that is the declaration of conscience's conviction, insofar as it succeeds, evokes other moments of failure. Let us look more closely at these failures.

Language and Objectivity

It is with respect to the problem of incommensurability, that is, the incommensurability of conscience with its acts, that language is introduced in Hegel's chapter on conscience, for while conscience as sheer conviction cannot exist for others in action, language is in contrast "the existence [*Dasein*] of Spirit" where existence entails actuality, presence, and being-for-others. "I" is not merely one word among other words in language, in this account. Rather, language is the self or the "I" that has become objective to others.[18] In language is where the self reflexively becomes "for itself" and thereby also "for others," as opposed to remaining sheerly in-itself. In Hegel's earlier chapter on culture, language performs the same function of bringing into existence and thus into being-for-others and presence the essence of self-consciousness: "In speech, self-consciousness, *qua independent separate individuality*, comes as such into existence, so that it exists *for others*. Otherwise the 'I,' this *pure* 'I,' is non-existent, is not *there*" (308/376). Through language a consciousness therefore speaks itself into objective existence. The objectivity of conscience's self, produced in language, brings to conscience the recognition of others; conscience can be brought precisely to the place where it is supposed to be, with the declaration serving as a guarantee of dutifulness alongside conscience's acts. Thus the declaration of conscience should resolve the problem of displacement—of the incommensurability between conscience and the expression of its duty in concrete acts.

Like the act of conscience, however, which should in effect translate conscience's individual certainty into an objectivity that others can acknowledge and recognize, the declaration of conscience acquires its own being and objectivity, which render it incommensurable with the subjective conscience it is supposed to objectify. The declaration of conscience's conviction takes on the character of an in-itself; for the declaration is it-self also an act from whose particularity conscience is removed by con-science's own universality. Like the act of conscience, the spoken assur-ances of conscience are now too much on the side of objectivity. With the assurance's performatively successful actualization, that assurance be-comes foreign to the self-consciousness to which it is supposed to belong. Hence the account of conscience's declaration of its duty repeats the fail-ures of the act of conscience, in which the objectivity of the act of duty ren-ders conscience ultimately incommensurable with duty and hence free from it.

Insofar as the declaration of conscience has taken on existence, it is too objective to be the speech of an immediately self-certain conscience: "The absolute certainty of itself thus finds itself, *qua* consciousness, changed immediately into a sound that dies away [*Austönen*], into an ob-jectification of its being-for-itself" (399/483). Similarly in the *Phenome-nology*'s section on "Culture," when an "I" utters itself, "that it is *perceived* or *heard* means that its *real existence dies away*" (309/376). The "sounding out" of conscience is the objectification of conscience in language, but as *objective* this sound does not hold to the *subjective* being of conscience. The *Austönen* of conscience is its performance of speech, but insofar as con-science produces speech, that speech takes on a being of its own and thus only its echo, not the performance itself, returns to conscience.[19] Con-science speaks and hears its own speech immediately, and yet this speech act, once performed, is not entirely its own because it is a being-for-others as well. But as we have seen, conscience's speech was *supposed* to ensure the presence of conscience in its act. The problem of conscience being *in* its acts is thus repeated with respect to conscience being *in* its speech; and the speech that should be conscience's being-for-self as well as its being-for-others is in fact performed so successfully that it is alienated from the conscience that it should objectify and actualize.

Language and Universality

As sense-certainty discovered early in the *Phenomenology of Spirit*, any at-tempt by consciousness to take a "this" ends up not with a specific object but with a universal.[20] In the declaration of conscience, this problem ap-pears as the problem of conscience taking its own certainty immediately by calling itself "I." For "I"—like the "this" of sense-certainty—is a univer-sal. The "I" of conscience names each and every self-consciousness as well as the particular conscience that tries to say it. Like the "this" of sense-certainty, conscience's "I" also refers to each and every "I," thus in the word "I" they coalesce (*zusammenfließen*) and the particular dissolves into the universal. The same quality by which conscience makes itself objective to itself in language by saying "I" belongs not to that self but to the language by which the self is made objective. It thereby exceeds that self and belongs to the language that may issue from any self; it is not exclusive to any one "I."[21] Thus conscience cannot say the "I" that it means, given the universalizing character of language, and thus cannot make itself and only itself objective, which is its intention.

A further problem arises insofar as conscience's declaration succeeds in rendering its act of duty universal—that is, in actualizing the act's universal character as duty.[22] Nonetheless conscience is a *particular* certainty of its conviction, and the declaration of conscience fails to put the particular conscience into that universal. To this degree, then, the declaration is too universal to be the actualization of particular conscience. Moreover, the declaration by conscience of its conviction turns out to be not just a declaration about its own act. The declaration itself, as the declaration that conscience attributes to itself *as* conscience, recognizes other consciences (by means of the universality of the word "I"), demands their recognition, and actualizes the recognition that they are the same.

> The declaration of this assurance in itself supersedes the form of its particularity. . . . In calling itself *conscience*, it calls itself pure knowledge of itself and pure abstract willing, i.e., it calls itself a universal knowing and willing which recognizes and acknowledges others, is the same as them—for they are just this pure self-knowing and willing—and which for that reason is also recognized and acknowledged *by* them. (397/480, translation modified)

The declaration of conscience is thus a universalizing and performative act of speech; it makes the deed of conscience actual as duty but also rhetorically recognizes the universality of duty and its existence in other consciences, which are by this universality rendered "the same" as itself. By "calling itself conscience," conscience demands the recognition of its acts as universal duty and simultaneously recognizes, albeit implicitly, that others who are called conscience merit the same recognition. This "calling itself conscience" is thus not merely a referential but indeed a performative calling, for it both demands and effects recognition by others of the universality that it is. In calling itself conscience, conscience thereby cancels out its own particularity and lays claim to a purity and universality that undermine the very particularity that does the calling. The rhetorical effects of conscience's declaration foil its performative accomplishment.

Figures of Failure

As the previous sections have shown, the declaration of conscience's conviction does not thoroughly bind conscience to its act and does not win conscience the recognition of other consciences. Instead it gives rise to further levels of one-sidedness and contradiction. Hegel portrays these moments of one-sidedness and contradiction in the *Phenomenology* in a series of figures, namely, the voice of conscience, the community of consciences, the beautiful soul, the hypocritical conscience, and the judging and confessing consciences. Through these exemplary figures Hegel's account unfolds various dimensions of failure spawned by the performative success of conscience's declaration of its certainty of its duty.

The Moral Genius

Hegel's depiction of the voice of conscience presents the form of conscience which is too subjective, and therefore too one-sided, to be truly one with the universal of which it is convinced as its duty. Although conscience's language validates the act of conscience by bringing its conviction into concrete existence, the declaration of conscience does not solve the problem of conscience's evil—its embrace of the arbitrariness of its own particularity—for conscience remains particular and thus opposed to universal laws and duties.[23] Hegel therefore calls it a "moral genius," the inventor of its own rules, the source of its own obligations.[24] This spontaneous and arbitrary conscience, arbitrary because it adheres to *itself* as duty, is the voice (*die Stimme*) of conscience. The voice of conscience is conscience's inward certainty of itself and thus falls on the side of its being-for-self; it represents conscience's immediate self-certainty. It stands in contrast to the performative declaration of conscience by which conscience should become actual for others and win their recognition. The figure of the voice of conscience models conscience as immediate and interior, in opposition to the external, performative language of conscience that functions as its being-for-others. This is not, however, an inadvertent moment of phonocentrism on the part of Hegel. For it is not Hegel, but rather conscience, that falls into a phonocentric fantasy of immediacy. Conscience's phonocentrism lies in its clinging to the ideal of immediacy, to the fantasy of an "interior voice" that would be both its own and an unmediated presence of universal duty.

We can see here a reference to Kant's "genius" in the *Critique of Judgment*, which invents the rule for its own art. Conscience is a "moral genius" because it takes itself as the source of its rule, of universal duty, rather than looking to anything else or any other consciousness for a universal rule of morality. For Kant, genius is "the innate mental disposition [*ingenium*] through which *nature gives the rule to art.*"[25] Moral genius would then be an *ingenium* prior to any concrete content of morality; it would be the rule-making capacity constitutive of morality. Moreover, Kant's artistic "genius" is famously described as inimitable; the genius gives the model that others can only imitate. In this vein, Hegel's moral genius may be understood as creating its own model, following no example, and inventing its own rules. It knows duty from out of itself, following no predetermined rule or pattern.

Hegel connects Kant's notion of artistic genius to what Hegel describes as the "divine" character of this voice: "[Conscience] is the divine creative power which in its Notion possesses the spontaneity of life" (397/481). Conscience does not adhere to any predetermined *definition* of duty but rather creates on its own the act of duty. This ability to create the duty of which it is the knowing is a divine ability, the power to give itself the rule of duty and follow no rule or example. Thus Quentin Lauer says of this divinity, "Conscience makes anything right; it cannot be questioned; its prerogatives are 'divine.' Gradually conscience becomes God, not merely for the one who acts according to it but also for the community; it is the only force that has any right to dictate conduct at all; it is all that counts."[26] The "voice" of conscience in its inward immediacy and divinity cannot be the same as the declaration that conscience must perform in order to win the acknowledgment of other self-consciousnesses as proof of its universality. The voice of conscience is in fact too interior and too subjective to achieve the universality that conscience as the self-certainty of duty should achieve. It is instead the simple worship and contemplation of itself.[27]

The Community of Consciences

The emergence of the voice of conscience and its divinity are the first clear evidence of how Spirit unfolds by way of conscience from morality into religion. The one-sided "solitary divine worship" of the single conscience turns out to be "the divine worship of a community" (397/481) of individual consciences, each member of which joins in "the rejoicing over this mutual purity," the contemplation of itself and others as universal selves (398/481). This community of consciences also finds itself to be in multifarious contradictions. For one, the outward manifestation of this worship is the "utterance of the community concerning its own Spirit" (398/482). The character of this utterance, however, is not immediate, but is instead still an utterance "*concerning* [*über*]" itself, and to this extent the utterance is incommensurable with conscience's immediacy. In addition, although each conscience inwardly knows itself to be universal self-consciousness, assures others of this, and rejoices over it with others, this community of consciences does not share the objectivity of duty through their declarations, but rather each rests content with its subjective consciousness.[28] This community does not share an objective consciousness; it is rather a collection of self-certainties, each of which derives its duty from itself. Thus Hegel indicates that this conscience must "[withdraw] into its innermost being, for which externality has vanished . . . into the contemplation of the 'I' = 'I,' in which this 'I' is the whole of essentiality and existence" (398/482). This withdrawal from all externality renders conscience pure but utterly poor, such that "consciousness exists in its poorest form, and the poverty which constitutes its sole possession is a vanishing" (399/482–83). In sticking so intensely to itself, conscience vanishes into itself, for what it is certain of is no content but an inward withdrawal.[29]

The Beautiful Soul

As we have seen, while on the one hand the inwardness of conscience's self-certainty leads it to founder within itself, on the other hand the speech of this pure conscience becomes too much being-for-others, too alien from the conscience that performs the utterance. In this respect conscience recapitulates the *Phenomenology*'s earlier chapter on the unhappy consciousness.[30] In the face of this contradiction, "and, in order to preserve the purity of its heart, it flees from contact with the actual world. . . . In this transparent purity of its moments, an unhappy, so-called 'beautiful soul'" (399–400/483–84). In the beautiful soul "duty is only a matter of words [*liegt nur in den Worten*], and counts as a being-for-another" (400/484). The words that mediate between consciences and thereby should assure each of each other's dutiful being are in the end *merely* words, a form of universality and being-for-another that is *not* also and immediately conscience's own being-for-itself. The words of conscience are sundered from conscience's particularity and self-certainty; as universals they are abandoned by the individual being-for-self of conscience. Hence when conscience has to come up with some specific content for the duty of which it is supposed to be immediately certain, "the content which it gives to that knowing is taken from its own self, as *this specific* self" (401/484–85). Conscience's declaration of its relationship to binding duty is still on the side of universality, but the acting conscience in its evil moment acts as a matter of its particularity and individuality.[31]

Language should be the mediating element of conscience, should serve as the assurance to other self-consciousnesses of conscience's conviction and thus become the means whereby each could acknowledge the others and be acknowledged. With the fleeing of conscience into itself, however, the language of conscience becomes a matter of each conscience's being-for-itself.

Hypocrisy and Its Unmasking

In attempting to win the recognition of others through its declaration and yet remaining evil in clinging to its own particularity instead of to the universal, conscience falls into hypocrisy. Evil is, as we have seen, defined by Hegel as a state of disparity between conscience's certainty of itself and the universal. In contrast to evil as a state of such disparity, hypocrisy occurs when evil conscience *declares* that it is in conformity with binding universal duty, and its declaration serves to cover over the disparity and even antithesis between its particular self-certainty and binding universal duty. Whereas evil is therefore a "state," namely, the situation of this disparity, hypocrisy is a concealment of such a state by means of a declaration. The hypocritical declaration claims a state of conformity with duty. The hypocritical declaration thus denies the disparity with and even antithesis from duty that is conscience's evil. Hypocrisy is therefore a characteristic of consciousness solely when consciousness speaks, for in hypocrisy conscience's language covers over the evil of the consciousness whose individuality is antithetical to the universal.[32]

But the declaration of hypocritical conscience is not merely a tool used to misrepresent conscience. It, too, has rhetorical effects. Conscience's hypocritical declaration gives conscience an existence, that is, a being-for-others, that lays claim to dutifulness. The language of conscience is not just a concealment of its evil from other consciousnesses but even from itself, for hypocrisy "demonstrates its respect for duty and virtue just by making a show of them, and using them as a mask to hide itself from its own consciousness, no less than from others" (401/485–86). This dutifulness to which conscience lays claim in its hypocritical declaration of conformity with duty is itself antithetical to conscience's evil essence. Even in enacting a hypocritical declaration that covers over conscience's disparity from its duty, conscience evokes the binding character of duty upon conscience. Because the language of hypocritical conscience actualizes conscience as dutiful—although conscience is not as dutiful as it claims—this language must be countered in order for hypocrisy to be unmasked.[33] The unmasking requires that the *show* of virtue and duty be revealed as excessively being-for-others and thus as a contempt for duty and virtue as an essence.[34] Hypocrisy must be shown to be a show, a show that covers over the fact that evil conscience puts its own law above the universal.

Judging Conscience

Evil does not disappear from the dialectic of conscience at the moment that hypocritical conscience is unmasked by a judging universal conscience. For not only the evil consciousness but also the universal consciousness, insofar as it judges evil consciousness, is itself evil, clinging to its subjective will as law.[35] Judging consciousness, in opposing evil consciousness in its particularity, is according to Hegel just as particular as that which it opposes. In holding to its own law in order to judge evil conscience, and in opposing the particularity of that evil conscience, judging consciousness endorses the evil of holding to one's own law; thus "this zeal does the very opposite of what it means to do" (402/487). In its condemnation it does what it simultaneously condemns.[36] Thus conscience in Hegel's account rhetorically accomplishes in its performance that which it does not intend and moreover that which contradicts its intention.

Judging consciousness is thus not only evil but also hypocritical, for "it is the hypocrisy which wants its judging to be taken for an *actual* deed, and instead of proving its rectitude by actions, does so by uttering [*aussprechen*] fine sentiments" (403/487). Judging consciousness makes a "show" or performance of virtue and duty in passing off its condemnation of evil consciousness as an action, where in fact judging consciousness remains merely thought and therefore does not suffer the antitheses of individuality and universality. In declaring its "fine sentiments [*vortrefflich(e) Gesinnungen*]," judging consciousness is "altogether the same as that which is reproached with making duty a mere matter of words" (403/487). In other words, in its mere utterance of a condemnation of the evil consciousness, judging consciousness makes a show of being virtuous and dutiful, and to this extent evokes the appearance of its dutifulness. This utterance, however, is nothing other than a one-sided evil, an adherence to the judging consciousness's particularity. The utterance of judging conscience is not a performative actualization of duty but rather a performative actualization of the *show* of duty. Judging consciousness talks of duty, but "duty without deeds is utterly meaningless [*(die Pflicht) hat ohne Tat gar keine Bedeutung*]" (403/488). Thus in judging conscience's hypocritical declaration, the utterances of conscience constitute once again a rhetorical failure precisely insofar as they are performatively successful, that is, precisely insofar as they actualize the show of judging conscience without actualizing the duty and universality that conscience should be.

Confession and the Hard-Hearted Conscience

The fact that judging conscience is as evil as the conscience it condemns provides the possibility to resolve the division of consciousness at this stage between universal consciousness and individual consciousness. The evil consciousness "*through this likeness,* comes to see its own self in this other consciousness" (403/487). The likeness between the evil conscience and the judging conscience is, according to the text, something to be *confessed;* it is here that language will perform a revelation and reconciliation that accomplishes a transition from the sphere of conscience to that of religion. Hegel writes of the evil acting conscience:

> Perceiving this identity and giving utterance to it, he confesses this to the
> other, and equally expects that the other, having in fact put himself on
> the same level, will also respond in words in which he will give utterance
> to this identity with him, and expects that his mutual recognition will
> now exist in fact. (405/489–90)

The evil conscience declares or expresses (*aussprechen*) the identity it perceives between itself and the judging conscience. Through the likeness with the judging conscience, acting conscience regains its immediate identity as Spirit, and thus the language of the confession is the "*existence of Spirit as an immediate self*" (405/490).[37]

The language of conscience's confession does not straightforwardly actualize the likeness of acting and judging conscience, however. Instead, the judging conscience has a "hard heart" and rejects the confession, which according to Hegel means that this consciousness "refuses to let his own *inner* being come forth into the *outer* existence of speech" (405/490). In rejecting the confession, judging conscience clings to its one-sidedness and particularity, even in the face of the other's supersession of its own particularity.[38] Hence this supposedly universal consciousness falls into a performative contradiction based on speech (*Rede*) and the recognition that it should win. On the one hand, judging conscience does not recognize the words of confession of acting conscience; on the other hand, it gives its judgment of acting conscience in words (*in der Rede*), and this judgment is the expression of its self-certainty as Spirit, the "outer existence of this inner being." In other words, while judging conscience gives itself existence as Spirit through speech, it does not grant the other existence as Spirit through speech.[39] Because judging conscience "cannot attain to an identity with the consciousness it has repulsed, nor therefore to a vision of the unity of itself in the other, [it] cannot attain to an objective existence" (406/491). Judging conscience's rejection of the evil acting conscience and its refusal to recognize its unity and identity with that conscience means that universal consciousness cannot become objective, cannot exist outwardly, but rather can only cling to its immediacy, "wasting itself in yearning and pining away in consumption [*zerfließt in sehnsüchtiger Schwindsucht*]" (407/491). The hard heart of judging conscience must, according to Hegel, be broken.

How can this hard-hearted conscience be broken and thus reconciled with the confessing conscience? Hegel reminds us that this is a process, that the process has its own existence, that is "only a *moment* of the whole." Because they are but moments of a whole, evil conscience "has to surrender its one-sided, unacknowledged existence of its particular being-for-self," and judging conscience "must set aside its one-sided, unacknowledged judgment" (407/492). The force of the word "must" here is ambiguous. Up until this point in the dialectic of conscience, this form of consciousness could be seen as unfolding by what appears to be its *own* necessity; that is, the contradictions within consciousness led to the antitheses of conscience. Here, however, Hegel seems to appeal to the fact that simply because this *is* Spirit, this culminating antithesis between the confessing conscience and the hard heart has to be resolved. In other words, the "must" and "has to" reflect the fact that it is Spirit in which these contradictions occur, and because there *is* Spirit, these elements are reconciled, since that is what Spirit *is*.[40]

Reconciliation and the Yes of Conscience

Given the objectifying character of conscience's declaration, as indicated earlier, reconciliation between these two consciousnesses must also take place in and as a word, for this reconciliation must exist objectively as the *Aufhebung* (sublation) of the antithesis of confessing conscience and the hard heart.[41] In forgiving the other, universal consciousness renounces its stubborn being-for-self and its subjectively determined judgment, just as acting conscience has in confessing renounced its subjectively determined action and its one-sided actuality.[42] But this reconciliation must have objective existence; it *is* and therefore occurs in a word, in a word of reconciliation.[43] Absolute Spirit is, then, this antithesis existing as a unity and moreover as a word. The word *is* Spirit "which beholds the pure knowledge of itself *qua universal* essence, in its opposite, in the pure knowledge of itself *qua* absolutely self-contained and exclusive *individuality*" (408/493). Spirit sees the pure knowledge of itself in its opposite, sees the universality and essentiality in the self-absorbed individuality; Spirit is that form of consciousness that sees the equality of these two moments. The objective existence of this seeing, of this recognition by Spirit of itself in the reciprocal recognition of universal and acting consciousness, is the word of reconciliation.

The yes with which the two consciousnesses are reconciled is, according to Hegel, the appearance of God in the midst of those who know themselves to be pure knowing, and thus morality becomes religion. As the objective existence of Spirit, the word is neither an act nor a thought, and hence it is not caught up in an antithesis of action and universality. The word, precisely as particular *and* universal, *is* itself the reconciliation of individual acting consciousness and universal judging consciousness; the word is the actuality of the unity that Spirit is, the unity of the antithesis of the previous consciousnesses. The "I" that emerges is the existence of a new form of consciousness, the "expanded" consciousness that is dual and contains the antithesis of the acting and judging consciousness. In saying yes, the existence (which means being-for-others, exteriority, and actuality) of the antithesis of acting and judging consciousness is *aufgehoben* (sublated).

There are at least two, perhaps not incompatible, ways to read the final two pages of the section on conscience and its reconciliation. On the one hand, it seems that Hegel shifts the scope of the whole procedure, such that reconciliation does not happen between these two consciousnesses as they have been described. Rather, these two consciousnesses are instead "retroactively" defined as moments of Spirit, and because they are moments in Spirit, they come to be reconciled: "The *self* that carries out the action, the form of its act, is only a *moment* of the whole, and so likewise is the knowledge, that by its judgement determines and establishes the distinction between the individual and universal aspects of the action" (407/492). Because there *is* Spirit, these consciousnesses are only moments of it. The text is in the position to remind us of this, to invoke the necessity of the *Aufhebung* on the basis of our knowledge as onlookers that this is an account of Spirit. On the other hand, the second explanation for the breaking of the hard heart is not a teleological one but rather depends on the dynamic intrinsic to judging and acting consciousness alone: because the acting consciousness perceives and confesses its likeness to universal consciousness, its particularity is "superseded" (*aufgehoben*), and it "displays itself as in fact a universal [*stellt sich . . . in der Tat als Allgemeines dar*]" (407/492). As universal, it is no different than the universal consciousness that judges it; hence "it returns from its external actual existence back into itself as essential being and therein the universal consciousness thus recognizes itself [*es kehrt aus seiner äußeren Wirklichkeit in sich als Wesen zurück; das allgemeine Bewußtsein erkennt also darin sich selbst*]." Because the evil acting conscience renounces its particularity, and "turns its back on its actual existence [*seine Wirklichkeit wegwirft*]," the universal conscience, which is withdrawn from actuality into universality, is able to see itself in it, and mutual recognition is achieved.[44] Since both consciousnesses are now essential rather than actual, their equality is accomplished.

Saying Too Much and Too Little

In each of the aforementioned figures of conscience, words and language both succeed and fail to do what conscience would have them do; insofar as they succeed performatively, they fail rhetorically, in terms of that which they enact. The declaration of conscience appears on the scene in order to resolve conscience's alienation from its own acts and its dissemblance, both of which reflect the absence of conscience in its acts, which take on independent existence and thus are not immediately one with the dutiful conscience that performs them. The declaration of conscience should bind conscience to its acts, but in fact the declaration also acquires concrete and particular existence. It becomes an in-itself just as the act of conscience became an in-itself. The declaration is something distinct from conscience, thereby confounding rhetorically the binding that conscience sought to achieve performatively. Moreover, the declaration of conscience should bring conscience the recognition of other consciences, but precisely in becoming actual for others, conscience's declaration becomes a performance in its own right—it becomes too objective, a mere sounding out and echo. While on the one hand the declaration of conscience is too objective to embody the universality of conscience, on the other hand the language of the declaration of conscience succeeds in performatively actualizing conscience's universality but does not thereby allow conscience to say the "I" that it alone is. Furthermore, the duty that conscience calls its own is rendered too universal to be binding upon such a subjective form of consciousness.

These complicated constellations of conscience's performative success and rhetorical failure, as we have seen, are unfolded in terms of a series of exemplary figures. The voice of conscience is the moral genius, immediate and self-certain but too subjective to live up to the universal character that conscience should have as the consciousness of duty. The beautiful soul speaks mere words and is withdrawn from acting out its duty, and thus it cannot win the recognition of others, a recognition that conscience requires as a reflection of its universality. The hypocritical conscience, in contrast, covers over the discrepancy between its self-certainty and binding universal duty—that is, covers over its evil—by means of its declarations, and it is for-others in a way that the beautiful soul is not. The confession of evil, however, breaks conscience into two forms, namely, the one that confesses its evil and the one that judges the confessing conscience. Hypocrisy, however, also belongs to the judging consciousness, for in "uttering fine sentiments" it gives its judging to be taken as an actual deed rather than mere thought. The identity between judging conscience and judged conscience is declared and thus rendered actual for others by the confession of the judged conscience, but the hard-hearted judging conscience rejects the confession and thereby refuses that exteriorizing utterance that is conscience's being-for-others. The hard heart of judging conscience breaks, it grants forgiveness to the judged conscience, and the two are reconciled at the end of the chapter on conscience. This reconciliation is made objective, once more, in a word, in a yes. However, with this binding yes, conscience is no longer conscience but religion, the Spirit that knows Spirit, the consciousness of absolute being. Thus even the reconciling yes is no longer simply the yes of conscience but the actualization of the next moment of Spirit, namely, religion.

Is there a rhetoric of conscience that would not collapse into the contradictions of being either too much for-it-self or too much for-others, too particular and too universal, too subjective and also too objective? What could make a universal duty binding on conscience, or make a declaration binding on the concrete existence and acknowledgment of that conscience and its duty? Insofar as Hegel's *Phenomenology* is a philosophy of the subject, even a philosophy where substance becomes subject and Absolute Spirit unfolds into concrete existence, the problem of interiorized conscience and exteriorized others bedevils the conscience of the *Phenomenology*. Hegelian conscience is a contradictory moment of subjectivity, for subjectivity is itself contradictory insofar as it is viewed in one finite moment, in the finitude of a particular aspect of its unfolding as Absolute Spirit. What would be a conscience that would not fall into the contradictions of subjectivity, interiority, and exteriority, and that would not, in the end, have to be religion? As we will see in the following chapter, Heidegger formulates an enigmatic conscience that ecstatically exceeds subjectivity in *Sein und Zeit* (*Being and Time*).

Performativity and the *Phenomenology of Spirit*

As we have seen, the performative declaration of conscience stymies the very actualization and recognition for which conscience strives, by virtue of what conscience inadvertently says and effects in its declaration. In this regard Hegel's chapter can be read as dramatizing what Denise Riley refers to in *The Words of Selves* as the "set of mechanical effects which spring up, felicitously or miserably, as that inescapable unconscious of language."[45] But questions of enacting, effecting, rhetoric, and performativity are not at issue here with respect solely to conscience's declaration. They are an issue for us as well, insofar as for Hegel we are ourselves forms of Spirit. As Jean-Luc Nancy writes, "[The word] 'We' [in the *Phenomenology*] designates neither a corporation of philosophers nor the point of view of a more elevated knowledge—and this, quite precisely, because this 'we' *is us,* us all."[46] The kinds of failures that conscience undergoes owing to excessive and unwitting discursive effects are also failures constitutive of our experience as speakers. Thus Hegelian conscience allegorizes the vulnerability of our own speech acts to unforeseen results.

The difficulties that befall conscience as a result of its performative declaration dramatize the imperfection of our own performatives. The failures of conscience's speech act are, in addition, instructive with regard to the *Phenomenology* as a whole, when taken as a speech act in its own right.[47] Before considering how conscience's speech act is instructive with respect to the *Phenomenology* as a whole, let us first ask this: How can the *Phenomenology* be considered a speech act? Hegel's preface suggests that the *Phenomenology* is not simply *about* the unfolding of Spirit but instead *enacts* the unfolding of Spirit. The book should thus be binding upon the world in a peculiar way, as the very movement and unfolding of Spirit *in the world.* The narration of Spirit's progress in the *Phenomenology,* according to Hegel, is strangely inseparable from, and perhaps even performs, that progress itself.

The possibility of reading the *Phenomenology of Spirit* as a speech act, as a performative text with binding force, hinges in large part on the *darstellen,* or presenting, to which Hegel refers when he writes, "It is this becoming of Science as such, or of knowledge, that this Phenomenology of Spirit . . . presents [*darstellt*]" (15/31, translation modified). *Darstellung* has several valences in German that are analogous to those associated with the English word "presentation." It connotes an element of description (as it is translated by A. V. Miller) as well as an element of performance, that is, the *action* of presentation.[48] The question of how to think the *Darstellung* of the *Phenomenology* is inseparable from that of how to think the "becoming of Science" that Hegel claims is *dargestellt,* or "presented," in the text. If *darstellen* is a form of description, then the *Phenomenology* would be a text *about* the becoming of Science, and thus should fulfill the constative task of describing that becoming. The *Phenomenology* would thus represent and describe "actual knowing" as the unfolding, fluid character of truth itself. According to Hegel, however, "actual knowing" involves understanding "the diversity of philosophical systems as the progressive unfolding of truth" rather than concentrating on the "antithesis of truth and falsity" (2/12). Such "actual knowing" requires attention to unfolding, to the "fluid nature" (*flüssige Natur*) of truth, to the "organic unity" of the forms of truth. In this regard John McCumber writes that Hegel gives us

> his own great original contribution, that of narrative development, so that the Concept, like everything "true" in his sense, is not something existing in a static state to be inspected but develops itself dynamically, as the systematizing of a company of words which themselves, as utterances sounding in time, are radically dynamic.[49]

When Hegel demands a philosophical attentiveness to "the real issue [*die Sache selbst*]" of a philosophical work, this "real issue" is not a static depiction resulting from the work but instead the process by which the aim becomes actual, for "the aim by itself is a lifeless universal [*der Zweck für sich ist das unlebendige Allgemeine*]" (2/13). Thus the life of a concept, rather than its representation, is of philosophical concern; "life" refers to process, movement, and the event of becoming—each of which Hegel associates with the *Phenomenology* itself.

The relationship between the "life" of texts and concepts to the "life" that is attained by self-consciousness in the text of the *Phenomenology* is a question. Can we speak of living words or living texts in the same way that we speak of the life of Spirit? Can the life of Spirit unfold apart from the words of the *Phenomenology*? Is the *Phenomenology* descriptive, or is the "life" of the concept of Spirit there unfolded, and what would be the epistemological criteria for deciding this question?[50] In the chapter of the *Phenomenology* on "The Truth of Self-Certainty," Hegel considers the life of self-consciousness. He defines self-consciousness as a living being, rather than as a mere being, insofar as self-consciousness is "reflected into itself," and is the "passive separating-out of the shapes [that] becomes, just by so doing, a movement of those shapes or becomes Life as a *process*" (107/141). Thus the life of Spirit is like the life Hegel describes in the preface; it is a process, a becoming, "the self-developing whole which dissolves its unfolding and in this movement simply preserves itself" (108/142, translation modified). But life is also at stake, according to Hegel, for the philosophical text. Hegel claims that without life, a philosophical work is dead, it consists of an aim severed from the process of its becoming, and "the bare result is the corpse which has left the guiding tendency behind it" (3/13). The process of Spirit's becoming in the *Phenomenology of Spirit* is its life, whereas mere results are but corpses, as they are devoid of the process and self-movement that is the life of Spirit.[51] If the *Phenomenology* is truly a philosophical text, then it does not merely narrate and describe the becoming of Science but instead unfolds and posits the progress of Spirit in a performative fashion.

The eventlike, dynamic character of Hegel's work has been thematized in twentieth-century phenomenology. Eugen Fink offers a description of Hegel's nonrepresentational, nondescriptive way of philosophizing, where this philosophizing consists not of "thinking-about" but instead of what Fink calls a "thought-event":

> Hegel's philosophy cannot simply be extracted from its text like other kinds of events and incidents are extracted from a report, —this philosophy is a thought-event, which exactly breaks open and destroys our sealed-up knowledge of the world, —which dissolves our embedded, habitual ways of speaking.[52]

Likewise Heidegger focuses on the positing and experiential components of the *Phenomenology*. Heidegger's claim that in Hegel "the presentation of phenomenal knowledge in its appearing is itself science" suggests that *Darstellung,* or presentation, is not merely a representation of *Wissen,* or knowledge, but is instead the positing of *Wissen,* for *Wissenschaft* (Science) does not occur without *Darstellung.*[53] Hence the *Phenomenology* is not separate from the becoming of Spirit that it presents and represents. For this reason Heidegger emphasizes that the *Phenomenology* is an *experience* of consciousness, as proclaimed in fact by the original title of the *Phenomenology,* "Science as the Experience of Consciousness."[54] This emphasis on experience, rather than on representation or description, is also present in Heidegger's emphasis on the interrelatedness between *Darstellung, Erfahrung* (experience), and *Wissenschaft:* "Experience, in presenting, is Science . . . [T]his title heads a work that performs [*ausführt*] the reversal of consciousness by presenting it." Likewise, "experience is the movement of the dialogue between natural and absolute knowledge."[55] The experience of the *Phenomenology* is here a performing, positing movement, a linguistically mediated and constituted movement of "conversation"—itself a doing that consists only of saying.

Hegel's discussion of the speculative proposition in the preface provides another approach to the question of the performativity of the *Phenomenology of Spirit.* There Hegel indicates that the propositions of the *Phenomenology* do not predicate of a subject, they are not simply "about" Science and Spirit. Rather, the speculative propositions of Hegel's text unfold from subject to predicate, they unfold the subject *as* or *into* the predicate, so that the subject by the end of the sentence is not the same subject as it was to begin with.[56] For this reason the "is" of the predicative propositions of the *Phenomenology* is a dynamic one, and the propositions them-selves are better understood not as predicative but as unfolding, where the "is" marks a movement of the Concept or *Begriff,* its becoming-other, rather than being a tool for attaching predicates to static subjects.[57] Per-haps the very difficulty of Hegel's writing derives from the way in which it is not merely a text *about* Spirit but rather is, or claims to be, the event of Spirit's unfolding.[58] In this regard Hegel also indicates the limitations of the proposition as a means of carrying out Science; for in rendering static the subject and accidental the predicates, the predicative proposition loses or at least eclipses the quality of movement and fluidity that knowl-edge requires, as well as eclipsing the self-movement that belongs to the Concept.[59] Science is thus entirely different than predication, representa-tion, and propositions "about," for each of these degrade philosophy into what Hegel calls "lifelessness." The enactment of Hegel's "scientific" method "consists partly in not being separate from the content, and partly in determining the rhythm of its movement on its own" (35/55, transla-tion modified).[60] The scientific method is, for Hegel, an enactment of its content—in short, it is performative.

Insofar as Hegel's *Phenomenology* claims not to be *about* but instead to *accomplish* the becoming of Spirit that it narrates, it appears to claim for itself a form of bindingness and performativity. But within the *Phenome-nology* the account of conscience offers an allegory of the potential for mis-carriages and failures of performatives. Thus in the very text that seems to claim for itself a performative character, the dialectic of conscience unfolds rhetorical failures that derive from the successes of conscience's performative language. The contradictions that arise in the chapter on conscience evoke some of the same questions of bindingness and perfor-mativity as the text of the *Phenomenology* as a whole, namely: Is language an act? Can saying make something so? How is a genuine declaration to be distinguished from empty words? Can words alone accomplish binding?

I have argued that conscience in the *Phenomenology* allegorizes the susceptibility of performatives to actualizing the unexpected and to ac-complishing more than, less than, or something other than what is in-tended or foreseen by the agent ostensibly responsible for the speech act. Do the failures associated with conscience's performative declaration within the *Phenomenology* reflect upon the performativity and bindingness of the *Phenomenology of Spirit* as a whole? In other words, if the *Phenome-nology* should be somehow binding on the world, as the performative un-folding of Spirit, and yet in the chapter on conscience we observe the mul-tifarious misfires of performatives, what do those misfires illuminate for us with regard to the bindingness of Hegel's text? The conscience chapter illuminates the pitfalls of attempts to bind words and declarations to a single, definitive content and thereby to foreseeable results. Likewise the *Phenomenology* may claim for itself to be the unfolding of Spirit that it also narrates, but it cannot conclusively bind itself as text to that act. In other words, the *Phenomenology* cannot be definitively and only that which it claims for itself, for there are insuperable discrepancies between what it says it says, what it says it is, and what it is beyond what it says it is. Just as conscience in the *Phenomenology* does not win recognition of its dutiful character, so too the *Phenomenology* has not won universal recognition of that which it claims for itself. Readers may and do refuse the claims for the text's unfolding of absolute Spirit in this world. The chapter on conscience in the *Phenomenology* allegorizes our human vulnerability to the excessive, unpredictable effects of performatives, and it also allegorizes the *Phenomenology*'s own impossibility of guaranteeing that it is and does that which it claims to be and to do.

3

Heidegger's *Being and Time:*
Not "About" Being

In the last chapter we saw that the *Phenomenology of Spirit* is in Hegel's own description not simply *about* the development of Spirit but instead enacts, or even is, this development. In Hegel's understanding, the *Phenomenology of Spirit* does not primarily *represent* but rather *performs* the unfolding that it describes. Heidegger's *Being and Time* (1927) also has a "not-about" quality, but for different reasons than the *Phenomenology of Spirit* claims for itself. Insofar as Heidegger articulates the goal as to understand being in terms other than those of beings, there are no correct or proper words with which to talk about being and hence with which to pose or to answer the question of the meaning of being. The text *Being and Time* is therefore profoundly figurative and specifically catachrestic, for it necessarily borrows words from the language of beings when in fact these words are necessarily inappropriate to being, its topic. It is my claim in this chapter that the inquiry into being continually defamiliarizes its terms in the manner of unhandy tools, precisely as a matter of fidelity to its object, and that it operates in a field of tension between performance and "aboutness" or constatation.

Within the text of *Being and Time* Heidegger also attempts, in an unhandy, defamiliarizing way, to articulate how conscience is primordially binding upon Dasein. The analysis of the call of conscience is not, however, merely one topic among others in the book. I will show toward the end of this chapter that the discussion of conscience constitutes a unique nexus between the function of conscience as described *within* the text and the function of *Being and Time* with respect to readerly Dasein. Hence I will argue at the end of this chapter that the very book *Being and Time* performs the call of conscience, insofar as the text is an attestation of Dasein's ownmost ability to be itself. The question of attestation with respect to the function of conscience *within Being and Time* helps explain, as I will show, how the book *Being and Time* comes to be binding upon its reader.[1]

Not "About" Being

In his retrieval of the question of being, Heidegger prescribes an onto-logical-phenomenological method, in which "the first philosophical step . . . consists in avoiding the *muthon tina diegeisthai*, in not 'telling a story' [*keine Geschichte erzählen*]" (6).[2] Specifically, Heidegger warns against determining being "as if being had the character of a possible being" (6). Why is the step back from storytelling the first step in under-standing the problem of being? Storytelling requires a matter, an object, if not a concrete entity, with which the story deals. Moreover, telling has the structure of "being about"; it deals with something and thereby im-plicitly ascribes entitativeness or actuality to its topic. In this regard, Gün-ter Figal writes,

> Every talking is a talking about something. Whoever talks about some-thing makes it present, in that he expressly distinguishes it or even does not distinguish it from other things. It is impossible to speak, without that which is spoken about becoming something specific.[3]

Precisely because being is not to be confused with beings, actualities, and even possible beings, it is in every case inaccurate to tell "about" being; in-deed the danger of telling a story wherein being is characterized as an en-tity lies not so much in the possibility of explicitly making such a charac-terization but instead in the very structure of telling.[4] Every telling *about* being, including theorizing, arguing, describing, and explaining, thus en-tails a sort of storytelling, insofar as it engages directly or indirectly in the determination of being as an entity.

Arguing, claiming, describing, and explaining are inappropriate ap-proaches to Being. Accordingly, readers of Heidegger have used a pleth-ora of terms for the kind of telling that is at stake in Heidegger's text. "Tran-sitivity" is one such term that is used by Hannah Arendt, in an explicit rejection of the "about":

> This thinking has a digging quality peculiar to itself, which, should we wish to put it in linguistic form, lies in the transitive use of the verb "to think." Heidegger never thinks "about" something, he thinks something.[5]

With reference to Heidegger's discussion of poetic speech, power, and language in *An Introduction to Metaphysics*, David Krell uses the word "ef-fecting": "The exercise of power in language, especially the language of poetizing-thinking, actualizes the Being (or presence) of a thing and makes it effectively real: the exercise of power in language is the 'effect-ing' of the thing."[6] Krell also describes Heidegger's account of anxiety in terms that emphasize the lack of distance between the saying and the said and that approaches the classic definition of performativity: "In the de-scription of the phenomenon of anxiety Heidegger's existential analysis reaches that crucial point where disclosure and the being disclosed con-verge."[7] David Wood calls *Being and Time* an "exemplary performance," namely, with regard to the accomplishing, executing, performative ele-ment of language that Heidegger attempts to evoke. In Wood's words, Heidegger "seeks to awaken a new experience of language, not a new view of it. And he does so by an exemplary performance. He writes in such a way as to demonstrate such a new relation."[8] Wood's characterization sug-gests that Heidegger's text, as an example, occupies a peculiarly impor-tant place between figure and performance.[9]

The nonconstative element of Heidegger's writing has also been figured in terms of movement. Ronald Bruzina describes Heidegger's writing and thinking in terms of a "wording movement" in order to em-phasize the absolute intertwining of Heidegger's thought and the words he uses.[10] Christopher Fynsk points to the necessity that reading be open to the movement of thought in Heidegger's writing, a movement which takes place in the very "shaking" or trembling of that writing's "surface in-telligibility."[11] What is to be followed if Heidegger is to be actually *read* is not an argument or content; what genuine reading does is to follow the becoming of thought—which, because it follows a *becoming*, requires that thought become other to what it is. This becoming of thought thus re-sembles, in a limited way, the logic of the Hegelian speculative sentence, where the subject becomes other than or more than what it was as subject as the sentence unfolds. Hence Samuel Ijsseling reminds us that the "is" in Heidegger's titles *What Is Philosophy?* and *What Is Metaphysics?* must be understood as transitive, which, as Ijsseling points out, Heidegger himself indicates in *What Is Philosophy?*[12] It is in each case not a matter in Heideg-ger of moving from one position in an argument to another via logical steps, but instead—again, in one respect similar to the speculative propo-sition of Hegel—of the very undoing of thought by itself, an undoing wherein thought becomes what it is not.

From Rhetoric to Performance: *Being and Time* as a Catachrestic Text

This brief catalog of terms—"transitivity," "effecting," and "movement"—reflects the nonexpository, nonrepresentational element to which Heidegger refers in his warning concerning storytelling "about" being. Heidegger indicates that "what" *Being and Time* is about is not some thing or concept that can be written about in an expository fashion and suggests the need to depart from *muthos* and from representational exposition. On the other hand, the book nonetheless formally and grammatically does resemble a book "about" being. *Being and Time* as a work *is* structured as an argument and exposition.[13] The formidable table of contents alone, in its rigorous outline form, reflects the densely structured character of the text, and however obscure or difficult the analysis may be, it nevertheless claims to function according to a method and thereby to philosophize "about" its theme.[14] In addition, the selection of Dasein—and not being— as the *Befragte* ("what is interrogated," 5) of the investigation into the meaning of being, namely, as that which it inquires into, allows the text a viable about-structure, given that Dasein is an entity and thus, unlike being, one can in some respects discuss, characterize, describe, and theorize about it. Insofar as the *Gefragte* ("that which is asked about," 5) is being itself, however, the problem of storytelling and the about-structure of argumentation remains. Moreover, insofar as Dasein is not just any entity, but the entity for which being is an issue, the problem of telling "about" being also concerns the inquiry into Dasein and how it is articulated.[15]

Finally, any question *about* being or investigation *into* being cannot but treat being as an entity, for it is impossible to thematize being without recourse to an entitative and thus actualizing vocabulary and grammar.[16] For instance, the very preposition "about" necessarily takes an object, which becomes substantivized in its grammatical role, seeming to name an entity or actuality. Likewise the very words "being" and "conscience" implicitly suggest entitativeness simply by virtue of their nominal forms. Thematization in the context of an argument depends on formal laws of grammar and on predication, both of which demand in turn a subject or nominative, and thus these also involve a grammatical substantivization and an ascription of entitativeness. Hence the investigation of the question of being and of the call of conscience cannot bring to language what they ought to, insofar as the nominalization, substantivization, and predication that a phenomenological-ontological investigation requires entail some implicit ascription of entitativeness to its object.

This tension between, on the one hand, the demand that Heidegger raises for a nonentitative understanding of being and, on the other hand, the systematic, argumentative structure of the text, can be described in terms of rhetoric. That is, insofar as *Being and Time* does discuss or offer arguments about being and to this extent adheres to the formulations of grammar and predication, the words with which the question of the meaning of being are investigated are inevitably in some way wrong or borrowed, which helps explain why they appear so often in italics or underlined, in scare quotes, or otherwise bracketed by means of particular printing strategies. In this regard Istvan Fehér cites the following statement of Heidegger:

> Christian theology and the philosophical "speculation" which stands under its influence and the anthropology which always also develops within such contexts all speak in borrowed categories, categories which are alien to their own field of Being.[17]

The "borrowed" character of the categories with which theology and philosophy operate, as highlighted by Heidegger himself, indicates the figurative element that is essential to these discourses. And although Heidegger here appears to distance his philosophizing from Christian theology and philosophical speculation influenced by it, his thought can hardly be said to be without connection to that theology and thus to the borrowed categories of which it makes use.[18]

While *Being and Time*'s superficial conventions and structure resemble those of a conventional inquiry, namely, an attempt to formulate the question of being and the analytic of Dasein in representational, expository and literal terms, in fact I would argue that Heidegger's account merely *stands in* for the representational, expository—or storytelling—account while being barely distinguishable from it. Specifically it is the problem of the not-about, nonstorytelling, nonrepresentational character of the text that raises the question of tropes—that is, of figures of speech in which words are used in borrowed, nonliteral, and purportedly nonnatural fashions—and rhetoric. For in view of the borrowedness, nonliteralness, and supposed nonnaturalness of the words for being and other related questions under investigation in *Being and Time,* the text may be seen as a complex figuration. This is not to embark on a discussion of Heidegger's metaphors or the metaphors in *Being and Time*. Rather, it is to show that insofar as *Being and Time* both concerns and operates at the limit of representation (i.e., insofar as representation is representation-of), the book cannot unproblematically utilize representative devices, including metaphor.[19] Nonetheless *Being and Time* is consummately figurative, for it must in each case borrow from entitative terms in order to discuss being, which is not an entity. Thus the claim here is that the text is not strictly metaphoric, but more precisely catachrestic, that is, it employs figures in which borrowed words serve to fill in where there is no proper term and where accuracy of representation is out of the question because there is no entity to be represented. Hence John McCumber writes of *Being and Time* that in it "knowing becomes the experiencing of gaps."[20] Insofar as the text is in any way about being, the argumentation of *Being and Time* is necessarily figurative, and specifically catachrestic; it makes use of inappropriate and borrowed words where proper words are lacking, and, what is more, it must indicate the inappropriate nature of its words for its nonsubstantive "subject matter" if it is to attempt a fidelity to the question of being at the same time that it pursues its inquiry.[21] According to this argument, the question of the meaning of being is a rhetorical question—not in the sense of a nonquestion, such as "How do you do?"—but rather insofar as the question cannot in proper words ask what it should ask, because *das Erfragte* ("what is to be ascertained" 5) and *das Gefragte* are not entities, and thus one cannot properly ask "about" them (5–6). The investigation is therefore located at the limit of meaningfulness, for every word and every expression for being is inappropriate to its task. These characteristics in part are what intrigue Heidegger's enthusiasts, frustrate new or unsympathetic readers, and account for many of the text's difficult and enigmatic locutions.[22]

There are numerous studies of Heidegger and metaphor, some of which deal with this limit of meaningfulness and appropriateness. My goal is to consider this limit first with regard to the figure of catachresis, in order to show that with Heidegger's catachrestic discussion the text oscillates between figuration and performance, insofar as it becomes something other than a storytelling text, but nonetheless without abandoning the conventions proper to a phenomenological investigation. That is, insofar as anything whatsoever *about* being is asserted, or similarly, insofar as the analysis of the call of conscience asserts something *about* the call of conscience, the text can provide only an *unfitting* representation. Its words disclose a great deal about the question of being, not by representing it but in continually defamiliarizing the terms of the account. In this respect the investigation of the meaning of being not only is a philosophical text *about* the meaning of being but, in its catachrestic operation, it also highlights, in a performance-like fashion, the impossibility of thematizing being in proper or literal words. Moreover, insofar as the words by which the investigation proceeds are borrowed, bracketed, and essentially inappropriate, it is a tropological and thus rhetorical inscenation of the impossibility of properly thematizing being. The text resembles an account of being and even an argument about it, but in fact that argument stands in the place of the impossibility of directly or literally saying something about being.

Figuration and rhetoric refer here to the borrowing, bracketing, and suspension that mark Heidegger's terminology; the performative character of the text is in my argument inseparable from this figurative-rhetorical element, for at the limit of the rhetorical elasticity of its words, the text evokes the impossibility of a proper language of being. Likewise, I will argue subsequently, the analysis of conscience evokes the impossibility of representing the call of conscience. That is, I will suggest that the description of the call of conscience consists in a rhetorical evocation of the impossibility to represent the "what" or topic that conscience is. Indeed, the words of the explanation are so catachrestic that accuracy and clarity are difficult to come by, and thus the critical element of this philosophizing consists more in its evocative and performative dimension than in some explicit argument. In other words, *Being and Time* is not *about* the meaning of being and the horizon of time; indeed, it performatively displaces or undoes the referential boundaries that make the comfortable distance between a text and what it is "about" possible.

The use of the language of performance or inscenation to describe *Being and Time* is supported by Heidegger's own claims that, unlike beings, being cannot be discovered but must instead be shown or demonstrated.[23] Heidegger also uses a vocabulary of *Durchführen* (execution or performance) in describing the task of *Being and Time*.[24] Indeed, the transition from rhetoric to performance is hinted at by Karl Jaspers in his notes on Heidegger, when he writes: "The truth of the rhetorical—and slipping into empty gestures."[25] Gesture (*Gebärde*), which is itself a form of performance, here is set alongside the truth of the rhetorical in Heidegger, by means of the ambiguous em-dash (—). The text's representational character, its expository "aboutness," is disrupted and exceeded by its performance, for insofar as *Being and Time* does not simply explain or argue about but instead performs or demonstrates at a catachrestic limit, the text shows that being—as the very condition of being-about—is not something that can be written about in an expository fashion. For this reason there is a tension between the dependence on wrong words and the requirement of phenomenological fidelity to point to their inadequacy. This tension, because its source cannot be explained in right words, is not explicated but rather performed by the text. Thus what I am calling the figurative and rhetorical character of the argument is at the same time the indicator of the excess of its theme, an excess whose impossibility of being represented and written "about" is performatively indicated.

Words as Unhandy Tools

Heidegger's analysis of the unhandy tool offers one way to approach the catachrestic and performative nature of *Being and Time,* insofar as the analysis of the unhandy tool applies to the use of words in *Being and Time* itself. I will show here that what Heidegger writes about the unhandy tool also provides an explanation of the functioning of the very words of his argumentation, which, as discussed earlier, cannot actually argue "about" being, because being is not an entity.[26] In this respect Heidegger's explanation of the broken, missing, or useless tool is not merely one theme of his text; rather, in *Being and Time* Heidegger engages in a practice of unhandy equipment. The text inscenates, by means of its figurative character and in its handling of and thematization of words, precisely what the analysis of the unhandy tool describes. Moreover, the discussion of the textual performance of the unhandy tool, together with a discussion in the next section of Heidegger's own description of theoretical comportment, indicates to what extent the performative element of the text depends on the tension between its theoretical comportment and the rhetorical limitations on theorizing about being.

According to Heidegger's famous discussion of equipment the tool in use is *zuhanden,* "ready-to-hand," which means that it is involved in circumspect, utilitarian dealing (*gebrauchender Umgang;* 73), whereas the characteristic of the unhandy tool is that it is "un-ready-to-hand," unhandy, or *unzuhanden.*[27] The analysis of the tool focuses on conspicuousness, obtrusiveness, and obstinacy as specific forms that *Unzuhandenheit* (unhandiness) takes. The broken tool is conspicuous insofar as it simply lies there (73); it stands out from the equipmental context and becomes a mere present-at-hand thing instead of remaining a ready-to-hand tool in use. The missing tool is obtrusive in being absent from a context in which it would be handy. The obstinate tool lies "in the way"; it is obstructive and a hindrance to Dasein's involvements. According to Heidegger, the broken, missing, or obstructive tool disrupts Dasein's referential totality (*Verweisungszusammenhang;* 75). The broken, missing, or obstructive tool no longer belongs merely to the equipmental context but becomes unhandy; when the tool becomes suddenly unhandy, the phenomenon of handiness is itself disclosed along with the unhandy tool.

It is my argument that *Being and Time* performs precisely what it says about the unhandy tool, in that many of the key words of the text function like unhandy equipment. Indeed while *Being and Time* takes the form of a text on the meaning of being or the temporality of Dasein, it remains notoriously inaccessible to everyday understanding. Its expositions and clarifications are often not particularly helpful or explanatory. The words of *Being and Time* are, on the one hand, the "equipment" of the text, for they are the necessary vehicles and tools of the book as a written text. On the other hand, the words of the book are often frustratingly unhandy as *words.* They are conspicuous, obtrusive, and even obstinate in the unhelpful and strange uses Heidegger makes of them.[28] Heidegger famously coins words, breaks words up with hyphenation, and uses words oddly and in sentences that seem contorted, such that they are remarkably unhelpful in performing the exposition they are supposed to accomplish.[29] It is precisely this unhelpfulness that recalls the discussion of the unhandy tool.

Conspicuousness is the mode of being-present of a thing at hand that is unusable; obtrusiveness is the mode of being of a thing that is missed, in the sense of being not at hand; and obstinacy is the mode of being of a thing that is unhandy and moreover in the way. With these elements of Heidegger's analysis of the unhandy tool in mind, we can consider the way in which the manipulations, inventions, and typical transformations of Heidegger's vocabulary can be understood as allegorizing, or even performing, what he describes with regard to the disclosure of unhandy tools. We can even map these designations onto various kinds of unhelpfulness in the exposition of *Being and Time*. The strange usage of particular words and the text's contorted sentences are conspicuous insofar as they are there but nonetheless unhelpful to our understanding of the book. The absence of appropriate, helpful, or even understandable words and formulations renders the words on the page, and the absence of more helpful ones, obtrusive—imagine the frustrated reader asking herself or himself why Heidegger couldn't have simply set his claims out in a straightforward fashion. In terms of our efforts to understand the text, Heidegger's invented terminology and odd formulations are obstinate and obstructive.[30] Such words as "being," "time," "world," and even the simple word "in" become unfamiliar, unhandy in Heidegger's writing.

The argument that Heidegger's words operate like pieces of unhandy equipment does not imply that language itself has an equipment-like character; on the contrary, the point is that individual words are inadequate to the task of raising—much less answering—the question of being.[31] As the inappropriate, catachrestic words of the analytic of Dasein shift into presence-at-hand, the words are denatured, defamiliarized. In their redeployment a new context of meaning is brought into being.[32] The word loses its comfortable equipmental role and becomes conspicuous and obstinate. In this respect, words of the text behave like the unhandy tool described in the text. Heidegger's uses of italics, hyphenation, and scare quotes are likewise techniques by which the words of the text are rendered broken, hence visible, and are brought into presence-at-hand rather than being merely used as handy tools.[33] In other words, the very words of the investigation into being are wrested out of readiness-to-hand, in part by devices such as italics, scare quotes, hyphenation, invention, and etymology, which thematize or make conspicuous the word-character of the words. Heidegger's writing can be frustratingly difficult, precisely because the text is not to be understood sheerly literally and constatively. Moreover, insofar as constative can be distinguished from performative with regard to a text, where constative refers to the "about" character of words and performative refers to the "doing" quality of a text, Heidegger's text is performative rather than constative, for Heidegger's argument operates with a level of force that goes beyond the literal and constative meanings of the sentences.

The Unhandy "Not"

Being and Time contains many statements in the negative—for instance, where Heidegger states that being is not an entity, that the call of conscience is not an utterance, or that temporality is not clock time. This sort of negative formulation can make for irritating reading, because Heidegger seldom supplies what the "not"-statement refuses. Like the unhandy tool, the many negative formulations are frustratingly unhelpful as explanation. In this regard, however, the "not"-statements of *Being and Time* are, with respect to the performative character of *Being and Time, necessarily* unhelpful. In their performances of a refusal of everyday understanding, they evoke the perplexity to which Heidegger exhorts us in the prologue's reference to Plato's *Sophist*. Hence Bruzina writes:

> Leading from one to the other are statements of negation: For example, warning that some formulation is *not* to be taken as a statement, insisting that metaphysical schemas must be neutralized and set out of play in one's thinking, denying the relevance of the designation "metaphorical," and so on. The situation seems to be, then, one in which rational explication turns upon itself within its own schema of determination and affirms a closure for its field of competence in negating its own performance, in order to allow another way of moving to work which in no way is to be recuperated in terms of that negated field and schema of performance.[34]

In their very negativity and in their disruption of everyday understanding, the "not"-statements perform an important function; they preclude or disrupt any simple transition from everyday understanding to the unthematizability of being. The "nots" do not merely point readers away from a particular interpretation, toward some other easily grasped interpretation, but rather in performing the refusal of rational understanding, they indicate the limits of thinking with respect to being. Rational explication thus negates its own performance, but this negation is *itself* a performance, and the "not"-statements of *Being and Time* perform in this fashion.

The analysis of the unhandy tool within *Being and Time* can be applied to the text at large in order to understand how the "not"-statements refuse straightforward understanding and evoke perplexity, for they highlight and thus remove from the handy context of reading particular elements or words in the manner of unhandy tools. The following lines from *Being and Time* are one instance in which words are rendered unhandy in a "not"-statement and for how the "not"-statement, in its very unhelpfulness and in the resistance it offers to understanding, provides the impetus for a different hearing:

> To be ontological does not yet mean to develop ontology. Thus if we reserve the term ontology for the explicit, theoretical question of the meaning of beings, the intended ontological character of Dasein is to be designated as pre-ontological. That does not signify being simply ontical, but rather being in the manner of an understanding of being. (12)

The opening "not"-statement rejects the "everyday" interpretation of the phrase "to be ontological" (everyday for those, presumably, who deal with the term "ontological" at all) as referring to Dasein's work on the field or subject matter of ontology. The phrase "to be ontological" and the word "ontology" are brought into view as words that we must notice, that we cannot simply read over in a handy context of understanding a text. The words are thereby rendered unhandy by the "not"-statement that refuses a straightforward understanding and yet provides no alternative. The word "pre-ontological," which Heidegger proposes to more carefully describe Dasein's relation to ontology, is in turn made unhandy by means of a "not"-statement that brings into view—in the form of refusal—the possibility of understanding the word "pre-ontological" as meaning "ontic." The negative statements in Heidegger's discussion of Dasein's relationship to ontology are the unhandy path by which Heidegger turns the meaning of "pre-ontological" into something other than "before ontology" and by which he suggests that the term "ontological" does not refer only to a field of study but rather to a manner of being.

The "not"-statements of *Being and Time* could be seen as simple pauses in an argument, as mere rhetorical rest stops on the way to a definitive thesis. As performatively rendering words unhandy, however, they can be seen to constitute one element of the not-about or performative path of *Being and Time*. The "not"-statements are thus not *merely* rhetorical but are rhetorical in a different sense of rhetoric, one that does not reduce to *mere* rhetoric or superfluity but rather refers to the production of effects, to a rhetorical force. The rhetorical force of the "not"-statements, like the brokenness of individual words, derives from the very resistances that the "not"-statements offer to understanding. The "not"-statements re-fute a particular understanding and thus are a necessary element in turn-ing thinking otherwise; they unmake or undo a thinking that would be se-cure in its understanding, they are a necessary step in the transformation of thinking and the evocation of perplexity. The "not"-statements per-form and ensure the continual dislodging of thinking from a smooth and secure path.

Theory and the Thematization of Being

In view of Heidegger's insistence that being is neither an entity nor a topic, it is on the one hand correct to say that Heidegger does not provide a theory *about* being, since every theory requires some sort of object about which it theorizes, and in this respect theory engages in thematizing as well as hypostatizing storytelling. A faithful characterization of *Being and Time* could not claim that the text offers a theory *of* being or a theory *about* time, although Heidegger declares that the explicit aim of *Being and Time* is to inquire into the meaning of being and into time as the horizon within which to understand being (1). Accordingly, *Being and Time* cannot produce a theory about that which it is supposed to be about, for being, death, conscience, time, and the other central topics of *Being and Time* cannot be made into proper objects of thematization. Moreover, as the previous sections have shown, the words for being are catachreses and function in the manner of unhandy tools.

What I am calling the performative character of *Being and Time* arises out of the tension between, on the one hand, the impossibility of theorizing about being and, on the other hand, the theorizing character of *Being and Time*. Indeed theorizing does take place in *Being and Time*, ac-cording to what the text itself says about theoretical comportment.[35] Al-though the text does not produce a theory, and according to its own prin-ciples could not produce a theory or theorizing *about* being, *Being and Time* nevertheless takes a "theoretical comportment" toward the *words* it brings into view, insofar as a theoretical comportment involves bringing everyday, mostly unseen, functions into view. Based on Heidegger's own characterization of theoretical comportment, the text of *Being and Time* is in fact a theorizing text—not with respect to being itself but with respect to the unhandy words of the text. The investigation into being cannot ful-fill the theoretical demand to explicate its theme, owing to the cata-chrestic and unhandy-tool character of its words.[36] Ultimately what I am calling the performative character of the text in fact depends precisely on the tension between the theoretical gesture of the text and the resistance of being to theorizing. The performance of the text takes place between the theoretical stance it takes and the rhetorical limitations on the terminology of theorizing that are available to a faithful investigation into the meaning of being. The text operates in a field of tension between a rhetoric of argumentation and the limitations of a rhetoric of being.

What is theorizing in *Being and Time,* and how does the text itself measure up with respect to the criteria of theorizing? Heidegger characterizes "theoretical behavior" as "just looking, noncircumspectly" (69), that is, in a way that is not subordinated to the in-order-to of a referential totality. Noncircumspect looking looks at a thing without the referential totality of equipmental purpose. This is not to say, as Heidegger explains in section 69b, that theory takes place where there is simply an absence of praxis and of circumspection.[37] Rather, theory involves *thematization* and making present; theory and thematization accompany the reversal of the entity's mode of presencing from *Zuhandenheit* (handiness) to *Vorhandenheit* (presence at hand).[38] Hence Krell writes: "All theory—including phenomenological theory—presupposes a nonthematized lapse from handiness to presence at hand."[39] Theory is a form of thematization, and thematization is a kind of making present and objectification, and likewise does not handle its objects in a ready-to-hand fashion. Theory therefore has something in common with the presence of the damaged tool, because with theory a referential context is disrupted, and specific items are thematized and disclosed.[40]

Thematization objectifies and hypostatizes, but as I have indicated, being cannot properly be thought of as an object. How then can being itself be thematized, such that it is an object of theory? Based on the argument in the previous section about broken tools and the withdrawal of the nonactual phenomena from thematizability, I would suggest that not being but the word "being" is objectified, thematized, brought into view. The word "being" is thematized, made present, objectified, and contemplated, and this is the case precisely insofar as being itself *cannot* be made present, objectified, and contemplated. Translated into Heidegger's discussion of the unhandy tool, one could say that *Being and Time* pries the word "being" from its referential totality as a ready-to-hand term and brings this word closer to presence. The word "being" is in this respect a damaged tool. Insofar as it takes a theoretical comportment toward the word "being" rather than toward being, *Being and Time* is a theoretical investigation.

This is not at all to suggest that being itself is made present at hand, or that language in general is made present at hand; indeed the bringing of particular *words* closer to presence at hand and the theoretical comportment toward these words must be distinguished in each case from a theorizing about what might be called the primordial "phenomena" (in scare quotes because they are not objects and withdraw from any "is"-centered definition) at stake in *Being and Time*. In fact the word "being" is made present precisely insofar as being itself withdraws from the possibility of thematization. Likewise "death," "conscience," and other words are considered from a theoretical stance insofar as they are extracted from a ready-to-hand context and brought closer to presence at hand for investigation. Furthermore, it is precisely the making-present of certain words that coincides with the withdrawal or enigma of the "phenomena" that Heidegger is attempting to evoke—such as being, death, and conscience—and the performative dimension of the text can be located precisely in the coincidence of the making present of a word *in its inadequacy* with the withdrawal of the phenomenon from description.[41]

There is therefore a tension between the attempt to express something that is impossible to express properly and the theoretical and argumentative character of *Being and Time*. Insofar as *Being and Time* displays a theoretical comportment but cannot fulfill the objectifying criteria for theory while remaining faithful to its hypostatized "object," it is an argument made with unhandy tools. Thus *Being and Time* performs in the tension between the theoretical gesture and the limitations of terminology, as suggested by Samuel Ijsseling's reference to the "strategic meaning" of Heidegger's key terms.[42] What Ijsseling refers to as "strategic meaning" belongs to what I call the performative quality of the text; as Ijsseling points out, these words do not refer to a positive content, they are rather gestures.[43] Thus inasmuch as the "topic" or *Gefragte* of *Being and Time* precisely *cannot* be made present at hand—since it concerns the very conditions and possibility of making present—*Being and Time* cannot fulfill even Heidegger's own characterization of theory. This is not to say that the text does not employ methodical, theoretical strategies. Yet despite such methodical gestures—for example, the elaborate breakdown of sections, the concern with the starting point, and the frequent claims to the necessity of particular lines of investigation—*Being and Time* does not derive its impact primarily from its argumentative method or procedure. The text does not execute a *theory* or a new *idea,* but rather it executes a perplexing performance as a "method" of philosophizing that exceeds theory and yet resembles it. Thus both Heidegger's *demonstration* of the necessity of an elliptical approach to the question of being and the way the text draws itself into an inquiry as to the meaning of being take place not by way of argument and theory; rather, they take place by way of a demonstration of the limitations of theory and of the words and tropes by means of which an argument about being can be conducted. The text's impact might be said to derive from the undermining force that it has *upon* theory, *upon* method, and *upon* the distinction between them.

If the recoil of *Being and Time* upon theorizing is not adequately rec-
ognized, it might be possible to treat *Being and Time* as a book with a theory, as a book *about* being and time—that is, to approach *Being and Time*
with the goal of translating the odd locutions that arise, to deal with them
as terms to be unpacked and ordered into straightforward paraphrase, to
assess the book's failure or success in achieving its goal of inquiring into
the meaning of being. This sort of reading would look primarily to the *argument* of *Being and Time* and must therefore see the difficulty of the text's
locutions as that which must be surmounted and overcome, and the argument contained therein as that which must be evaluated, criticized, and
corrected. In such a reading, the movement, showing, and performance
of the text are to be encapsulated and frozen. But Heidegger is central to
philosophy—and also to other disciplines, including literary studies—
not because he constructs a theory or theories but on account of the way
he instead displaces the theoretical gaze—not from some things to other
things, or from things to ourselves; rather, his work displaces theorizing
itself.

The Elision of Meaning in the Introduction
to *Being and Time*

The opening of the text of *Being and Time* is, to use David Wood's term, an
"exemplary performance" of how the word "being" is initially rendered
unhandy. That is, there is a peculiar elision that occurs with regard to the
phrase "the question of the meaning of being," an elision that renders it
instead "the question of being" (*Seinsfrage* or *die Frage nach dem Sein*). Indeed, the focus of the opening pages of *Being and Time* oscillates between
"the question of being" and "the question of the *meaning* of being" (my
emphasis). The titles and subtitles of the introduction seem to unproblematically conflate and equate them: the prologue raises "the question of
the *meaning* of being" and suggests that what follows will introduce "the
reasons for making this our aim, the investigations which such a purpose
requires, and the path to its achievement"; whereas the titles of the introductory sections that follow, and which should therefore accomplish this
introduction, are "The necessity of an explicit retrieve of the question of
being," "The formal structure of the question of *being*," "The ontological
priority of the question of *being*," and "The ontic priority of the question
of *being*" (all emphases mine). Moreover, while the introduction to *Being
and Time* is entitled "The exposition of the question of the meaning of
being," the titles of the introduction's two subsections refer instead to the
Seinsfrage; the word "meaning" disappears in the term *Seinsfrage*.

As with the section headings, within the introduction there is also oscillation between "the question of being" and "the question of the meaning of being." The first subsection, entitled "The necessity, structure, and
priority of the question of being," does not formulate "the question" to
which it refers; rather, in reviewing the prejudices about being, it indicates
the necessity for a retrieval of the question of being, rather than the question of the *meaning* of being referenced in his prefatory discussion of the
Sophist quotations. Heidegger famously argues for "the fundamental necessity of repeating the question of the meaning of 'being,'" for "the *answer* to the question of being [is] lacking" (4). The apparently unproblematic oscillation between "the question of being" and "the question of
the meaning of being" is also conspicuous when Heidegger writes, "The
question to be *formulated* is about the meaning of being. Thus we are con-
fronted with the necessity of explicating the question of being with regard
to the structural moments cited" (5). In his explanation of the ontological priority of the question of being, Heidegger repeats the demand that
we understand "what we really mean by this expression 'being'" and opens
the next paragraph with reference to "the question of being" (11).

Given that Heidegger seems unproblematically to use the phrase
"the question of being" with reference to the inquiry into the *meaning* of
being, it seems perhaps a matter of hairsplitting to distinguish Heidegger's references to "the question of the meaning of being" from his references to "the question of being." Nevertheless, precisely the elision of
meaning—that is, the elision of the fact that the question guiding *Being
and Time* is one of meaning—is significant. My claim is that the oscillation
between the question of being and the question of the meaning of being
is in fact an oscillation between two projects—one concerning being and
the other concerning the meaning of being, that is, of the *word* "being."
Because being itself is no thing, and thus being cannot be written or
talked *about,* being itself is eclipsed, and the *word* "being" comes to the
fore as a catachresis in the manner of an unhandy tool.[44] In this way the
enterprise that seeks to show that and how being is not an entity depends
on a word whose meaning it eviscerates. This evisceration does not dis-
pense with the word but rather leaves it intact as a question mark, as a location of perplexity. Because Heidegger cannot write *about* being as one
writes about an entity, the text must repeatedly evoke the catachrestic
character of being, the unhandy character of the *word* "being," in order to
distance the text from being *itself.* The project "about" being transforms
into a project that can be "*about,*" at most, the *word* "being," for unlike
being itself, the word "being" has an entitative character and *can* be thematized directly. The projects are in a way shadows of each other, the one
project concerning the word "being," playing at the edge of the other that
concerns being "itself."

The phrase "the question of" is in this regard no mere, unproblematic abbreviation or shortcut for "the question of the meaning of" but rather is an elision that strategically makes the term "meaning" problematic precisely in eliding it. A semiological issue arises here; to suggest that there is a difference between the meaning of the *word* "being" and the meaning of being "itself" appears to invoke a semiology, that is, it appears to assume that the *word* "being" is a signifier and that being "itself" is signified by the *word* "being." However, this semiological distinction is problematic inasmuch as Heidegger belabors the nonentitative character of being, and thus to talk of "being itself" is to contravene much of the argument of the text. The abbreviation "the question of being" for "the question of the meaning of being" serves to elide the rhetorical dimension of the inquiry, for the character of "being" as a *word* is also elided.

As a consequence of this elision, the question of *Being and Time* then appears to be a question concerning being itself. That is, having elided the fact that the inquiry is in its inaugural moment an inquiry into the *word* "being," the entire text constantly risks appearing too literal, appearing to be *about* being, which would entail understanding being in terms of entities. Heidegger must therefore constantly and repeatedly retrieve being in *Being and Time* from such an understanding. He must reevoke precisely the rhetorical element of the discussion, that is, reevoke the *tension* between the rhetorical project surrounding the *word* "being" and the impossible literal project concerning being itself. Thus the text's repeated insistence on the nonentitative character of being prevents being from appearing as an entity and forecloses successful constative statements about it. Heidegger must protect the word "being," in part by means of difficult locutions, from entering into a discussion *about* being, at the same time that he exposes it to such discussion. *Being and Time* must therefore forget or cover over its central concern for the meaning of the word "being," in the process of its own unfolding. It must reread itself as always in danger of being *about* being and thus must repeatedly defamiliarize the word "being" in such a way that being itself is constantly distanced from entitativeness.

Making a Word Unhandy

Another way to approach the problem of the possible conflations of being and the word "being" would be through an observation of Heidegger's use of scare quotes, italics, and other unhandy-making strategies. For instance, in the prologue, the word "being" appears in scare quotes when it is explicitly discussed as a term; Heidegger writes "the word 'being,'" "the expression 'being.'" The word "being" also appears to be at issue with the italics in Heidegger's phrase "the meaning of *'being'*" (1).[45] Thus in these instances the scare quotes indicate that the word "being" is the object of discussion. The first section of the introduction, which enumerates the prejudices of philosophy with respect to the concept of being in order to show the necessity of an explicit retrieval of the question of being, also frequently employs scare quotes around the word "being"—precisely because in these instances a *concept* of being is at stake, hence, "'Being' is the most universal concept," "the concept of 'being' is indefinable," "'being' is a self-evident concept" (3–4).[46] Being taken as a concept, however, is incompatible with the defamiliarized, nonentitative being that *Being and Time* evokes. Thus in each prejudice that Heidegger describes, and then dismisses, being is taken for granted as a concept (even where the concept is described as undefinable), and the meaning of the word "being" is not questioned. Each conceptual understanding of being predefines the boundaries by which being is to be understood; it relegates being to a realm of concepts, and thus does not draw us into the *Verlegenheit,* or embarrassed perplexity, that our ignorance of the *meaning* of being and of the very question of the meaning of being should evoke, according to the prologue of *Being and Time.*

The prologue and the introduction do have the word "being" in scare quotes, albeit inconsistently, when discussing the question of the meaning of being.[47] For example, Heidegger in the introduction writes, "We do not *know* what 'being' means. But already when we ask, 'What is "being"?' we stand in an understanding of the 'is' without being able to determine conceptually what the 'is' means" (5).[48] The scare quotes here indicate the status of the words "is" and "being" as objects of consideration, and thus they point to the understanding of the *words* themselves as a problem. The scare quotes interrupt a handy reading of the sentence and make the word "is" and the word "being" fleetingly present to us. When Heidegger discusses the question of the meaning of being, the phrase "the meaning of" functions to mark the word "being" as equipment, as a tool that is conspicuous or obtrusive. When Heidegger drops the phrase "the meaning of" and refers instead to "the question of being," it is ambiguous whether the word "being" is in question or whether *being* is at stake. But this indicates precisely what I have suggested, namely, that the elision of the word-character of the word "being" lets it appear as if being "itself" were at stake in the investigation. And yet, *Being and Time* is not *about* being, because being is not some *thing* that a text could be *about;* it defies "aboutness." Words, in contrast, can be made objects of study, they can be questioned, investigated, considered in their use. But the word "being" ought not be conflated with being "itself," which cannot be manipulated, questioned, investigated. Of course, the word "being" is not without any relation to being "itself," but what is this relation? How could we know it or say it?

The fact that "the question of the meaning of 'being'" is so easily elided with "the question of being" indicates precisely what I have claimed with respect to Heidegger's method, namely, that he *breaks* or damages words so that their handiness is disrupted and they appear in the manner of unhandy tools. The disappearance of scare quotes around "being," however, in the first few sections of *Being and Time*, suggests that first the word "being" slips out of thematization into handiness. Perhaps this is necessary in order for the inquiry, that is, the working out of the question of being, to proceed. Heidegger uses scare quotes around the word "being" consistently when portraying the prejudices of philosophy. In his next section, however, concerning the formal structure of the question of being, the scare quotes have almost completely disappeared around the word "being" and instead appear around the thematized topics of "investigation" (*Untersuchen;* 5), "just-asking-around" (*Nur-so-hinfragen;* 5), and "circular reasoning" (*Zirkel im Beweis;* 7–8). In other words, scare quotes appear when the word "being" is thematized, as demonstrated in the lines already cited: "We do not *know* what 'being' means. . . . we ask 'what is "being"?'" (5), but then disappear again in other contexts. But if the scare quotes are the marks of thematization and problematization, why is the word "being" not enclosed in them throughout all of *Being and Time*, which is after all an investigation into being? I suggest that the withdrawal of being itself from any word for it, as marked by the scare quotes employed in the early sections of *Being and Time*, itself withdraws from obvious view with the disappearance of the scare quotes as the text proceeds. The word "being" in scare quotes marks, at best, the withdrawal of being from the investigation.

The Attestation of Conscience

What I have described with regard to the unhandy, catachrestic, and defamiliarizing character of Heidegger's formulation of the question of being appears over and over throughout *Being and Time* with regard to many elements of the analytic of Dasein. The call of conscience is one more point of tension or oscillation between the text's expository, analytic approach and the rhetorical-tropological limitations on the possibility of exposition with respect to its theme. In Heidegger's analysis of conscience the content, the caller, and the one who is called are defined in terms of possibility rather than in terms of entity or actuality, and therefore the analysis of the call of conscience repeats in miniature the very difficulty of saying that pervades *Being and Time* as a whole. Nonetheless, out of all the analyses of Dasein in *Being and Time,* the account of conscience is not only one instance among others of the dynamic between figuration and performance described in earlier sections of this chapter. Instead, I would argue, the call of conscience occupies a peculiar place in the performative constellation of the text, for it is a point of reversal wherein the text as a whole allegorizes what is said *in* the text about the call of conscience. I will show shortly that while the call of conscience in *Being and Time* serves as a performative attestation, the text's discussion of the call serves as an attestation of that attestation. In doubling the attestation that it describes, *Being and Time* may be read as a performance of what is argued in the analysis of conscience. While the call of conscience is an exemplary performance with respect to the rhetorical limitations it exhibits, *Being and Time* can itself be seen as an exemplary performance of the call of conscience.

Let us unpack these claims more slowly. *Being and Time*'s turn to conscience is governed by a demand for a specific kind of performance, namely, for an attestation, in answer to the question whether an attestation of Dasein's ability to be can be found: "We are looking for an authentic potentiality-of-being of Dasein that is attested by Dasein itself in its existentiell possibility. First of all, we have to find this attestation itself" (267). The function of the analysis of the call of conscience thus consists in showing that no "exterior" entity calls Dasein to its ownmost ability to be, but rather the possibility already belongs to Dasein to be called by conscience. The call is not important as a call *about* something but instead in that it *performs* an attestation. In its very occurrence, rather than in what it might say, the call of conscience performs its function for Dasein—and also for the text as a whole, as I will show.

Why is an attestation necessary? It seems, on the one hand, to be a matter of proof, that is, the attestation offers to the inquiry into being a proof that the authentic ability to be is not possible just *for* Dasein, but rather is "in Dasein itself" (288). In this respect, *Being and Time*'s account of conscience serves to show that it is not any external entity that calls Dasein to its ownmost ability to be, but rather the possibility of being called by conscience belongs already to Dasein and is not foreign or other to it. The call of conscience coincides with Dasein in its possible authenticity and shows it to Dasein. However, conscience's specific way of being "not-other" to Dasein, while also belonging to Dasein, is not a straightforward matter. Indeed the attestation that conscience provides is defined by a series of "nots," which, to return to Fynsk's words, shake the surface intelligibility of the very notion of an attestation. In other words, the attestation that the call of conscience evokes is characterized by a series of negative statements, which transform the notion of attestation into an unhandy tool.

First, the attestation that conscience provides is an attestation of an *ability* to be and thus is not an attestation of a thing or actuality: "It is the summons of the self to its potentiality-of-being-a-self, and thus calls Dasein forth to its possibilities" (274). Second, the "self" whose ability to be is attested in conscience is, as section 25 concerning the "who" of Dasein indicates, not an ontic "who" or "what" but instead a way of existing (267). "What" is attested in conscience is thereby several times removed from "things," for what is attested to is a possibility of being a "way." Heidegger further points out that conscience "'is' only in the kind of being of Dasein" (269). That is to say, conscience *is* not in the manner of a thing, but *is* in the manner of a *way*. Hence conscience is, like Dasein, a *way* of being, and it discloses to a way of being (i.e., to Dasein) its ability to be itself, namely, to be its possibilities. Conscience discloses, but "disclosure" does not mean that conscience is a thing that discloses another thing. For this reason the new experience of the words surrounding conscience (e.g., "call," "guilty" [*schuldig*], "resoluteness" [*Entschlossenheit*]) belongs to an evocation of Dasein in terms of possibility, an evocation that cannot be accomplished sheerly literally, in hypostatizing terms, nor sheerly constatively, in the manner of being-about. Attestation is in everyday life one way in which a fact is made present, but in the case of conscience, that which makes present and that which is made present are not facts or things but possibilities and ways, and thus they cannot be made present in the way of actualities. In this respect the analysis of the call of conscience depends upon what was referred to earlier as the withdrawal of the phenomena from the words that are supposed to describe them but cannot refer to them, given their nonactual nature.

This complicated, double instance of attestation (and also of disclosure, which of course is discussed at length throughout *Being and Time*) makes for difficulty in writing *about* conscience in a direct way, apart from "not"-statements. Heidegger's account of conscience epitomizes the not-about character of the investigation into the meaning of being. The call is said to say nothing and to report no occurrences, and the caller is no one and is not determinable by anything. The call is not determinable as a "what" and is not uttered by a "who"; it is indeed silent, and from this call nothing follows.[49] How can Heidegger designate as a call something that is silent, says nothing, and issues from no one? To designate this as a call at all seems to be contrary to the very notion of a call. To once more invoke the performance of the unhandy tool: the sections of *Being and Time* on conscience are conspicuous in their enigmatic character; the lacking "fitting" or accurate explanation makes the text obtrusive through the very absence thereof; and the negative statements through which Heidegger does characterize the call are comparable to the tool that lies obstinately in the way, for they offer no particular assistance.[50]

In line with the foregoing discussion of "not"-statements, I suggest that the analysis of the call of conscience, as with the discussions of being, consists in part in a performance of what Heidegger says about the unhandy tool, and moreover performs or operates to frustrate everyday explication, for each "not" refuses a possible understanding of the call of conscience and renders everyday terms useless for understanding what conscience is. Moreover, and in accordance with Bruzina's discussion of the rejection of metaphor, Heidegger also refuses an understanding of this call in metaphoric terms, for Heidegger explicitly states that the call is not to be understood as a mere figure.[51] In this respect, the discussion of the call of conscience is catachrestic and hence rhetorical, for it operates at the limit of appropriate and understandable words.

Given the use in Heidegger's sections on conscience of "not"-statements, I would suggest that the account of conscience is an example of the performatively perplexing "not." Furthermore, with the analysis of conscience there is also a doubling of not-about discourse, for the call of conscience is itself not-about, because it has no message, and also because it talks in the manner of being silent:

> But how are we to define *what is spoken* in this discourse? *What* does conscience call to the one summoned? Strictly speaking—nothing. The call does not say anything, does not give any information about events of the world, has nothing to tell. . . . The call is lacking any kind of utterance. It does not even come to words. (273)

Specifically, the call does not give any "what" in its calling. The primordial phenomenon of the call of conscience is not a constative utterance, to use Austin's terminology. Thus within the text of *Being and Time,* which I am claiming is not *about* being, there is a discussion of conscience, which itself is said not to talk *about* some factical event or matter of guilt to Dasein. Nevertheless, this call discloses. Thus the disclosure that the call of conscience accomplishes cannot occur as a communication of something or about something. The call of conscience is itself a not-about instance of Logos, and the analysis of the call of conscience runs up against the catachrestic limit of theorizing about conscience. The new experience of language that Heidegger's difficulty serves is inextricable from a new experience of thinking conscience and also of thinking potentiality-for-being.

The difficulty of being-about that pertains to being and conscience therefore also holds for temporality, historicity, and other words in the constellation of difficult words that function like unhandy tools.[52]

Being and Time as a Performance of the Call

The discussion of the call of conscience is one instance wherein "not"-statements and unhandy words operate performatively, in the sense of Fynsk's "movement of thought in its becoming-other" or Wood's "exemplary performance." However, with respect to a discussion of bindingness, the call of conscience merits special attention for another reason, having to do with what would seem to be its singular performative role in *Being and Time*. That is, while we have considered the call of conscience as one performance within *Being and Time*, in addition *Being and Time* can itself be read as performing for the reader that which the analysis of the call of conscience describes with respect to Dasein. For while on one hand the discussion of the call of conscience repeats in miniature the catachrestic, negative, and performatively perplexing character of *Being and Time* as a whole, on the other hand, *Being and Time* as a whole can be read as a performance of conscience, writ large, in the following fashion: the attestation that is the call of conscience breaks off Dasein's listening to the they-self. An everyday, fallen sort of listening is broken off if conscience is successful, that is, if another kind of hearing is aroused (271). But is that not the very task of *Being and Time*, which in its enigmatic and difficult language forces another kind of hearing, a hearing not dominated by ontic and everyday expectations and things? What Heidegger writes about conscience's call can also be said of the text *Being and Time*, that is, "it reaches him who wants to be brought back" (271).[53] The text *Being and Time* binds readerly Dasein in its disclosure of the function of conscience. The inquiry that is *Being and Time* calls Dasein to its ownmost ability to be, and thus the inquiry discloses the demand that Dasein makes of itself with respect to its authentic ability to be.

To put it another way, insofar as *Being and Time* includes a "phenomenal demonstration [*Aufweis*]" of the attestation that is conscience, *Being and Time is* the attestation *of the attestation* of the potentiality-of-being of each of our Daseins; it performs what it explains. It discloses an authentic interpretation of conscience, which discloses Dasein's ownmost ability to be itself. In this reading, it would seem that *Being and Time* is our conscience, an "other" that is with us.[54] *Being and Time* draws us out of the they-self, and out of the common interpretation of temporality, and binds us to the conscience that it portrays. As Heidegger writes, "In order to find *itself* at all, [Dasein] must be 'shown' to itself in its possible authenticity" (268). Thus it is not only the attestation of conscience within *Being and Time* but in addition the book *Being and Time* that shows *our* Dasein to itself in its possible authenticity. This is not to simply say that *Being and Time is* conscience; for the "is" in the text is disrupted by Heidegger's "not"-statements and perhaps even more so by the "positive" characterizations of Dasein, and it is of course also the epicenter of the trembling of intelligibility of *Being and Time,* so that such a straightforward equation is implausible and moreover would hide the very difficulty of the connection between being and disclosure. Nonetheless *Being and Time* should be, according to its own terms, in some way binding on readerly Dasein in the same way that conscience is binding on the Dasein described in *Being and Time;* for the attestation performed *in* the text is also an attestation of our own bond, as Dasein, *to* the text.

Both *Being and Time* and the account of conscience within it enact—in different and yet overlapping ways—an encounter with possibility that is irreducible to any specific encounter or any specific possibility. Precisely owing to the "nature" of the withdrawn possibility at issue in Dasein's *Seinkönnen,* there is an irreducibility to "it," which renders every performance an example of it, and yet for which there is no single exemplar. *Being and Time* may be read as the performance of the operation of conscience, namely, the showing to Dasein of its ownmost ability to be itself. Heidegger's account of the call of conscience is not *merely* description, for *Being and Time* should *be* the attestation *of the attestation* that conscience is. Attestation would thus be doubled in the account of the call of conscience in *Being and Time.* In this respect, *Being and Time* seems to perform the attestation of which it is also the account, binding us as readers to the attestation that it is. Owing to the nonentitative aspect of Dasein it must evoke, the text therefore acts as a repetition and a performance of what it cannot say and what, owing to its catachrestic character, cannot be properly said. And yet we return here to the conclusion of the previous chapter: What guarantees that *Being and Time* may be binding upon anyone or anything? How is *Being and Time* to attain recognition of what it says and what it does? Does the fact that Heidegger does not claim that the text is binding upon the world, in the way that Hegel seems to, mitigate the uncertainty and possibility for performative misfire?

Conclusion: The Frailties of Guarantee

In the preceding chapters I have considered how conscience is characterized as binding *within* texts of Hobbes, Hegel, and Heidegger, and I have also examined those characterizations as paradigmatic for a consideration of how texts may be binding upon their readers and the world. Given the emphasis placed in the preceding readings on the nonconstative, "not-about," and binding aspects of texts, it is a discomfiting task to formulate a conclusion or finding. For to advance in a constative mode a finding *concerning* bindingness is to risk a gesture of hypostasis and substantivization, and thus to risk flattening the scope of the question of how texts may be binding upon their readers. Let me attempt to reformulate the issue. Each of these accounts of conscience provides a claim for what conscience *truly* is. The persuasiveness of these claims, however, does not subsist only at the level of argumentative strength but also at the level of *encounter.* It originates, that is, at the level of one's encounter with the text—for example, with Hobbes's exquisitely figured rejections of figurative language; with Hegel's text that claims to unfold what it describes; and with Heidegger's *Being and Time* that performs for us what conscience is said to perform for Dasein. Such encounters exceed the intratextual components of style and argumentation. This excess belongs to what I have called the "bindingness" of words, by means of which they reach out of the dimension of constatation and aboutness in order to effect or even compel.

In the case of Hobbes, I have shown that his account of conscience as a metaphor purports to explain how private conscience comes into being and turns out to be less binding, more corruptible, and more unreliable than shared, witnessed knowledge. In *Leviathan,* conscience can be seen as not merely an example of the dangers of metaphor but instead as *the* most dangerous metaphor, the metaphor that institutes the realm of private opinion, making error, deception, and the corruption of knowledge possible. Hobbes's account of the metaphoric transformation of the word "conscience" operates as a model of the performative positing of subjectivity and of the internalization by which a subjective "inside" is fabricated rather than simply represented. The dangers of metaphor that

Hobbes recounts in the story of conscience, however, turn out to be profoundly ineluctable because we *may* in every case position words in sentences against their conventional meanings and thus *may* at every moment perform a corruption of the truth that is defined by Hobbes as the correct ordering of words. The corruption of names that Hobbes so fears in metaphor is a function of the inherent corruptibility of the verb "to be," which may connect in an utterly labile fashion words that, in Hobbes's nominalist model of truth, do not belong together. Hence Hobbes's question "Why may we not say . . . ?" is indeed no merely rhetorical question but is rather precisely the question that points to the binding force of figuration. Hobbes's own figures exemplify and thus demonstrate the possibility and danger that metaphor performatively inaugurates a shift in the order of names and thus in truth.

Hobbes's account of conscience exemplifies performative positing by a rhetorical figure, but in addition his understanding of speech as predication and of truth as the order of names opens the way to limitless performative effects. What we are able to say determines the range of possible usages and of possible corruptions of truth. The order of names is in its very nature open to corruption by the simple performance of figurative speech. The component of rhetoric that pertains sheerly to figuration is thus performative with regard to its shaping of truth, that is, of the usages which define the order of names. The Hobbesian account of the instability of the order of names both explains and exemplifies the difficulties of achieving incontrovertible bindingness through words, and yet we do nonetheless promise, write, and rely on this very bindingness that cannot be guaranteed.

Hegel's *Phenomenology of Spirit* raises the question of the performative possibilities of a philosophical text, for the *Darstellung* (representation) of Spirit in that text, as Hegel explains it in the introduction, is not a mere description but *enacts* Spirit's very unfolding and becoming, in all its contradictions. The text of Hegel is also supposed to be performative, in that it is itself to *accomplish* the very unfolding which it narrates. The book *Phenomenology of Spirit* should thus be binding on our world, for it not only narrates but also posits the appearance of Spirit in its successive forms. Within Hegel's text, however, the chapter on conscience occupies a distinctive role, for it is in this chapter that Spirit encounters the possibility of failure with respect to performative language. The contradictions in terms of which conscience unfolds in the *Phenomenology* derive largely from conscience's attempt at a performative declaration: where conscience actualizes for others its objectivity in its declaration, it shows itself as both too objective and too subjective; and where conscience states its particularity, it shows itself as too particular and too universal, and so on.

The declaration of conscience which should in fact solve the problem of conscience's *Verstellung* (dissemblance or displacement), that is, of conscience's need to be "in" its actions, repeats and intensifies conscience's contradictions. These contradictions are played out in the figures of the voice of conscience, the moral genius, the community of consciences, the beautiful soul, hypocrisy, judging consciousness, and the yes of reconciliation. In each case words and language both succeed and fail to do what conscience would have them do. Thus, to borrow again a phrase from Judith Butler, conscience's declaration "rhetorically confounds precisely what it is supposed to show."[1] The frustration and misfire that beset conscience are the result of the performative successes of conscience's declarations, for inasmuch as conscience declares, its declarations evoke and accomplish effects which frustrate conscience's attempt to actualize itself in language.

The failure of conscience to guarantee the bonds among itself, its acts, and its duty is exemplary for the question regarding whether and how the *Phenomenology* as a whole may be binding—that is, whether the text can truly *be* the actualization of the Spirit whose unfolding it narrates. In the conscience chapter Hegel dramatizes how the effects of performative saying cannot be controlled by any point from which they are issued. What is produced in performative saying may be less, more, or other than that which is explicitly said, for the saying itself takes on an existence of its own. Whether this existence is a binding one is not determinable in advance by the agency governing the performance, nor by the performance itself. This insight may also be applied to the text of the *Phenomenology*. Hegel suggests that Spirit is not only described but also *unfolds* in this text; insofar as we accept this suggestion, then we must view the text as in some respect a saying—like that of conscience—that should produce universal recognition of its true character and thus achieve the full actualization of what it means to be. But of course *within* the *Phenomenology*, conscience's declaration of its actuality does not produce such a univocal actuality nor the universal recognition it requires. Its failures are illustrative of the potential for aberration and failure at the level of any text or any saying that would claim to be the actualization of what it describes.

Heidegger, unlike Hobbes, notoriously embraces the polysemy of words and the nonunivocity of statements, specifically allowing for intonations wherein other resonances and etymological possibilities come to be heard.[2] Thus in the course of investigating the performative and rhetorical aspects of *Being and Time,* I argue that the tension between the rhetorically determined formulations concerning being and the impossibility to treat being in proper terms is itself performative in various respects. In this regard, the ontological enterprise is a performance of Heidegger's account of the unhandy tool, where the words of the very text are shown to be "unhandy" and yet in their unhandiness to constitute a theorizing. In addition, the "not"-statements of *Being and Time* perform a repeated refusal of straightforward or literal understanding. Likewise the elision in the introductory sections of *Being and Time* of the words "meaning of," as the investigation into the meaning of being is conflated with the investigation into being, is itself crucial for the repeated defamiliarization, thematization, and problematization of the word "being" throughout the text. The analysis of the call of conscience is also an unhandy analysis, constructed around the word "not" and the refusal of specification, for conscience in *Being and Time* is deeply withdrawn from entitativeness and into possibility. The description of conscience as calling Dasein to its ownmost ability to be itself, moreover, raises the possibility of reading *Being and Time* as such an attestation and even as such a call, and thereby calls into question the exemplary status of conscience within the larger text. In fact, if Heidegger's text in some respects attempts to let language speak, as opposed to using language as a tool, then in fact it could be argued that Heidegger is attempting to yield his place as author to the performativity of language itself, to give place to the unfolding, performing, inscenation that takes place in his text.

There are intrinsic problems with invoking, as I have here, a rhetorical positing or a bindingness of words. Any reference to a binding that has been accomplished by means of a saying is always after the fact, that is, after the fact of the alleged positing, and thus it *confirms* as much as it *tells* a story of performativity. This means that the stories of performativity's effects can never be told in a language or with a grammar that would be appropriate to them, for the narrative requirements of beginning each story are founded upon each story's outcome. For these reasons, while this book traces several instances or stagings of the connections among conscience, figuration, and bindingness, this connection cannot be defined or delineated in a generalized fashion but instead occurs in each case in a singular fashion.[3] Indeed, I would suggest that it is the case that *only* examples can be offered for bindingness—examples that may, indeed, be judged to *fail* to exemplify it and thus may raise the question as to whether it even exists.

There is thus an undecidability at the center of the question of performative or binding texts. That is, it seems impossible to definitively prove that there *is* such thing as a performativity or a bindingness that could be ascribed to texts. In the end, one of course *may* say of a text that it is only a text, that it does not perform anything at all. Hegel's *Phenomenology of*

Spirit, for example, is not universally applauded or even admired by philosophers, and some *may* argue that what is characterized as its "living" and "unfolding" instead reflects Hegel's misunderstandings of the nature of predication and of truth as correspondence. Likewise, what I have attempted to characterize as the performative difficulty of Heidegger's text *may* be said to be simple obscurantism, and Hobbes *may* be said to commit a simple performative contradiction, in condemning rhetoric while writing in a highly rhetorical fashion. There is no guarantee that a text can be a performance or that there is such thing as a performative text. This is perhaps owing to the very nature of a guarantee. Is a guarantee a constative confirmation or a performative promise—in this case, a promise that there is such a thing as textual performativity? The dangerous possibility at the heart of Hobbes's worry about metaphor is instructive here, namely, precisely that one *may say,* may connect words, and thereby may say-into-being a new order of names and thus a new truth. The *being* produced by a saying-into-being is a tenuous one at best. Nevertheless, any text, including this book, in its own way may exemplify it, but this exemplification is without guarantee of an independent ontological subsistence.

Is a text performative? Can a text *do* something, and especially can it do what it says? We circle in these questions around the problem of the rhetoric of agency, for in our everyday notion of doing, texts do not *do* anything at all. And nonetheless there is the question of whether texts, works of art, or objects can be spoken of as agents and as binding. Of course, we are *able* to speak of them as such; we simply put the name of the text or the work of art in the grammatical subject position and commence talking and writing. But is it *permissible?* Is this a *true* account of what happens? Just because we are able to say that a text is performative and are able to describe it as binding, does that mean that it is so? Perhaps in writing and talking in this way we simply displace our own agency as readers, or an author's agency as an author, onto texts that are constitutionally innocent of all agency.

Nonetheless, some kinds of doing are attributed to texts by means of figurative formulations that are so familiar that they do not raise the eyebrows even of the staunch literalist. We are comfortable with the expression that a text "says" this or that. Perhaps that is because we are comfortable with the particular metonymic gesture in which we substitute author for work, or vice versa, such that we can say that we are reading an author instead of her or his work. In each of these cases, the location of agency slips easily and comfortably between author and work. It is only when we are caught in the unfamiliarity of a phrase, when we focus, for instance, on something like "textual doing," that this problem seems to arise. For this reason it is not particularly helpful to be admonished that texts are not agents. Luther's, Marx's, and Freud's texts may not have *done* anything at all; but then again, *didn't* they? Aren't the metonymies of producer/product acceptable because they allow us to express the effectual character of products, of things, without having to take responsibility for the ambiguous agency that they pronounce?

Perhaps we are simply bewitched by our own prosopopoeic description of textual agency. Perhaps we unfairly literalize a metonymy of producer/product or a prosopopoeic ensoulment of the text when we attribute actual agency to a text. If the problem is that we are confusing a linguistic expression with natural reality, that would mean that the text can be said to *do* things only *if* we prosopopoeically displace the operations of readers, writers, and effects—perlocutionary or otherwise—onto the text and rhetorically *make* it the agent. What is interesting is that we *can* perform this displacement, both in our concepts and in our grammar. We can because the formulation by which we take the text as an agent is extremely close to, if not indistinguishable from, the very same kind of formulation by which we take ourselves as agents. But for this very reason epistemological certainty with regard to where agency lies is foreclosed; we have no epistemological guarantee, we can never be *entirely* sure whether the text is an agent only by prosopopoeia or whether it is in fact *literally* an agent. For from what position outside figuration is the directionality of agency perceivable? To make the judgment once and for all that it is truly and unequivocally *we* that are the side of agency, and not the text, is to assume a position of unmediated, extrafigural observation. This would assume, then, that there is an uncontaminated normative position from which to judge and disqualify the prosopopeic breach of the literal/figurative boundary.

The apparent slippage between literal and figurative that we are seeing with regard to a rhetoric of textual bindingness or performativity could be approached in terms of the figure syllepsis, which is a trope wherein a word is used both literally and figuratively at the same time. In other words, syllepsis is a trope with one foot—so to speak—in the figurative realm and the other in the literal realm. One classic example of syllepsis is Racine's line from *Andromache,* "Brûlé de plus de feux que je n'en allumai" ("Burning in fires far worse than ever I set"). It evokes at the same time both the heat of fires lit and of passions felt.[4] What is especially remarkable about syllepsis is that it absorbs the literal into the tropological system along with the figurative; it is a *trope* in which the very exchange or leap *between* literal and figurative is reinscribed into the tropological system. Syllepsis validates, within the system of tropes, the slippage between literal and figurative.

In a sense syllepsis marks the institutionalization within the system of tropes of the coexistence and commingling of literal and figurative, confounding our attempts to say which is which. The figure of syllepsis could thus be said to foreclose any definitive decision *between* literal and figurative and thus to foreclose our decisions here regarding metaphoric, metonymic, prosopopoeic, or otherwise figurative agency. The very existence of syllepsis—the mere possibility that a phrase such as "textual agency" *might* be used sylleptically and thus at least *partly* tropologically— imperils the normative position from which a decision could be made with regard to the figurativeness of any attribution of agency or bindingness. A sylleptic reading releases the requirements of meaning from the either/or of literal versus figurative reading and takes on the pervasive possibility that renders undecidable the ultimate status of claims that might otherwise be said to confuse natural reality with a figurative expression. Syllepsis is a spoiler with regard to the charge of confusion of literal and figurative agency; because it in effect accounts for the potential literalization of tropes (e.g., of prosopopoeia, metaphor, or metonymy with regard to "textual agency") *within* the same tropological system upon whose boundaries depends any charge of unwarranted displacement of agency. For these reasons the epistemological guarantee of our own agency and of the text's apparent lack of agency is also foreclosed, however obvious either of those may seem. The pervasive possibility of which syllepsis takes account, namely, of a commingled literalness and figurativeness, means that a guarantee cannot be enforced as to where performance or binding takes place, nor as to whether a figurative textual agency is being confounded with or merely compared with a literal human agency, nor as to who or what is being personified, nor as to who or what is the true agent. A sylleptic reading sustains a potential irony that renders any definitive—that is, binding—answer incomplete. Precisely because we both read and are subject to the effects of the texts we read, we are ineluctably vulnerable to a sylleptic disruption of a definitive account of textual agency and binding.

Notes

Introduction

1. Victor Hugo, "La conscience," in *La Légende des Siècles* (Paris: Pléiade, 1950), 25–26. Herman Melville, *Moby-Dick, or The Whale* (New York: Penguin, 1992), 255.

2. Jacques Derrida's "White Mythology: Metaphor in the Text of Philosophy," in *Margins of Philosophy*, trans. Alan Bass (Chicago: University of Chicago Press, 1982), is central for contemporary considerations of metaphor and catachresis. See also Patricia Parker, "Metaphor and Catachresis," in *The Ends of Rhetoric: History, Theory, Practice*, ed. John Bender and David E. Wellbery (Stanford, CA: Stanford University Press, 1990). My approach to the question of figuration is also indebted to Ernesto Grassi's discussions of "rhetorical philosophizing" in "The Rehabilitation of Rhetorical Humanism: Regarding Heidegger's Anti-Humanism," *Diogenes*, no. 142 (Summer 1988): 136–56; as well as Grassi's *The Primordial Metaphor*, trans. Laura Pietropaolo and Manuela Scarci (Binghamton: Medieval & Renaissance Texts & Studies in collaboration with the Italian Academy, 1994). For a discussion of how literality is itself a metaphor, see Bill Readings, "The Deconstruction of Politics," in *Reading de Man Reading*, ed. Lindsay Waters and Wlad Godzich (Minneapolis: University of Minnesota Press, 1989).

3. The question of whether and in what fashion conscience exists is clearly a question that can be approached from many angles. One recent attempt to reconsider the metaphysics of conscience is Douglas C. Langston, *Conscience and Other Virtues* (University Park: Pennsylvania State University, 2001). Langston redescribes conscience as a "relational entity" rather than a faculty or a "substantial entity."

4. With the use of the term "bindingness" I risk substantializing the processual character of "binding" in addition to sacrificing euphony. On the other hand, I hope that the awkwardness of adding a nominalizing suffix to the participle might prevent the nominalization from smoothly assimilating the processual and dynamic element of "binding" to the conceptual realm of substantial entities. The impossibility of keeping such metaphysical considerations apart from matters of "mere" terminology illustrates larger issues at the intersection of philosophy and rhetoric. For similar reasons—that is, in hope that a certain awkwardness may help keep the terms in question from too easily falling into our established categories of thought—I use "figurativeness" and "literalness" in lieu of the more euphonic and customary terms "figurality" and "literality."

5. This book is indebted to scholarship on conscience in the fields of intellectual history, theology, and literature. I list here some of the sources that I found very useful, but clearly a bibliography of relevant materials would be much longer. Heinz D. Kittsteiner's monumental study, *Die Entstehung des modernen Gewissens* (Frankfurt am Main: Suhrkamp, 1991), is invaluable. Johannes Stelzenberger offers philological and historical analyses of conscience in *Syneidesis, conscientia, Gewissen: Studie zum Bedeutungswandel eines moraltheologischen Begriffes* (Paderborn, Germany: Ferdinand Schöningh, 1963). See also Johannes Stelzenberger, *Das Gewissen* (Paderborn, Germany: Ferdinand Schöningh, 1961). Uta Störmer-Caysa's introduction to and collection of texts entitled *Über das Gewissen: Texte zur Begründung der neuzeitlichen Subjektivität* (Weinheim, Germany: Beltz Athenaeum, 1995) is also an important contribution to the cultural and literary history of conscience. Jürgen Blühdorn's *Das Gewissen in der Diskussion* (Darmstadt: Wissenschaftliche Buchgesellschaft, 1976) is particularly valuable for its bibliography. Hendrik Gerhardus Stoker's *Das Gewissen: Erscheinungsformen und Theorien* (Bonn: Cohen, 1925), mentioned by Heidegger in *Being and Time*, is a useful, albeit very dated, source. The question of the early modern divergence between consciousness and conscience—mainly in French thought but with applicability to the English distinction—is treated in helpful detail by Catherine Glyn Davies, *Conscience as Consciousness: The Idea of Self-Awareness in French Philosophical Writing from Descartes to Diderot* (Oxford: Voltaire Foundation at Taylor Institution, 1990).

On Hegel and conscience, the following sources have been particularly useful for this book: Margery Rösinger, *Die Einheit von Ethik und Ontologie bei Hegel* (Frankfurt am Main: Peter Lang, 1980); Guido Heintel, "Moralisches Gewissen und substantielle Sittlichkeit in Hegels Geschichtsphilosophie," in *Geschichte und System: Festschrift für Erich Heintel zum 60. Geburtstag*, ed. Hans-Dieter Klein and Erhard Oeser (Munich: R. Oldenbourg, 1972), 128–43; Karlheinz Well, *Die "schöne Seele" und ihre "sittliche Wirklichkeit": Überlegungen zum Verhältnis von Kunst und Staat bei Hegel* (Frankfurt am Main: Peter Lang, 1986); Udo Rameil, "Sittliches Sein und Subjektivität: Zur Genese des Begriffs der Sittlichkeit in Hegels Rechtsphilosophie," *Hegel-Studien* 16 (1981): 123–63; Albert Reuter, "Dialektik und Gewissen: Studien zu Hegel" (Ph.D. diss., Albert-Ludwigs-Universität Freiburg, 1977).

For works on Heidegger and conscience, see Jean-Francois Courtine, "Voice of Conscience and Call of Being," in *Who Comes after the Subject?* ed. Eduardo Cadava, Peter Connor, and Jean-Luc Nancy (New York: Routledge, 1991), 79–93; Karsten Harries, "Fundamental Ontology and the Search for Man's Place," in *Heidegger and Modern Philosophy: Critical Essays*, ed. Michael Murray (New Haven, CT: Yale University Press, 1978), 65–79; Michael J. Hyde, "The Call of Conscience: Heidegger and the Question of Rhetoric," *Philosophy and Rhetoric* 27, no. 4 (1994): 374–96; Alphonso Lingis, "Authentic Time," in *Crosscurrents in Phenomenology*, ed. Ronald Bruzina and Bruce Wilshire (The Hague: Martinus Nijhoff, 1978), 276–96; Hans-Georg Gadamer, "Martin Heidegger und die Marburger Theologie," in *Heidegger: Perspektiven zur Deutung seines Werks*, ed. Otto Pöggeler (Weinheim, Germany: Beltz Athenaeum, 1994), 169–79; Frank Schalow, "The Topography of Heidegger's Concept of Conscience," *American Catholic Philosophical Quarterly* 49, no. 2 (1995): 255–73; J. M. Hollenbach, *Sein und Gewissen: Über den Ursprung der Gewis-*

sensregung. Eine Begegnung zwischen M. Heidegger und thomistischer Philosophie (Baden-Baden: Bruno Grimm, 1954); and Dominic Kaegi, "Die Religion in den Grenzen der blossen Existenz: Heidegger, religionsphilosophische Vorlesungen von 1920/21," *Internationale Zeitschrift für Philosophie,* no. 1 (1996): 133–49.

6. Martin Heidegger, *The Principle of Reason,* trans. Reginald Lilly (Bloomington: Indiana University Press, 1991), 47–49. In their influential *Metaphors We Live By* (Chicago: University of Chicago Press, 2003), George Lakoff and Mark Johnson offer the following blend of analogy and figure with regard to the question of whether sensory perception may be delimited from interpretation: "It is as though the ability to comprehend experience through metaphor were a sense, like seeing or touching or hearing, with metaphors providing the only ways to perceive and experience much of the world. Metaphor is as much a part of our functioning as our sense of touch, and as precious" (239).

7. Heidegger's lecture course does not replace the literal/figurative schema with some other schema, nor does it eradicate it and leave in its place nothing at all. Instead Heidegger demonstrates in his reading over several lectures of Silesius's verse "The rose is without why, it blooms because it blooms" that the verse can be read not only as a figure but also as a statement about the groundlike character of being. Heidegger's lecture course carries out the unfolding of a series of thoughts and offers itself as exemplary for other investigations. In other words, the alternative that the text offers to a literal-figurative schema is merely itself, not another system, polarization, or dialectical resolution of the posited divergence of literalness and figurativeness.

8. Immanuel Kant, *Critique of Practical Reason,* trans. Lewis White Beck (New York: Macmillan, 1993): "For pure [practical] reason, once it is demonstrated to exist, is in no need of a critique; it is pure reason itself which contains the standard for the critique of its entire use" (15–16, translation modified). Kant explains just above this that "if we now can discover means to show that freedom does in fact belong to the human will . . . then it will have been proved not only that pure reason can be practical but also that it alone, and not the empirically conditioned reason, is unconditionally practical" (15).

9. Judith Butler's *The Psychic Life of Power: Theories in Subjection* (Stanford, CA: Stanford University Press, 1997) focuses on the performative power of tropes (e.g., 176–77) and specifically on the tropological inauguration of the subject, conscience, and the fabulation of a psychic topography. My book takes up questions of the performative power of tropes with regard to conscience and the binding and performative power of texts; it is in this sense less oriented toward the "psychic" life of power and more toward the question of how texts may be described as performative or as having "binding" power.

10. Shannon Jackson, in *Professing Performance: Theatre in the Academy from Philology to Performativity* (Cambridge: Cambridge University Press, 2004), offers a comprehensive analysis of the disciplinary and institutional developments around performance and performativity. Andrew Parker and Eve Kosofsky Sedgwick offer in their editors' introduction to *Performativity and Performance* (New York: Routledge, 1995), 1–18, an examination of the intersection of philosophical and literary conceptions of performativity with theatrical and social performances.

11. J. L. Austin, *How to Do Things with Words,* ed. J. O. Urmson and Marina Sbisà (Cambridge: Harvard University Press, 1975), 6.

12. See, for example, John R. Searle's *Speech Acts* (Cambridge: Cambridge University Press, 1969) and his "How Performatives Work," *Linguistics and Philosophy* 12 (1989): 535–58.

13. Judith Butler, "Performative Acts and Gender Constitution: An Essay in Phenomenology and Feminist Theory," in *Performing Feminisms: Feminist Critical Theory and Theatre,* ed. Sue-Ellen Case (Baltimore: Johns Hopkins University Press, 1990), 273.

14. Josette Féral, "Performance and Theatricality: The Subject Demystified," *Modern Drama* 25 (1982): 173.

15. For connections between enactment, theater, and philosophy, see James N. Edie, "Appearance and Reality: An Essay on the Philosophy of the Theatre," in *Phenomenology: Dialogues and Bridges,* ed. Ronald Bruzina and Bruce Wilshire (Albany: SUNY Press, 1982), 339–52; and Bruce Wilshire, "Theatre as Phenomenology: The Disclosure of Historical Life," in Bruzina and Wilshire, *Phenomenology: Dialogues and Bridges,* 353–61.

16. Augustine, *Confessions,* trans. William Watts (Cambridge: Harvard University Press, 1989), 8.7, 1:441–43. References are to book, chapter, volume, and page numbers.

17. This productive conflation of love and conscience is apparent when Augustine begins his *Confessions* 10.6 with "Not out of a doubtful, but with a certain conscience [*non dubia, sed certa conscientia*] do I love thee, thou hast stricken my heart with thy word" (Augustine, *Confessions,* 10.6, 2:87). Here conscience and love are mingled; conscience *loves* rather than witnesses.

18. Ibid., 2.4, 1:79.

19. Ibid., 10.3, 2:81.

20. Ibid., 1.2, 1:5.

21. Ibid.

22. Ibid., 10.2, 2:75, translation modified.

23. Such suspicion is apparent, for example, in Hegel's *Phenomenology of Spirit* and *Philosophy of Right* and in Emmanuel Levinas's disparaging references to good conscience. Chapter 2 of this book will deal in detail with Hegel's account of conscience. For references in Levinas to good conscience, see, for example, *Beyond the Verse: Talmudic Readings and Lectures,* trans. Gary D. Mole (Bloomington: Indiana University Press, 1994), xii and 3; and *Time and the Other,* trans. Richard A. Cohen (Pittsburgh: Duquesne University Press, 1987), 117–18.

Chapter 1

Unless otherwise noted, page numbers in running text refer to Thomas Hobbes, *Leviathan, or The Matter, Form, and Power of a Commonwealth Ecclesiastical and Civil,* in *The English Works of Thomas Hobbes of Malmesbury,* vol. 3, ed. Sir William Molesworth (London: Bohn, 1839). Where it is not clear that this text is being referenced or where multiple texts are referenced, page numbers for *Leviathan* are preceded by the abbreviation *L*. Other works of Hobbes will also be cited from the Malmesbury edition (*The English Works of Thomas Hobbes of Malmesbury*, 11 vols., ed. Sir William Molesworth [London: Bohn, 1839]), abbreviated *EW*, followed by volume and page numbers.

1. Hobbes research also connects to questions of performativity and performance around Hobbes's metaphorics of the stage, theater, and personation. See, for instance, Louis Roux, *Thomas Hobbes: Penseur entre deux mondes* (Saint-Étienne, France: Publications de l'Université de Saint-Etienne, 1981), 245–88; Christopher Pye, "The Sovereign, the Theater, and the Kingdome of Darknesse: Hobbes and the Spectacle of Power," *Representations* 8 (1984): 85–106; and George Shulman, "Metaphor and Modernization in the Political Thought of Thomas Hobbes," in *Political Theory* 17, no. 3 (August 1989): 392–416, in which Shulman argues that "Hobbes writes the script people have followed as they have authorized modernity" (393).

2. Hobbes's emphasis on "acts of language" has been cited as justification for placing him at the origin of Anglo-Saxon philosophy; see André Robinet, "Pensée et langage chez Hobbes: Physique de la parole et *translatio*," *Revue internationale de Philosophie* 129 (1979): 452–83, esp. 452. Hobbes's focus on how the sovereign's declarations make laws binding was also frequently compared to Austin's model of performativity in the decade following the appearance in 1962 of Austin's *How to Do Things with Words*. See Geraint Parry, "Performative Utterances and Obligation in Hobbes," *Philosophical Quarterly* 17 (1967): 246–52; David R. Bell, "What Hobbes Does with Words," *Philosophical Quarterly* 19 (1969): 155–58; and Martin Bertman, "Hobbes and Performatives," *Critica* 10 (December 1978): 41–52. See also J. W. N. Watkins, *Hobbes' System of Ideas* (London: Hutchinson University Library, 1965); Gershon Weiler, "Hobbes and Performatives," *Philosophy* 45 (July 1970): 210–20; W. von Leyden, "Parry on Performatives and Obligation in Hobbes," *Philosophical Quarterly* 23 (1973): 258–59; and Eerik Lagerspetz, "Hobbes's Logic of Law," in *Hobbes: War among Nations*, ed. Timo Airaksinen and Martin A. Bertman (Aldershot, England: Avebury, 1989), 142–53, which discusses the ways in which Austin adopts Hobbes's theory of law. Anat Biletzki, in "Thomas Hobbes on 'The General Use of Speech,'" *Hobbes Studies* 7 (1994): 3–27, raises the issue of speech-act theory with respect to semantics and pragmatics. Robert Bernasconi, in "Opening the Future: The Paradox of Promising in the Hobbesian Social Contract," *Philosophy Today* 41 (Spring 1997): 77–86, argues that "the Hobbesian social contract is better understood as the means by which the individual is produced and given identity than as the product of individuals whose identities are presupposed by the contract" (83).

3. See Samuel Mintz, "Leviathan as Metaphor," *Hobbes Studies* 1 (1988), 8: "Hobbes had a sense of language as action, of performative utterances, of sentences that are themselves the act they are reporting. . . . But Austin had a low opinion of the fictional or literary uses of performative utterance. He called them 'infections,' 'parasites,' 'the etiolations of language.' For Hobbes they are creative acts, they resemble the speech acts that constitute the Creation." Performativity is in this context bound to divine creation and to the act of decree.

4. Hence Strong argues that "the task that *Leviathan* performs is the writing

of an actual Scripture" (Tracy Strong, "How to Write Scripture: Words, Authority and Politics in Thomas Hobbes," *Critical Inquiry* 20, no. 1 [Autumn 1993]: 128–59, quotation at 131). Thus *Leviathan* is not merely a text *about* authority, sovereignty, and the establishment of the commonwealth; rather, "*Leviathan* is the Scripture necessary to the understanding of sovereignty that Hobbes has established" (158). Textuality is here not exterior to the establishment of the sovereignty essential to the commonwealth, for the sovereign "is the text in which we can at the same time find ourself and each other. That is, in setting up the Leviathan we have represented ourself to our self" (158). David Johnston claims, in a similar vein, that the text *Leviathan* is itself a political act. See David Johnston, *The Rhetoric of Leviathan: Thomas Hobbes and the Politics of Cultural Transformation* (Princeton, NJ: Princeton University Press, 1986), esp. 91 and 119. Johnston investigates the performative quality of *Leviathan*, emphasizing "what Hobbes was attempting to *do* in that work as well as, in a narrow sense, what he was trying to say" (ix). Johnston also provides historical evidence for how in Hobbes's time the distinction between saying and doing was a problematic one. As Johnston observes, "The notion that speech and the written word are forms of action . . . was a commonplace to Hobbes and his Renaissance forebears" (ix). Jeremy Rayner ("Hobbes and the Rhetoricians," *Hobbes Studies* 4 [1991]: 76–95) claims, "However we choose to read *Leviathan*, it must surely be seen as a performance intended to have practical consequences, a performance made or broken by the persuasive powers of Hobbes himself" (91).

5. Exceptions to this are Jürgen Habermas, *Strukturwandel der Öffentlichkeit: Untersuchungen zu einer Kategorie der bürgerlichen Gesellschaft* (Neuwied, Germany: Luchterhand, 1962), 113–14, and Reinhart Koselleck, *Kritik und Krise* (Frankfurt am Main: Suhrkamp, 1997), 18–32 and 161–64. Hobbes also makes important appearances in Heinz Kittsteiner, *Die Entstehung des modernen Gewissens* (Frankfurt am Main: Suhrkamp, 1991), 235f, and Johannes Stelzenberger, *Syneidesis, conscientia, Gewissen: Studie zum Bedeutungswandel eines moraltheologischen Begriffes* (Paderborn, Germany: Schöningh, 1963), 113 and 115. See also Keith C. Pepperell, "Religious Conscience and Civic Conscience in Thomas Hobbes' Civic Philosophy," *Educational Theory* 39 (Winter 1989): 17–25, and Margaret Sampson, "'Will You Hear What a Casuist He Is?' Thomas Hobbes as Director of Conscience," *History of Political Thought* 11, no. 4 (1990): 721–36.

6. For these reasons Hobbes recommends that "a Counselor . . . ought to propound his advice, in such form of speech, as may make the truth most evidently appear; that is to say, with as firm ratiocination, as significant and proper language" (*L* 246).

7. *EW*, 2:137–38.

8. Victoria Kahn, *Rhetoric, Prudence and Skepticism in the Renaissance* (Ithaca, NY: Cornell University Press, 1985), 158.

9. For an example of these reductive accusations, see Frederick G. Whelan, "Language and Its Abuses in Hobbes's Political Philosophy," *American Political Science Review* 75, no. 1 (1981): 59–75. Whelan claims that "Hobbes's work is plagued throughout by the contradiction between the alleged self-evidence of its

principles and the prevalence of the kinds of errors and discords against which those principles militate" (71).

10. James Martel, "Strong Sovereign, Weak Messiah: Thomas Hobbes on Scriptural Interpretation, Rhetoric and the Holy Spirit," in *Theory and Event* 7:4 (Baltimore: Johns Hopkins University Press, 2004).

11. William Mathie, in "Reason and Rhetoric in Hobbes's *Leviathan*," *Interpretation* 14 (May–September 1986): 281–98, shows that Hobbes claims that moral science must in the end combine reason and eloquence rather than entirely exclude eloquence. See Quentin Skinner, *Reason and Rhetoric in the Philosophy of Hobbes* (Cambridge: Cambridge University Press, 1994), 356–75, on the place of *Leviathan* as a reevaluation in Hobbes's thought on rhetoric. See also Martin Bertman, "What Is Alive in Hobbes," in Airaksinen and Bertman, *Hobbes: War among Nations*, 1–14, for a discussion of differences between "black rhetoric" and "white rhetoric." Johnston, *Rhetoric of Leviathan*, 107–14, argues that in Hobbes's thought there is a shift from a reason/rhetoric opposition to a reason/superstition opposition. Jeffrey Barnouw, in "Persuasion in Hobbes's *Leviathan*," *Hobbes Studies* 1 (1988): 3–25, discusses the respects in which persuasion holds a more ambiguous status than eloquence in Hobbes.

12. *EW,* 1:22–23.

13. See Marie-Madeleine Martinet, "La notion de perspective et les métaphores de l'espace," in *Hobbes et son vocabulaire: Études de lexicographie philosophique,* ed. Yves Charles Zarka (Paris: J. Vrin, 1992), 125–38, present reference at 138. Martinet points out in her study of spatial metaphors in Hobbes's "Answer to Sir William Davenant's Preface before *Gondibert*" that, in that text, syntactic metaphors are not only accepted but also praised.

14. *EW,* 2:161–62.

15. Metaphor is not alone among figures: "And, therefore, they have in their speeches, a regard to the common passions and opinions of men, in deducing their reasons; and make use of similitudes, metaphors, examples, and other tools of oratory, to persuade their hearers of the utility, honour, or justice of following their advice" (*L,* 243).

16. Johnston, *Rhetoric of Leviathan,* 67, points out that the style of *Leviathan* is more rhetorically vivid than that of the earlier *Elements of Law* and *De Cive.* Conal Condren, in "On the Rhetorical Foundations of *Leviathan*," *History of Political Thought* 11, no. 4 (1990): 703–20, also offers a more differentiated understanding of rhetoric in his argument against reductive claims for the merely rhetorical or merely scientific character of *Leviathan.*

17. Ross Rudolph, "Hobbes et la psychologie morale: l'obligation et la vertu," in *Thomas Hobbes: Philosophie première, théorie de la science et politique,* ed. Yves Charles Zarka, with the collaboration of Jean Bernhardt (Paris: Presses Universitaires de France, 1990), 247–63, esp. 250–51.

18. See Alfred Schaefer, *Die Idee in Person: Hobbes's Leviathan in seiner und unserer Zeit* (Berlin: Arno Spitz, 1993), 134, for an argument that Hobbes shares with Cicero and Aristotle a notion that law concerns behavior and does not extend to the inner realms of conscience and thought.

19. *EW,* 2:162–63. Hobbes adds that "this they have from that sort of eloquence, not which explains things as they are, but from that other, which by moving their minds, makes all things to appear to be such as they in their minds, prepared before, had already conceived them."

20. *L,* xi.

21. See Kenneth Minogue, "From Precision to Peace: Hobbes and Political Language," *Hobbes Studies* 3 (1990): 75–88: "Words, then, are power, and must be subject, like all other forms of power, to the rules of the sovereign" (81).

22. Parry, in "Performative Utterances," argues that the validity of the covenant rests not on the power of the sovereign or on the fear out of which the covenant originates but rather on the performative aspect of the verbal formulas that are used to make the covenant.

23. *L,* 240. See Dorothea Krook, "Thomas Hobbes's Doctrine of Meaning and Truth," *Philosophy* 31, no. 116 (January 1956): 3–22; and Gayne Nerney, "Homo Notans: Marks, Signs, and Imagination in Hobbes' Conception of Human Nature," *Hobbes Studies* 4 (1991): 53–75.

24. The insignificance of words seems to pose a hazard most of all to philosophers, who in puzzling away with such notions as "incorporeal body" or "quiddity" operate without regard for the tenets of what Hobbes ascribes to first philosophy, namely, the "right limiting of the significations of such appellations, or names, as are of all others the most universal" (671). In *De Corpore,* Hobbes writes, "Now in all matters that concern this life, but chiefly in philosophy, there is both great use and great abuse of *abstract names; . . .* the abuse proceeds from this, that some men . . . speak of accidents, as if they might be separated from all bodies"(*EW,* 1:33). Interestingly, however, the examples that Hobbes provides of the sort of insignificance that derive from Aristotelian philosophy are in fact accusations of church doctrine and practice; see for example, *L,* 675.

25. For Hobbes, the names of which language is composed serve three functions: registration of thought in the thinker, recollection of thought by the thinker, and declaration of thought to others. Hobbes distinguishes the registering of thoughts to ourselves as marks from the communication of thoughts and passions to others that employs names as signs. See *L,* 19–20; and Nerney, "Homo Notans."

26. In stating that "error is but a deception" (*L,* 32), Hobbes suggests that the error by which one falsely records one's own conception is equivalent to self-deception and that the error by which one falsely makes knowledge public is deception of others. In this respect, what Hobbes describes as deception by metaphor is more closely linked to what in everyday terms would be considered mere error rather than a calculated deception of others. On metaphor and error, see Luc Foisneau, "Le vocabulaire du pouvoir: Potentia/Potestas, Power," in Zarka, *Hobbes et son vocabulaire,* 98–101. In *De Corpore,* Hobbes distinguishes falsity as one form of error, namely that wherein, "[i]n affirming and denying, when they call any thing by a name, which is not the name thereof" (*EW,* 1:55). Thus metaphor is in every instance an error of at least this sort. This sort of error is distinct from what Hobbes also considers tacit errors, or "errors of the sense and cogitation," which occur in the "passing from one imagination to the imagination of another

different thing; or by feigning that to be past, or future, which never was, nor ever shall be. . . . or lastly, when from any sign we vainly imagine something to be signified, which is not" (*EW,* 1:56). Deception and error are also connected with absurdity, hence Hobbes adds to his condemnation of metaphor in a chapter of *Leviathan* on reason and science, such that figurative language is described not as fostering deception, as I have just described, but rather as causing absurd conclusions. Each of seven causes of absurd conclusions listed by Hobbes involves mistakes in nomenclature. The sixth cause is "the use of metaphors, tropes, and other rhetorical figures, instead of words proper. For though it be lawfull to say, for example, in common speech, *the way goeth, or leadeth hither, or thither, the proverb says this or that,* whereas ways cannot go, nor proverbs speak; yet in reckoning, and seeking of truth, such speeches are not to be admitted" (34). Literally, assertions that "proverbs say" are absurd, for they use language improperly; the faculty of speech does not in fact belong to a proverb, hence the name "proverb" cannot be the subject of the verb "to say." Such assertions that abuse the literal meanings of the words they contain are for Hobbes inadmissible to the search for truth, for they themselves already depart from the proper ordering of names and thus already partake of error, deception, and absurdity. (The third and fourth abuses of speech pertain to intentional misleading and aggravation.)

27. "Briefly, in the state of nature, what is just and unjust, is not to be esteemed by the actions but by the counsel and conscience of the actor" (*EW,* note to 2:45–46).

28. See also *L,* 436, on private judgment.

29. See Schaefer, *Die Idee in Person,* 67, on the subordination of the anarchy of conscience to the commonwealth and on how the person of the sovereign is to be seen as the conscience of the commonwealth.

30. An interesting, theologically oriented reflection on the interiority of conscience appears in Hendrik Gerhardus Stoker, *Das Gewissen: Erscheinungsformen und Theorien* (Bonn: Cohen, 1925), 209: *"Das echte Gewissen ist die reelle innere Kundwerdung des Personalbösen. . . . Diese Kundwerdung ist . . . innere"* (Genuine conscience is the real, inner awareness of one's own evil. . . . This awareness is . . . inward). Stoker footnotes this definition of genuine conscience in order to mention that *innere* is used in a double sense (presumably as heart and interior) and to point out that each meaning supplements the other.

31. Emphases added. The spatial character of conscience that the "in" of conscience evokes is in some instances illustrated by the figure of conscience as a juridical court: "The law of nature doth always and everywhere oblige in the internal court, or that of conscience; but not always in the external court" (*EW,* 2:46), and "by spiritual power [the doctors of the Romish church] mean the power to determine points of faith, and to be judges in the inner court of conscience of moral duties" (*EW,* 6:171). The conjunction of the metaphorics of interiority and the judicial model of conscience as an internal court belong to a tradition of court metaphors with respect to conscience but are less relevant to the present consideration of the conjunction of conscience, privacy, and interiority, and their connection with the condemnation of figurative language.

32. Judith Butler, *The Psychic Life of Power: Theories in Subjection* (Stanford, CA: Stanford University Press, 1997), 19.

33. For discussions of the relationship between the words "conscience" and "consciousness," see Stelzenberger, *Syneidesis, Conscientia, Gewissen,* 107–10; Stoker, *Das Gewissen,* 5–24; and Catherine Glyn Davies, *Conscience as Consciousness: The Idea of Self-Awareness in French Philosophical Writing from Descartes to Diderot* (Oxford: Voltaire Foundation at Taylor Institution, 1990).

34. Self-love is also thematized in *Leviathan*'s epistle dedicatory. In case *Leviathan* would meet with disapproval from which Francis Godolphin, to whom the book is dedicated, would want to dissociate himself, Hobbes suggests that Godolphin make the excuse that Hobbes is simply in love with his own opinion (vi).

35. See Quentin Skinner, "The Study of Rhetoric as an Approach to Cultural History: The Case of Hobbes," in *Main Trends in Cultural History,* ed. Willem Melching (Amsterdam: Rodopi, 1994), 17–53; and Skinner, *Reason and Rhetoric,* 282–84 and 317–26.

36. Cited in Skinner, "Study of Rhetoric," 19.

37. Skinner, "Study of Rhetoric," 46–47. On the other hand, Skinner also points out the reference to what could later be called "paradiastole" in Hobbes's own translation of Thucydides' *History of the Peloponnesian Wars.*

38. *L,* 28; see Skinner, "Study of Rhetoric," 46.

39. For an excellent discussion of the relationship between examples and exemplum, see John Lyons, *Exemplum: The Rhetoric of Example in Early Modern France and Italy* (Princeton, NJ: Princeton University Press, 1989), 3–34.

40. It is fascinating to observe the abundant tropes by means of which Hobbes characterizes laws and their value for human society in his *Discourse of Laws,* including his explicit reference to Plato's and Heraclitus's characterization of laws. Laws are described as princes, bulwarks, defenses, sinews, and physicians, and justice as a knot and a guard. See Thomas Hobbes, "A Discourse of Laws," in *Three Discourses,* ed. Noel B. Reynolds and Arlene W. Saxonhouse (Chicago: University of Chicago Press, 1995), 105–19.

41. On obedience in Hobbes, see Simone Goyard-Fabre, "Loi civile et obéissance dans l'Etat-Léviathan," in Zarka, *Thomas Hobbes,* 289–304.

42. Hobbes sets similar requirements in his *Philosophical Rudiments Concerning Government and Society:* "The knowledge of the laws depends on the legislator; who must publish them; for otherwise they are not laws. For law is the command of the law-maker, and his command is the declaration of his will; it is not therefore a law, except the will of the law-maker be declared, which is done by *promulgation.* Now in *promulgation* two things must be manifest; whereof one is, that he or they who publish a law, either have a right themselves to make laws, or that they do it by authority derived from him or them who have it; the other is the sense of the law itself" (*EW,* 2:192).

43. Goyard-Fabre, "Loi civile," claims that laws are not coercive because they originate in the public itself (299).

44. "Whether all other nations of the world have in their several languages a word that answereth to it, I cannot tell; but I am sure they have not need of it" (673).

45. See Nerney, "Homo Notans," 56–58, on the role of the mediation of the imagination in the origins of appetite and aversion. See Arto Tukiainen, "The Commonwealth as a Person in Hobbes's *Leviathan*," *Hobbes Studies* 7 (1994): 44–55, on how the metaphor "strikes" between imagination and desire. See Rayner, "Hobbes and the Rhetoricians," 84–85, for discussion of how trains of thought are governed by passionate appetites.

46. *L*, 12.

47. Martel, in "Strong Sovereign, Weak Messiah," points out that Hobbes criticizes beliefs in ghosts, possession and exorcism as *overly* literal-minded; thus literal-mindedness is in such cases not preferable to figurative thought.

48. See Hobbes's discussion in *De Corpore:* "And though there may be fallacy in equivocal terms, yet in those that be manifestly such, there is none at all; nor in metaphors, for they profess the transferring of names from one thing to another" (*EW*, 1:62–63).

49. *L*, ix. Cf. Shulman, "Metaphor and Modernization," which contains an excellent discussion of the metaphorics of machines and theatricality associated with the artificial man. See also Mintz, "Leviathan as Metaphor"; Franck Lessay, "Le vocabulaire de la personne," in Zarka, *Hobbes et son vocabulaire*, 155–86; Tukiainen, " Commonwealth as Person"; and Schaefer, *Die Idee in Person*.

50. *L*, 307.

51. The actual site of resemblance, however, is unspecified; the train of thought is indeed free to assume—perhaps erroneously—exactly in what the resemblance consists.

52. *L*, x. See Strong, "How to Write Scripture," 140, for how the making of pacts imitates God's creation.

53. Martin Heidegger, in *The Basic Problems of Phenomenology*, trans. Albert Hofstadter (Bloomington: Indiana University Press, 1982), 183–92, focuses in detail on the copula in Hobbes. At 188, Heidegger shows how the "is" is both an identification of relatedness and an expression of being-true in propositions.

54. Aristotle, *Metaphysics* 7.1.1, 1028a.

55. Hobbes then adds, "For what is the *heart*, but a *spring;* and the *nerves*, but so many *strings;* and the *joints*, but so many *wheels*, giving motion to the whole body, such as was intended by the artificer?" (*L*, ix).

56. Cf. Michael Esfeld, *Mechanismus und Subjektivität in der Philosophie von Thomas Hobbes* (Stuttgart: Frommann-holzboog, 1995).

57. Cf. Bernasconi, "Opening the Future," on the promise that binds each person first to himself or herself.

Chapter 2

Unless otherwise noted, references in running text refer to G. W. F. Hegel, *Hegel's Phenomenology of Spirit*, trans. A. V. Miller (Oxford: Oxford University Press, 1977). Following a slash (/) appears the corresponding page number from the German text, *Phänomenologie des Geistes* (Frankfurt am Main: Suhrkamp, 1998). The abbreviation *PR* stands for G. W. F. Hegel, *Elements of the Philosophy of Right*, ed. Allen Wood, trans. H. B. Nisbet (Cambridge: Cambridge University Press, 1991). Following a slash (/) appears the corresponding page number from the German version, *Grundlinien der Philosophie des Rechts* (Frankfurt am Main: Suhrkamp, 1993).

1. Judith Butler, *Subjects of Desire: Hegelian Reflections in Twentieth-Century France* (New York: Columbia University Press, 1987), 31.

2. Cf. Daniel Cook, *Language in the Philosophy of Hegel* (The Hague: Mouton, 1973), esp. "Language as the Medium of Culture and Morality," 78–97. The role of language in sense-certainty, as illustrated by Hegel's "Now is night" example, has been an object of many studies. It is not clear, however, that the *Phenomenology*'s discussions of the phrase "Now is night" and the demonstrative "this" are intrinsically important to the consciousness that is sense-certainty in the text. They may be read instead as illustrations of what the language of sense-certainty, and sense-certainty itself, is for an *observing* consciousness—including for us who read the book. Does the consciousness depicted in those instances discover the limits of language, or is it *we* who thereby discover the impossibility of saying a particular in language? This raises larger questions about the relationship between an "observing consciousness" and sense-certainty in the text, as well as questions of whether consciousness unfolds of itself in the text, and to what extent the language of the text is itself the possibility of the reflexivity by means of which such unfolding proceeds. I restrict myself here to the question of how the unfolding of Spirit and its relationship to language are played out in the chapter on conscience, rather than on the scale of the entirety of the *Phenomenology*.

3. Charles Taylor, *Hegel* (Cambridge: Cambridge University Press, 1975), 108–9, offers an analogy based on a performance of gestures rather than declarations: "If someone makes a certain gesture which is aimed at a certain result and which negates it; if he wants to persist in this, then we can say that he is behaving in a contradictory fashion. And this is what *Geist* can be said to do, in that it cannot help but posit external finite reality, and yet this negates it and has to be in turn negated."

4. Cf. the *Philosophy of Right*, esp. "The Good and Conscience," 157–86/243–91. On the *Philosophy of Right*'s treatment of conscience, see Udo Rameil, "Sittliches Sein und Subjektivität: Zur Genese des Begriffs der Sittlichkeit in Hegels Rechtsphilosophie," *Hegel-Studien* 16 (1981): 123–63, esp. 127–39. For a discussion of conscience in Hegel's philosophy of history, see Guido Heintel, "Moralisches Gewissen und substantielle Sittlichkeit in Hegels Geschichtsphilosophie," in *Geschichte und System: Festschrift für Erich Heintel zum 60. Geburtstag*, ed. Hans-Dieter Klein and Erhard Oeser (Munich: R. Oldenbourg, 1972), 128–43.

5. The term "aufheben," as Hegel deploys it, presents notorious difficulties for translation. It connotes canceling, preserving, and raising. The English verb "to sublate" is a standard, albeit unilluminating, translation.

6. Cf. Hans-Georg Gadamer, *Wahrheit und Methode: Grundzüge einer philosophischen Hermeneutik*, vol. 1 (Tübingen: Mohr, 1990), 349.

7. In the *Philosophy of Right*, Hegel distinguishes briefly between the conscience of morality and the "true conscience" as "that which determines itself to will what is in and for itself the good and a duty" (PR 165/259). True conscience

has an "objective content," as opposed to the infinitely self-certain conscience that is the topic of these sections. See also Hegel, *Hegel's Philosophy of Mind, Being Part Three of the "Encyclopaedia of the Philosophical Sciences (1830), together with the "Zusätze" in Boumann's Text (1845)*, trans. William Wallace and A. V. Miller (Oxford: Clarendon Press, 1971), 252; and *Die Philosophie des Geistes, Enzyklopädie der philosophischen Wissenschaften im Grundrisse (1830), Dritter Teil* (Frankfurt am Main: Suhrkamp, 1986), 316.

8. Hence Albert Reuter, in "Dialektik und Gewissen: Studien zu Hegel" (Ph.D. diss., Albert-Ludwigs-Universität Freiburg, 1977), 94, emphasizes that Hegelian conscience is *convinced* of its duty, whereas Kantian conscience *respects* its duty.

9. Cf. Taylor's explanation of Hegel's critique of conscience as a critique of romanticism (*Hegel*, 192–94).

10. This certainty recapitulates the immediacy of previous stages of Spirit in which certainty was definitive. Heidegger points out that in the *Phenomenology of Spirit* "in every instance certainty means the entirety of the relation, in knowing, of a knower to what is known, the unity of knowing and what is known, the manner of being known and consciousness in the broadest sense of knowing and cognition" (Martin Heidegger, *Hegel's "Phenomenology of Spirit"* [Bloomington: Indiana University Press, 1988], 54).

11. Cf. Cook, *Language in the Philosophy of Hegel*, 91–94. See also Elliott L. Jurist, "Recognition and Self-Knowledge," in *Hegel-Studien* 21 (1986): 143–50.

12. Reuter, "Dialektik und Gewissen," 113, my translation.

13. *PR* 167/261; 168/263.

14. Cf. Miguel Giusti, "Bemerkungen zu Hegels Begriff der Handlung," *Hegel-Studien* 22 (1987): 51–71; see esp. 66f.

15. This point is made clearer in the *Philosophy of Right:* "Where all previously valid determinations have vanished and the will is in a state of pure inwardness, the self-consciousness is capable of making into its principle either *the universal in and for itself,* or the *arbitrariness* of its *own particularity,* giving the latter precedence over the universal and realizing it through its actions—i.e., it is capable of being *evil*" (*PR* 167/260–61).

16. "The duty which it fulfils is a *specific* content; it is true that this content is the *self* of consciousness, and so consciousness's *knowledge* of itself, its *identity* with itself. But once fulfilled, set in the medium of *being,* this identity [*Gleichheit*] is no longer knowing, no longer this process of differentiation . . . the action is a *specific* action, not identical [*ungleich*] with the element of everyone's self-consciousness" (394/477).

17. See David Wood, *Philosophy at the Limit: Problems of Modern European Thought* (London: Unwin Hyman, 1990), 77–78, for a comparison of the language of conscience with that of culture and with religion as art. See John McCumber, *Poetic Interaction: Language, Freedom, Reason* (Chicago: University of Chicago Press, 1989), 59–62, for a discussion of action and speech as forms of externalization and of language's unique property of universalizing the self of the utterer.

18. Cf. Margery Rösinger, *Die Einheit von Ethik und Ontologie bei Hegel* (Frankfurt am Main: Peter Lang, 1980), 34–35.

19. Hence Hegel writes, "This return, therefore, does not mean that the self is in essence and actuality present in its speech" (399/483).

20. "The 'I' is merely universal like 'Now,' 'Here,' or 'This' in general; I do indeed *mean* a single 'I,' but I can no more say what I *mean* in the case of 'I' than I can in the case of 'Now' or 'Here.' When I say 'this Here,' 'this Now,' or a 'single item,' I am saying all Thises, Heres, Nows, all single items" (62/87).

21. Denise Riley, *The Words of Selves: Identity, Solidarity, Irony* (Stanford, CA: Stanford University Press, 2000), in her section "'I' lies" (57–59), describes with eloquence the impossibility of saying the "I" that one means. On the paradoxes of sense-certainty, see also Slavoj Žižek, *Der erhabenste aller Hysteriker: Lacans Rückkehr zu Hegel* (Vienna: Turia & Kant, 1991), 20f.

22. "To make the deed a reality . . . means translating it . . . into the form of an *assurance* that consciousness is convinced of its duty" (396/479–80).

23. "Conscience, then, in the majesty of its elevation above specific law and every content of duty, puts whatever content it pleases into its knowing and willing" (397/481).

24. See also Joseph P. Vincenzo, "The Nature and Legitimacy of Hegel's Critique of the Kantian Moral Philosophy," *Hegel-Studien* 22 (1987): 73–87; esp. 76f. For a discussion of the relationship between Hegel's and Jacobi's "moral genius," see Emanuel Hirsch, "Die Beisetzung der Romantiker in Hegels Phänomenologie," in *Materialen zu Hegels "Phänomenologie des Geistes,"* ed. Hans Friedrich Fulda and Dieter Henrich (Frankfurt am Main: Suhrkamp, 1973), 253f.

25. Immanuel Kant, *Critique of Judgment,* tr. Werner S. Pluhar (Indianapolis: Hackett Publishing Company, 1987), 174.

26. Quentin Lauer, *A Reading of Hegel's "Phenomenology of Spirit"* (New York: Fordham University Press, 1976), 252. While this characterization fits the text in a broad sense, it also overlooks some of the more interesting complications. First, why does the divinity of conscience appear in terms of voice? Is voice is an expendable element in conscience's becoming divine? If it is expendable, then "voice" is an arbitrary figure of immediacy. In a section where language is so prominently at stake, however, "voice" may be not an arbitrary characterization but rather an essential element of conscience's becoming divine. Second, how does conscience "gradually become" God? Is it by being *like* God through giving itself prerogatives that conscience *becomes* God? If that is so, then likeness has a peculiar power, the power to make something into that which it is like. And if God is what conscience is first like, and then becomes, it appears that through imitation conscience becomes what it imitates. Thus conscience would be seen as becoming the inimitable—that is, God—by imitating God.

27. Howard Kainz, in *Hegel's "Phenomenology," Part II: The Evolution of Ethical and Religious Consciousness to the Absolute Standpoint* (Athens: Ohio University Press, 1983), says that conscience's moral conceptions are *"equivalent to* a divine voice" (115, emphasis added). Robert C. Solomon, in *In the Spirit of Hegel: A Study of G. W. F. Hegel's "Phenomenology of Spirit"* (New York: Cambridge University Press, 1983), writes, "The person of conscience comes to see him or herself *as* divine" (577, emphasis added). In each case, the commentators are perhaps reluctant to

say that conscience *is* God, because "God" will unfold differently later in the *Phenomenology*, and to say that conscience *is* God makes for a rather limited notion of God, given conscience's subjective and arbitrary character here. The "divinity" attributed to conscience and its voice must in any case be an inadequate one, for God cannot be such a subjective and one-sided divinity, and worship cannot truly be such contemplation of self.

28. Lauer, *Reading*, 252.

29. Hence Hegel calls this a "foundering of consciousness within itself [*(ein) Versinken innerhalb seiner selbst*]" (399/483, translation modified).

30. For an analysis of the oft-neglected sections of the *Phenomenology* on unhappy consciousness, see Judith Butler, *The Psychic Life of Power: Theories in Subjection* (Stanford, CA: Stanford University Press, 1997), 31–62.

31. "And, in speaking of the conscientiousness of its action, it may be well aware of its pure self, but in the *purpose* of its action, a purpose with an actual content, it is aware of itself as this particular individual, and is conscious of the antithesis between what it is for itself and what it is for others" (401/485).

32. The contradictions into which language falls in conscience, that is, as having both too much being-for-self and too much being-for-others, recapitulate the unfolding of language in "Culture." There, for instance, the universal name "monarch" actualizes the monarch's individuality and intensifies his being-for-self; and in addition the language of "base flattery" (315/384) asserts that wealth is an essence while knowing that it is instead inessential.

33. "It must be made apparent that it *is* evil, and thus its existence made to correspond to its essence; the hypocrisy must be unmasked" (401/485).

34. Hegel considers a hypothetical declaration of evil conscience, in order to show what it means for evil to be unmasked as opposed to being abolished (402/486). Evil consciousness cannot merely deny that it is evil—that is, declare that its conviction is in fact identical to duty—for a true universal consciousness would still differ from it. This difference or disparity alone would indicate that evil consciousness is *not* universal, and thus the assurance issued by evil consciousness does not overcome its nonidentity with universal consciousness. However, if evil were to deny its evil, the show of hypocrisy would cease, because it would *fail* as a show, insofar as virtue and duty would be clearly seen as antithetical to this evil consciousness. The declaration by evil consciousness that it is universal turns out to be a confession of its evil, for in its disparity with universal consciousness it clearly shows itself to conform only to its *own* law. This would not be the same, however, as "unmasking" evil as evil. It would be instead evil's direct abolition of itself, according to Hegel. In contrast, the resolution of hypocrisy requires not its cancellation or abolition but its unmasking—because hypocrisy is in its essence a show.

35. Cf. Žižek, *Der erhabenste aller Hysteriker,* 91f.

36. To understand judging consciousness as evil requires that we understand judging consciousness as an acting consciousness. The individual evil consciousness that judging consciousness judges acts; it is defined as evil inasmuch as the duty that it claims its action to be is determined by its individuality rather than

by a universal. It may appear that in contrast the judging consciousness merely apprehends the evil and thus "remains in the universality of thought [*bleibt in der Allgemeinheit des Gedankens*]" (403/487). Yet the judging it performs *is* an action, and precisely because it *is* an action—and indeed through this action—judging consciousness itself is evil, holding to itself as its own law in its activity of judging.

37. "His confession is not an abasement, a humiliation . . . he gives himself utterance solely on account of his having seen his identity with the other . . . and gives utterance to it for the reason that language is the *existence* of Spirit as an immediate self" (405/490).

38. See Hirsch, "Die Beisetzung der Romantiker," 261f, for a discussion of the hard heart with respect to Hölderlin.

39. "It does not recognize the contradiction it falls into in not letting the rejection which has taken place in *words*, be validated as a genuine rejection" (406/491).

40. Žižek, in *Der erhabenste aller Hysteriker*, 34 n. 24, points to the example of reconciliation as evidence for the retroactive character of the performativity of Hegelian dialectic. Erich Jung, in *Entzweiung und Versöhnung in Hegels Phänomenologie des Geistes*, ed. Hermann Röckel (Leipzig: Felix Meiner, 1940), argues for the centrality of the notion of reconciliation, or *Versöhnung*, in Hegel's thematic of the movement of recognition (20–21). According to Rösinger, *Die Einheit von Ethik*, the moment of final forgiveness consists in showing that forgiveness has *already* happened on both sides (42). J. N. Findlay, in *Hegel: A Re-examination* (New York: Oxford University Press, 1958), calls the appearance of forgiveness here a "compromise between judging and doing" without explaining the way in which this compromise is reached, that is, what it is that breaks the hard heart of judging consciousness (130). In his commentary *Hegel: Phenomenology and System* (Indianapolis: Hackett, 1995), H. S. Harris says simply that the hard heart "must *break*" and that forgiveness allows "us" to pass from morality to religion (78). Kainz, *Hegel's "Phenomenology,"* suggests instead that the madness and yearning "breaks up" the hard heart and thus suggests that this stubborn consciousness moves to forgiveness, rather than implying—as the other commentators do—that *we* are the ones who make this move, or that Spirit, as what this consciousness is, *must* make this move (122).

41. Hegel's mention of the nature of "the word" in his section on psychology in his *Encyclopaedia* (see *Philosophy of Mind*) has interesting resonances here, although what the word is is not entirely the same as it is in the *Phenomenology*. In an addition to the text concerning the difference between intelligence and will, Hegel notes that the will is engaged with resistant externalities and actualities and thus with utterly singular elements. In contrast, "intelligence as such in its manifestation, its utterance, only goes as far as the *word*, this fleeting, vanishing, completely *ideal* realization which proceeds in an unresisting element, so that in its utterance intelligence remains at home with itself, satisfies itself internally, demonstrates that it is its own end (*Selbstzweck*), is divine and, in the form of comprehensive cognition, brings into being the unlimited freedom and reconciliation of mind with itself" (*Philosophy of Mind*, 187/239). The word of intelligence is on

the one hand finite and less actual than the will, for it disappears the moment after it is uttered. The lack of endurance of the word and hence its lack of actuality lets intelligence remain comfortable in its nonactuality. On the other hand, the utterance proceeds without encountering any resistance from the time into which it disappears. The utterance, as intelligence's immediate declaration of itself, satisfies intelligence, gives it the divinity that we also see in the immediacy of the inner voice of conscience. As with the dialectic of conscience, the word also brings a "reconciliation."

42. See Žižek, *Der erhabenste aller Hysteriker,* 100–103.

43. See Peter Cornehl, *Die Zukunft der Versöhnung: Eschatologie und Emanzipation in der Aufklärung bei Hegel und in der Hegelschen Schule* (Göttingen: Vandenhoek & Ruprecht, 1971), 93–145, for a theologically oriented overview of forgiveness in Hegel and its relationship to eschatology. See Günter Wohlfahrt, *Denken der Sprache: Sprache und Kunst bei Vico, Hamann, Humboldt und Hegel* (Freiburg: Karl Alber, 1984), 221–22, on language as the actualization of religious Spirit's reconciliation.

44. Hyppolite therefore says that the hard heart must break, precisely because "equality has been established" between confessing consciousness and judging consciousness (Jean Hyppolite, *Genesis and Structure of Hegel's "Phenomenology of Spirit,"* trans. Samuel Cherniak and John Heckman [Evanston, IL: Northwestern University Press, 1974], 523). This equality having been established, the word of reconciliation "surges forth" as a necessary result.

45. Denise Riley, *Words of Selves,* 96.

46. Jean-Luc Nancy, *Hegel: The Restlessness of the Negative* (Minneapolis: University of Minnesota Press, 2002), 77.

47. For an interesting but flawed attempt to identify different kinds of performative texts, see Gwendoline Jarczyk, "Texte et hors-texte," in *Le texte comme objet philosophique,* ed. Institut catholique de Paris, Faculté de philosophie (Paris: Beauchesne, 1987), 173–82.

48. Hegel also writes, for example, that every moment of the individual "displays itself [*zeigt sich*] in the universal individual" (16/31) and that Science "sets forth" and "exposes [*stellt . . . dar*]" (17/33) the movement of Spirit and its moments.

49. John McCumber, *The Company of Words: Hegel, Language, and Systematic Philosophy* (Evanston, IL: Northwestern University Press, 1993), 111.

50. Gadamer, for example, refers to an "analogical" relation between life and self-consciousness (*Wahrheit und Methode,* 1:231–35, 256–57).

51. Death is not, however, what opposes the life of Spirit. Rather, as the power of the negative, death dissolves the idea into its moments, and this is what makes for the self-moving character of the idea. Cf. Andrzej Warminski, *Readings in Interpretation: Hölderlin, Hegel, Heidegger* (Minneapolis: University of Minnesota Press, 1987): "Natural consciousness . . . always carries a death within itself, always carries *its own* death within itself, and therefore can never achieve the rest (*Ruhe*) of self-sufficiency, for it is always suffering violence at the hands of itself to go beyond itself. Its staked out route, as well as its beginnings and ends, is nothing else than, can

be nothing else than, a way of doubt and despair on which it can do nothing but constantly die to itself in order that it may continue to follow the route of its dying to itself" (128). In order to consider how death is involved in the self-moving character of the concept, Hegel describes the function of understanding. Understanding, as the workings of analysis and as the creator of formalism and the dissolution of an idea into its moments, is the purveyor of nonactuality, for it breaks the concept into moments. On the one hand, the possibility of the understanding to dissolve the idea into moments is "the most astonishing and greatest of powers, or rather the absolute power" (18/36, translation modified). It breaks apart the circle of immediate relationship and frees the accident for a separate existence. This absolute power is the "tremendous power of the negative" (19/36); it is not itself any thing but is instead the nonactuality that dissolves the accident from whatever circumscribes it. This nonactuality can also be called death, as Hegel states: "Death, if that is what we want to call this non-actuality, is of all things the most dreadful [*Furchtbarste*], and to hold fast to what is dead requires the greatest strength" (19/36). To hold fast to what is dead (*das Tote*) requires strength precisely because according to this definition of death as the absolute power of the negative, what is dead *is not*, it is nonactual and free, absolute power—sheer potentiality, and yet thoroughly nonactual. Moreover, to hold fast to what is dead requires the greatest strength because what is dead has "acquired an existence of its own and a freedom" and thus is by definition independent and unbound. Thus "the life of Spirit is not the life that shrinks from death and keeps itself untouched by devastation, but rather the life that endures it and maintains itself in it" (19/36). As nonactuality the negative dissolves immediacy and thereby makes possible self-movement, the reflexivity by means of which consciousness progresses to self-consciousness.

52. Eugen Fink, *Hegel: Phänomenologische Interpretationen der "Phänomenologie des Geistes"* (Frankfurt am Main: Vittorio Klostermann, 1977), 3, my translation.

53. Martin Heidegger, "Hegel's Concept of Experience," in *Off the Beaten Track*, ed. and trans. Julian Young and Kenneth Haynes (Cambridge: Cambridge University Press, 2002). Heidegger, "Hegels Begriff der Erfahrung," in *Holzwege* (Frankfurt am Main: Vittorio Klostermann, 1977), citation from 143: "Die Darstellung des erscheinenden Wissens in seinem Erscheinen ist selbst die Wissenschaft." See also Wood, *Philosophy at the Limit,* 73, on how Hegel's texts "embody or exemplify" various theories of language, where such exemplification "allows the text to function as a local demonstration of the truth of its own claims."

54. Regarding "Science as the Experience of Consciousness" as the original title of the *Phenomenology*, see Otto Pöggeler, *Hegels Idee einer Phänomenologie des Geistes* (Freiburg: Karl Alber, 1973), 170–230; Otto Pöggeler, "Die Komposition der Phänomenologie des Geistes," in Fulda and Henrich, *Materialen zu "Phänomenologie,"* 329–90; and Warminski, *Readings in Interpretation,* 112–14.

55. Heidegger, "Hegel's Concept of Experience," 148, 152. Heidegger also writes, "Now this term ['experience'] names the being of beings" (150).

56. I refer here to 36–40/56–61. This discussion is indebted to Stephen Houlgate, "Hegel's Theory of the Speculative Sentence," in *Hegel, Nietzsche and the Criticism of Metaphysics* (Cambridge: Cambridge University Press, 1986), 141–56.

57. Houlgate, *Hegel, Nietzsche,* writes: "In the speculative sentence the predicate is itself a subject, in fact it is a statement of the substance of the initial subject-term. It is the predicate, therefore, that states what the subject intrinsically *is*. But this means that the subject-term loses the substantial determinacy that it initially appears to have. The subject-term is not the firm point of reference for the sentence because it is only the predicate that tells us what the subject in fact is" (147–48). Ernst Bloch writes in *Subjekt-Objekt: Erläuterungen zu Hegel,* vol. 8 of *Gesamtausgabe* (Frankfurt am Main: Suhrkamp, 1962), "Hegel's language violates customary grammar only because it has something unheard of to say, for which grammar up until now offered no assistance" (19, my translation). On the speculative sentence, see also Erich Heintel, "Der Begriff des Menschen und der 'spekulative Satz,'" *Hegel Studien* 1 (1961): 201–27, esp. 220–27; Heinz Hülsmann, "Der spekulative oder dialektischer Satz," *Salzburger Jahrbuch für Philosophie* 10/11 (1966–67): 69–80; and Jere Paul Surber, "Hegel's Speculative Sentence," *Hegel-Studien* 10 (1975): 211–30.

58. See Žižek's section "Die retroaktive Performativität, oder wie das Notwendige aus dem Zufälligen hervorgeht," in *Der erhabenste aller Hysteriker,* 29–46. Žižek ascribes a retroactive temporality to the performativity of Hegel's text. As other commentators have done, Žižek suggests that its performativity lies in the realization of what Spirit already must have been, rather than in Spirit becoming something else than the form of Spirit it was. Hence Žižek claims, "In a certain sense nothing 'happens' in the dialectical process, the transition from one stage to the next follows the logic 'it is already so'" (101, my translation). See also Warminski, *Readings in Interpretation,* esp. 133, for discussions of how the text of the *Phenomenology* reads itself and writes itself.

59. See L. Bruno Puntel's chapter on "Die Erfahrung als dialektische Maßstab," in *Darstellung, Methode und Struktur: Untersuchungen zur Einheit der Systematischen Philosophie G. W. F. Hegels; Hegel-Studien, Beiheft 10* (Bonn: Bouvier, 1973), 287–93.

60. Hence Gadamer writes in "Hegel—Vollendung der abendländischen Metaphysik?" in *Hegel, Hölderlin, Heidegger,* ed. Helmut Gehrig (Karlsruhe: Badenia, 1971), 11–23: "The 'speculative sentence' occupies a middle ground between tautology and self-abolition, in the endless determination of its meaning, and herein lies the highest actuality of Hegel: the speculative sentence is not so much statement as it is language. In the speculative sentence is not only the concretizing task of dialectical explication taken up, but at the same time the dialectical movement is in the speculative sentence brought to a halt" (note 21, my translation). According to Heinz Röttges, *Der Begriff der Methode in der Philosophie Hegels* (Meisenheim: Anton Hain, 1976), the question of method in Hegel is nothing other than the question of how Hegel can write about concepts that are at once pure essences *and* self-moving (92). Taylor, *Hegel,* rightly asserts with Heidegger that "Hegel is not proposing the use of a dialectical 'method' or 'approach'" (129). However, I disagree with Taylor's flattening characterization of the procedure of Hegel's text as "descriptive" because it overlooks this unfolding, performative element.

Chapter 3

Unless otherwise noted, references in running text are to Martin Heidegger, *Being and Time*, trans. Joan Stambaugh (Albany: SUNY Press, 1997) [hereafter cited in notes as *BT*]. Page numbers refer to the original German page numbering, noted in the margins of the Stambaugh translation and in contemporary Niemeyer editions of the German text. My references are from *Sein und Zeit* (Tübingen: Max Niemeyer, 1995).

1. References to *Being and Time* do not follow Stambaugh's hyphenation of the word "Dasein."

2. On the meaning of *muthos* with respect to Heidegger, see K. H.Volkmann-Schluck, "Das Problem der Sprache," in *Die Frage Martin Heideggers: Beiträge zu einem Kolloquium mit Heidegger aus Anlaß seines 80. Geburtstages,* in *Sitzungsberichte der Heidelberger Akademie der Wissenschaften, philosophisch-historische Reihe,* no. 4 (1969): 50–61. The translation of *muthos* as "story" (*Geschichtchen* or *Geschichte*) is but one possibility. Volkmann-Schluck suggests other German translations of the Greek, namely, *Rede, Erzählen,* and *Sagen,* each with a distinct resonance.

3. Günter Figal, *Martin Heidegger: Phänomenologie der Freiheit* (Frankfurt am Main: Athenaeum, 1988), 41–42, my translation.

4. Cf. John van Buren, "The Ethics of *formale Anzeige* in Heidegger," *American Catholic Philosophical Quarterly* 49, no. 2 (1995): 157–70. On *formale Anzeige,* see also Hent de Vries, "Formal Indications," *MLN* 113, no. 3 (April 1998): 635–88, esp. 663–76.

5. Hannah Arendt, "Martin Heidegger at Eighty," in *Heidegger and Modern Philosophy: Critical Essays,* ed. Michael Murray (New Haven, CT: Yale University Press, 1978), 296.

6. David Krell, *Intimations of Mortality: Time, Truth, and Finitude in Heidegger's Thinking of Being* (University Park: Pennsylvania State University Press, 1986), 158. Krell is referring to Heidegger's *Einführung in die Metaphysik* (Tübingen: Max Niemeyer, 1957), 122.

7. Krell, *Intimations of Mortality,* 157.

8. David Wood, *Philosophy at the Limit: Problems of European Thought* (London: Unwin Hyman, 1990), 144. Wood defines a performative reflexivity "in which the object of reflection is the nature and limits of writing itself, or of a particular practice of writing (such as philosophy)" (133). Performative reflexivity seems to differ from performativity in that the topic of the performance must be language or, more narrowly construed, writing.

9. See ibid., 71–73, for a discussion of exemplification as a mode of textual reflexivity.

10. Ronald Bruzina, "Heidegger on the Metaphor and Philosophy," in Murray, *Heidegger and Modern Philosophy,* 197: "By this time we should be ready to recognize that Heidegger is not attempting to formulate a position, but rather to execute a movement. If we realize now that this 'movement' he executes is not only always *in language,* but also in a highly original and strange kind of wording, then we are close to seeing that this very *immersion in a wording movement* constitutes thinking."

11. Christopher Fynsk, *Heidegger, Thought and Historicity* (Ithaca, NY: Cornell University Press, 1986), 15: "These sentences [from Heidegger's *Identity and Difference*] suggest that we do not begin to read Heidegger until the surface intelligibility of the language is shaken and we follow not the content, a series of propositions or theses (or even a series of what may seem to be poetic figures), but the very movement of thought in its becoming-other." The need for reading to follow a shaking and trembling intelligibility will be reformulated subsequently in my claim that the words of Heidegger's argument are defamiliarized and thematized in the manner of unhandy tools.

12. Samuel Ijsseling, "Das Ende der Philosophie als Anfang des Denkens," in *Heidegger et l'idée de la phénomenologie,* ed. F. Volpi et al. (Dordrecht: Kluwer Academic Publishers, 1988), 297. Ijsseling's Heidegger reference is to *Was ist das—die Philosophie?* (Pfullingen: Günther Neske, 1981), 22.

13. See Joseph J. Kockelmans, in *Heidegger's "Being and Time": The Analytic of Dasein as Fundamental Ontology* (Washington, D.C.: Center for Advanced Research in Phenomenology and University Press of America, 1989), 41 and 67–69, on Heidegger's argumentative and methodological style. Stanley Corngold, in "Heidegger's *Being and Time:* Implications for Poetics," in *Fate of the Self: German Writers and French Theory* (New York: Columbia University Press, 1986), 199, argues that although *Being and Time* may seem to operate poetically, it in fact is systematic. (Corngold also claims, unconvincingly, that *Being and Time* offers a theory of poetry.) Karl Löwith, *Heidegger—Denker in dürftiger Zeit: Zur Stellung der Philosophie im 20. Jahrhundert* (Stuttgart: J. B. Metzlersche Verlagsbuchhandlung, 1984), 128, differentiates the systematic structure of *Being and Time* from that of Heidegger's later works.

14. See *BT,* 6–8, for the question of the proper entity with which to begin the investigation; on the phenomenological method, see 27–28; see also sections 61, 63, and 83.

15. Thus Figal, in *Heidegger: Phänomenologie der Freiheit,* writes, "The 'comportment toward being' that Heidegger speaks about is accordingly not to be interpreted as a 'relatedness to something,' but rather means simply the experience of this comportment in all its limitation" (72–73, my translation).

16. The analyses in *Die Grundprobleme der Phänomenologie* (Frankfurt am Main: Vittorio Klostermann, 1927), are perhaps even more clearly relevant to this point than *Being and Time.* See especially the discussions of the problem of "is" as copula and of phenomenological expression, 291–304.

17. István M. Fehér, "Heidegger's Understanding of the Atheism of Philosophy: Philosophy, Theology, and Religion in His Early Lecture Courses Up to *Being and Time," American Catholic Philosophical Quarterly* 69 (1995): 189–228, citation at 227, originally in "Phänomenologische Interpretationen zu Aristoteles (Anzeige der hermeneutischen Situation)," in *Dilthey Jahrbuch für Philosophie und Geschichte der Geisteswissenschaften* 6 (1989): 237–69, citation at 263.

18. Cf. Hugo Ott, "Martin Heidegger's Catholic Origins," *American Catholic Philosophical Quarterly* 69 (Spring 1995): 137–56.

19. My arguments about Heidegger and metaphor are indebted to Bruzina,

"Heidegger on Metaphor"; Rodolphe Gasché, "Joining the Text: From Heidegger to Derrida," in *The Yale Critics: Deconstruction in America,* ed. Jonathan Arac, Wlad Godzich, and Wallace Martin (Minneapolis: University of Minnesota Press, 1983), 156–75; Joseph Kockelmans, "Heidegger on Metaphor and Metaphysics," *Tijdschrift voor Filosofie* 47 (1985): 415–50; and especially Jean Greisch, "Les mots et les roses: La métaphore chez Martin Heidegger," *Revues des Sciences Philosophiques et Théologiques* 57 (1983): 433–55.

20. Cf. John McCumber, *Metaphysics and Oppression: Heidegger's Challenge to Western Metaphysics* (Bloomington: Indiana University Press, 1999), 217. McCumber also discusses the "active, shaping gap" (14) that Heidegger offers as a challenge to Western metaphysics and the hegemony of the notion of substance.

21. See *BT,* 311. "Thus the existential analytic constantly has the character of *doing violence,* whether for the claims of the everyday or for its complacency and its tranquillized obviousness." ("Die existenziale Analyse hat daher für die Ansprüche bzw. Die Genügsamkeit und beruhigte Selbstverständlichkeit der alltäglichen Auslegung ständig den Charakter einer *Gewaltsamkeit.*")

22. Karl-Otto Apel says of Heidegger's style that it has a pretentiousness that is difficult to bear; see Karl-Otto Apel, "Wittgenstein und Heidegger: Die Frage nach dem Sinn vom Sein und der Sinnlosigkeitsverdacht gegen alle Metaphysik," *Philosophisches Jahrbuch* 75 (1967): 56–126, reference at 57. Löwith, *Heidegger— Denker in dürftiger Zeit,* 127, criticizes what he calls the "magic circle" of Heidegger's language and claims that the difficulty of Heidegger's text stems from the fact that it frowns upon argument and a logical development and sequential progress. In a certain sense Löwith is correct, namely, insofar as argument and logic presume the representability of their objects, *Being and Time* cannot engage in argument and logic in a straightforward fashion. This is in my view evidence for Heidegger's attempted fidelity to the object of the argument, not for an abandonment of argumentation per se.

23. "The path of the analytic of Dasein which we have traversed so far has led us to a concrete demonstration of the thesis only suggested at the beginning" (311, "Der bisher durchlaufene Weg der Analytik des Daseins wurde zur konkreten Demonstration der eingangs nur hingeworfenen These . . ."); "As what is asked about, being thus requires its own kind of demonstration which is essentially different from the discovery of beings" (6, "Sein als das Gefragte fordert daher eine eigene Aufweisungsart, die sich von der Entdeckung des Seienden wesenhaft unterscheidet"). Likewise Alfredo Guzzoni describes Heidegger's project as an attempt to carry out or perform (*durchzuführen*) the question of being. Alfredo Guzzoni, "Das Loch: Eine Ausführung über Sein und Seiendes," *Philosophisches Jahrbuch* 75 (1967): 95–106, reference at 106.

24. See *BT,* 26, 123, 184, 202, 310, 312, 332.

25. Karl Jaspers, *Notizen zu Martin Heidegger,* ed. Hans Saner (Munich: R. Piper, 1978): "Die Wahrheit des Rhethorischen [*sic*]—und die Abgleitung in leere Gebärde" (56, my translation). See David Halliburton, *Poetic Thinking: An Approach to Heidegger* (Chicago: University of Chicago Press, 1981), especially his conclusion, "The Play of the World," 200–224, for a discussion of the models of ges-

ture, play, and dance with respect to Heidegger's thought. The discussion in Krell, *Intimations of Mortality,* 162, of thinking within anxiety suggests that in the shattering against death, all assertion becomes gesture.

26. My focus on the centrality of the unhandy tool in Heidegger's thought is indebted to Graham Harman's extraordinary study, *Tool-Being: Heidegger and the Metaphysics of Objects* (Chicago: Open Court Press, 2002).

27. Cf. Kockelmans, *Heidegger's "Being and Time,"* 116–22, and Ernst Tugendhat, *Der Wahrheitsbegriff bei Husserl und Heidegger* (Berlin: de Gruyter, 1967), 286–88.

28. Gilbert Ryle, "Heidegger's *Sein und Zeit,*" in Murray, *Heidegger and Modern Philosophy,* 58: "Heidegger imposes on himself the hard task of coining, and on us the alarming task of understanding, a complete new vocabulary of terms—mostly many-barreled compounds of everyday 'nursery' words and phrases." Jaspers, *Notizen zu Martin Heidegger,* 37 n.12, comments that Heidegger's wordplays are "irritating."

29. See Erasmus Schöfer, *Die Sprache Heideggers* (Pfullingen: Günther Neske, 1962), 103–17.

30. P. Christopher Smith, *The Hermeneutics of Original Argument: Demonstration, Dialectic, Rhetoric* (Evanston, IL: Northwestern University Press, 1998), 326 n. 23, makes a similar point with respect to Heidegger's reading of Stefan George's poem "Das Wort" in "Das Wesen der Sprache." Smith suggests that Heidegger's reflections on the lacking word parallel those on the damaged tool and, moreover, that both analyses proceed negatively.

31. Cf. Hans-Georg Gadamer, "Mensch und Sprache," in *Wahrheit und Methode: Grundzüge einer philosophischen Hermeneutik,* vol. 1 (Tübingen: Mohr, 1990), 148 (my translation): "Language is not an instrument at all, not a tool."

32. Cf. Kockelmans, *Heidegger's "Being and Time,"* 159. See also Schöfer, *Die Sprache Heideggers,* especially "Die inhaltlichen Neubildungen Heideggers," 73–117. Schöfer's detailed study of Heidegger's language in *Being and Time,* carried out with a quantitative methodology, argues for the inventiveness of Heidegger's constructions, emphases, and breaking up of words rather than for their etymological validity. Schöfer claims that when Heidegger seems to use a word in a strange context (e.g., *Lichtung*) it is in fact not even the same word as the one it entirely resembles (108). In this respect, Schöfer offers a sort of rescue to Heidegger from accusations of faulty etymology and romanticism, for he recasts Heidegger's invention and manipulation of words as precisely *not* appeals to earlier meanings.

33. Cf. Manfred Schneider, "Halkyonische Töne: Nietzsche der Sprachkunstler," *Du* (June 1988): 84–85, with respect to the dashes, scare quotes, and other types of punctuation in Nietzsche, the purpose of which Schneider believes is to make Nietzsche's text musical.

34. Bruzina, "Heidegger on Metaphor," 199. Bruzina here also rightly ties the "not"-statements to the character of the text as nonmetaphoric and to its neutralization of the literal/figurative distinction.

35. Cf. William McNeill, in "The Genesis of Theory: *Being and Time* (1927),"

from his *The Glance of the Eye: Heidegger, Aristotle, and the Ends of Theory* (Albany: SUNY Press, 1999), 55–85, for important discussions of the relationship between *theoria* and praxis in Heidegger and Aristotle; the modification from circumspective to theoretical concern; and thematizing projection.

36. This comparison between theory and broken equipment is indebted to Harman, *Tool-Being*, 56–58.

37. "In characterizing the change-over from 'practically' circumspect handling and using and so on, to 'theoretical' investigation, it would be easy to suggest that merely looking at beings is something that emerges when taking care *abstains* from any kind of use. Then what is decisive about the 'origin' of theoretical behavior would lie in the *disappearance* of praxis. . . . But this is by no means the way in which the 'theoretical' attitude of science is reached. . . . To refrain from the use of tools is so far from 'theory' that staying, 'reflecting' circumspection remains completely stuck in the tools at hand taken care of. . . . And just as praxis has its own specific sight ('theory'), theoretical investigation is not without its own praxis" (357–58). See also McNeill, *Glance of the Eye*, 82: "Thematization does not first posit beings, but merely releases them or frees them in such a way that they can be subsequently interrogated and determined in a particular respect." See also Kockelmans, *Heidegger's "Being and Time,"* 280–83; and William J. Richardson, *Heidegger: Through Phenomenology to Thought* (The Hague, Martinus Nijhoff, 1967), 52.

38. "Thematization objectifies. It does not first 'posit' beings, but frees them in such a way that they become 'objectively' subject to questioning and definition. The objectifying being together with innerworldly things objectively present has the character of an *eminent making present*" (363).

39. Krell, *Intimations of Mortality*, 87.

40. Cf. Franco Volpi, "*Dasein* comme *praxis*: L'assimilation et la radicalisation heideggerienne de la philosophie pratique d'Aristote," in Volpi et al., *Heidegger et la phénomenologie*, 15–17, on how *Vorhandenheit* corresponds to the determination of *theoria*. Of course, theory does not have everything in common with the unhandy tool; however, the perhaps unexpected convergence of the noticing that is involved in theory and the obtrusiveness of the unhandy tool into the field of noticeability offer new possibilities for rethinking both theory and the tool. Harman, *Tool-Being*, points in new directions precisely in this sense.

41. In a similar vein, Apel, "Wittgenstein und Heidegger," 81, writes that Heidegger utilizes unusual, often violent and provocative abstractions and that his images and metaphors (I would call these catachreses) are so strange that they cancel out the metaphoric appearance of an ontology of objects that pervades language.

42. Ijsseling, "Das Ende der Philosophie," 292: "The matter of thinking is designated with many and diverse names by Heidegger, for example being itself, the event, aletheia, difference, clearing, difference as difference, *Austrag*, and many, many others. All these names and their manifoldness have on the other hand a strategic meaning, i.e., they do not refer to some positive content, but rather they merely point in a specific direction. They guide our view. They are hints or also ways." (My translation: "Die Sache des Denkens wird von Heidegger

mit vielen und verschiedenen Namen bezeichnet, wie zum Beispiel das Sein selbst, Ereignis, *aletheia,* Unterschied, Lichtung, Differenz als Differenz, Austrag und noch viele, viele andere. All diese Namen und ihre Vielheit haben wiederum eine strategische Bedeutung, d.h. sie deuten nicht auf irgendeinen positiven Inhalt hin, sondern sie weisen lediglich in eine bestimmte Richtung. Sie lenken das Blick. Es sind *Winke* oder auch *Wege.*")

43. See note 25 on Jaspers's reference to rhetoric and gesture in Heidegger.

44. I use the expression "being itself" to distinguish the question of the meaning of being from the question of the meaning of the word "being." Obviously the "itself" reinforces the hypostasis of being, which is what is to be undermined.

45. The English translation omits the scare quotes.

46. Even though the second prejudice, that is, that the concept of "being" is indefinable, is compatible with Heidegger's own exposition in holding that "'being' cannot be understood as a being," Heidegger opposes the conclusion that this prejudice appears to lead to, namely, a dispensing with the question of the meaning of being.

47. In marking the elision of the word-character of "being" in the move from "the question of the meaning of being" to "the question of being," it is worth noting that the phrase "the question of" does not directly precede the word "being" placed in scare quotes, that is, nowhere does Heidegger write "the question of 'being,'" which would mark the word "being" as the object of the question and thus would include or imply the problem of terminology and hence meaning.

48. I correct here the omission in the English translation of the initial scare quote around the word "being."

49. See *BT,* 273, 278, 276, and 279.

50. In addition, the analysis of the call of conscience thematizes the negativity upon which the analysis turns. That is, the indebtedness to which conscience attests, in giving Dasein to understand that it is guilty (287), turns out to involve being responsible *for* a notness (*Nichtigkeit*) (284–85). This thematization of notness with respect to conscience is significant for the following reason: If conscience is the basis for being a notness, indeed if conscience is *the* basis for notness, then conscience is also the ground of the notness that pervades the rhetoric of *Being and Time,* that is, in its many "not"-statements.

51. "What is characteristic about conscience as a call is by no means only an 'image,' like the Kantian representation of conscience as a court of justice" (271). See my introduction for a discussion of Kantian conscience at the crossroads of epistemological and ontological uncertainty and how this discussion pertains to the crossroads of literal and figurative language.

52. See Ijsseling, "Das Ende der Philosophie": "When one tries, with Heidegger, to approach philosophy as a work, as language . . . the words and sentences from which the work is constructed cannot and must not be viewed as signs or a network of signs that would designate a given extratextual actuality" (294, my translation).

53. "What" Dasein is brought back to, however, is of course no thing. The

call does not call the self back to itself as a unity but rather summons the self that is not a thing but a way, the way that is called being-in-the-world: "The summons of the self in the they-self does not force it inwards upon itself so that it can close itself off from the 'external world.' The call passes over all this and disperses it, so as to summon solely the self which is in no other way than being-in-the-world" (273).

54. See Fynsk, *Heidegger: Thought and Historicity,* 41–42.

Conclusion

1. Judith Butler, *The Psychic Life of Power: Theories in Subjection* (Stanford, CA: Stanford University Press, 1997), 49.

2. See, for example, Heidegger's two intonations of Leibniz's famous "Nihil est sine ratione" ["Nothing is without a reason,"] in Martin Heidegger, *Der Satz vom Grund* (Pfullingen: Günther Neske, 1953), later published as *The Principle of Reason,* trans. Reginald Lilly (Bloomington: Indiana University Press, 1991).

3. Each staging may be understood in terms of what Paul de Man refers to as "the passage from trope to performativity," a passage that he figures as a limit and as a residue. See Paul de Man, *Aesthetic Ideology* (Minneapolis: University of Minnesota Press, 1996), 133.

4. See Heinrich Lausberg, *Handbuch der literarischen Rhetorik: Eine Grundlegung der Literaturwissenschaft* (Stuttgart: Franz Steiner Verlag, 1990), 353. Syllepsis is defined as a *mixed* trope—where "mixing" itself may also be understood sylleptically. The translation is from Jean Racine, *Andromache,* trans. Richard Wilbur (New York: Harcourt Brace Jovanovich, 1982), 21.

Selected Bibliography

Airaksinen, Timo, and Martin A. Bertman, eds. *Hobbes: War among Nations.* Aldershot, England: Avebury, 1989.

Aler, Jan. "Heidegger's Conception of Language in *Being and Time.*" In *On Heidegger and Language,* edited by Joseph J. Kockelmans, 33–62. Evanston, IL: Northwestern University Press, 1972.

Allemann, Beda. "Martin Heidegger und die Politik." In Pöggeler, *Heidegger: Perspektiven,* 246–260.

———. "Metaphor and Antimetaphor." In *Interpretation: The Poetry of Meaning,* edited by Stanley Romaine Hopper and David L. Miller, 103–23. New York: Harcourt, Brace, 1967.

Althusser, Louis. "Ideology and Ideological State Apparatuses." In *Lenin and Philosophy and Other Essays.* New York: Monthly Review Press, 1971.

Apel, Karl-Otto. "Sinnkonstitution und Geltungsrechtfertigung: Heidegger und das Problem der Transzendentalphilosophie." In Bad Homburg Forum, *Heidegger: Innen- und Außenansichten,* 131–75.

———. "Wittgenstein und Heidegger: Die Frage nach dem Sinn vom Sein und der Sinnlosigkeitsverdacht gegen alle Metaphysik." *Philosophisches Jahrbuch* 75 (1967): 56–126.

Arac, Jonathan, Wlad Godzich, and Wallace Martin. *The Yale Critics: Deconstruction in America.* Minneapolis: University of Minnesota Press, 1983.

Arendt, Hannah. "Martin Heidegger at Eighty." In Murray, *Heidegger and Modern Philosophy,* 293–303.

Aristotle. *Metaphysics.* 2 vols. Trans. Hugh Tredennick. Cambridge, MA: Harvard University Press, 1989.

Aubenque, Pierre. "Hegelsche und Aristotelische Dialektik." In *Hegel und die antike Dialektik,* edited by Manfred Riedel, 208–24. Frankfurt am Main: Suhrkamp, 1990.

Augustine. *Confessions.* 2 vols. Trans. William Watts. Cambridge, MA: Harvard University Press, 1989.

Austin, J. L. *How to Do Things with Words.* Edited by Marina Sbisà and J. O. Urmson. Cambridge, MA: Harvard University Press, 1975 (first published in 1962 by Harvard University Press).

Bad Homburg Forum für Philosophie, ed. *Martin Heidegger: Innen- und Außenansichten.* Frankfurt am Main: Suhrkamp, 1989.

Bahm, Archie J. "Theories of Conscience." *Ethics* 75, no. 2 (1964): 111–20.

Barnouw, Jeffrey. "Hobbes's Psychology of Thought: Endeavours, Purpose and Curiosity." *History of European Ideas* 10, no. 5 (1989): 519–45.

———. "Persuasion in Hobbes's *Leviathan*." *Hobbes Studies* 1 (1988): 3–25.

———. "Prudence et science chez Hobbes." In Zarka, *Thomas Hobbes*, 107–17. Paris: Presses Universitaires de France, 1990.

Baumgarten, Eduard. *Gewissen und Macht: Abhandlungen und Vorlesungen 1933–1963.* Edited by Michael Sukale. 2 vols. Meisenheim, Germany: Anton Hain, 1971.

Beeley, Philip. "Right Reason and Natural Law in Hobbes and Leibniz." *Synthesis Philosophica* 24, no. 2 (1997): 445–59.

Beistegui, Miguel de. *Heidegger and the Political: Dystopias.* London: Routledge, 1998.

Belaval, Yvon. *Études leibniziennes.* Paris: Gallimard, 1976.

———. *Histoire de la Philosophie.* Edited by Raymond Queneau. 3 vols. Paris: Éditions Gallimard, 1973.

Bell, David R. "What Hobbes Does with Words." *Philosophical Quarterly* 19 (April 1969): 155–58.

Bender, John, and David E. Wellbery. "Rhetoricality: On the Modernist Return of Rhetoric." In *Ends of Rhetoric*, 3–39.

Bender, John, and David E. Wellbery, eds. *The Ends of Rhetoric: History, Theory, Practice.* Stanford, CA: Stanford University Press, 1990.

Berlinger, Rudolph. "Der höchste Gedanke des Gewissens." In *Philosophischer Eros im Wandel der Zeit,* edited by Anton Mirko Koktanek, 17–32. Munich: R. Oldenbourg, 1965.

Bernasconi, Robert. "Opening the Future: The Paradox of Promising in the Hobbesian Social Contract," *Philosophy Today* 41 (Spring 1997): 77–86.

———. *The Question of Language in Heidegger's History of Being.* Atlantic Highlands, NJ: Humanities Press International, 1985.

Bernet, Rudolf. "Phenomenological Reduction and the Double Life of the Subject." In *Reading Heidegger from the Start: Essays in His Earliest Thought,* edited by Theodore Kisiel and John van Buren, 245–67. Albany: SUNY Press, 1994.

Bernhardt, Jean. "Grandeur, substance et accident: Une difficulté du *De Corpore.*" In Zarka, *Thomas Hobbes,* 39–46. Paris: Presses Universitaires de France, 1990.

Bertman, Martin A. "Heidegger on Hobbes." *Hobbes Studies* 2 (1989): 104–25.

———. "Hobbes and Performatives." *Critica* 10 (December 1978): 41–53.

———. "Semantics and Political Theory in Hobbes." *Hobbes Studies* 1 (1988): 134–43.

———. "What Is Alive in Hobbes." In Airaksinen and Bertman, *Hobbes: War among Nations,* 1–14.

Bezzola, Tobia. *Die Rhetorik bei Kant, Fichte und Hegel: Ein Beitrag zur Philosophiegeschichte der Rhetorik.* Tübingen: Max Niemeyer, 1993.

Biletzki, Anat. "Thomas Hobbes on 'The General Use of Speech.'" *Hobbes Studies* 7 (1994): 3–27.

Black, David W. "Rhetoric and the Narration of Conscience." *Philosophy and Rhetoric* 27, no. 4 (1994): 359–73.

Black, Max. "Metaphor." *Proceedings of the Aristotelian Society* 55 (1954): 273–94.

Bloch, Ernst. *Subjekt-Objekt: Erläuterungen zu Hegel,* vol. 8 of *Gesamtausgabe.* 15 vols. Frankfurt am Main: Suhrkamp, 1962.

Blühdorn, Jürgen. *Das Gewissen in der Diskussion.* Darmstadt: Wissenschaftliche Buchgesellschaft, 1976.

Blumenberg, Hans. *Lebenszeit und Weltzeit.* Frankfurt am Main: Suhrkamp, 1986.

———. *Paradigmen zu einer Metaphorologie.* Frankfurt am Main: Suhrkamp, 1998.

Bock, Irmgard. *Heideggers Sprachdenken.* Meisenheim, Germany: Anton Hain, 1966.

Borot, Luc. "Le vocabulaire du contrat, du pacte et de l'alliance: Quelques enjeux lexicaux." In Zarka, *Hobbes et son vocabulaire,* 187–205.

Bosco, David. "Conscience and Court and Worm: Calvin and the Three Elements of Conscience." *Journal of Religious Ethics* 14 (Fall 1986): 333–55.

Browning, Gary K., and Raia Prokhovnik. "Hobbes, Hegel and Modernity." *Hobbes Studies* 8 (1995): 88–104.

Bruns, Gerald L. "Disappeared: Heidegger and the Emancipation of Language." In Budick and Iser, *Languages of the Unsayable,* 117–39.

Bruzina, Ronald. "Heidegger on the Metaphor and Philosophy." In Murray, *Heidegger and Modern Philosophy,* 184–200.

Bruzina, Ronald, and Bruce Wilshire, eds. *Phenomenology: Dialogues and Bridges.* Albany: SUNY Press, 1982.

Bucher, T. "Die heutige Einschätzung der Metapher in der Philosophie." *Tijdschrift voor Filosofie* 34 (1972): 704–60.

Budick, Sanford. "Tradition in the Space of Negativity." In Budick and Iser, *Languages of the Unsayable,* 297–322.

Budick, Sanford, and Wolfgang Iser. Introduction to *Languages of the Unsayable,* xi–xxi.

Budick, Sanford, and Wolfgang Iser, eds. *Languages of the Unsayable: The Play of Negativity in Literature and Literary Theory.* Stanford, CA: Stanford University Press, 1996.

Butler, Judith. *Bodies that Matter: On the Discursive Limits of "Sex."* New York: Routledge, 1993.

———. *Excitable Speech: A Politics of the Performative.* New York: Routledge, 1997.

———. *Gender Trouble: Feminism and the Subversion of Identity.* New York: Routledge, 1990.

———. *The Psychic Life of Power: Theories in Subjection.* Stanford, CA: Stanford University Press, 1997.

———. *Subjects of Desire: Hegelian Reflections in Twentieth-Century France.* New York: Columbia University Press, 1987.

Cadava, Eduardo, Peter Connor, and Jean-Luc Nancy, eds. *Who Comes after the Subject?* New York: Routledge, 1991.

Carlson, Marvin. *Performance: A Critical Introduction.* London: Routledge, 1996.

Carnap, Rudolf. "The Overcoming of Metaphysics through Logical Analysis of Language." In Murray, *Heidegger and Modern Philosophy,* 23–34.

Cassirer, Ernst. *Das Erkenntnisproblem in der Philosophie und Wissenschaft der neueren Zeit.* 4 vols. Berlin: Bruno Cassirer, 1911.

Chase, Cynthia. *Decomposing Figures: Rhetorical Readings in the Romantic Tradition.* Baltimore: Johns Hopkins University Press, 1986.

Chomsky, Noam. *Aspects of the Theory of Syntax.* Cambridge, MA: MIT Press, 1965.

Ci, Jiwei. "Conscience, Sympathy and the Foundation of Morality." *American Philosophical Quarterly* 28, no. 1 (1991): 49–59.

Cohen, Ted. "Figurative Speech and Figurative Acts." In *Journal of Philosophy* 72 (1975): 669–82.

Condren, Conal. "On the Rhetorical Foundations of *Leviathan.*" In *History of Political Thought* 11, no. 4 (1990): 703–20.

Conquergood, Dwight. "Ethnography, Rhetoric and Performance." *Quarterly Journal of Speech* 78 (1992): 80–97.

Cook, Daniel. *Language in the Philosophy of Hegel.* The Hague: Mouton, 1973.

Cornehl, Peter. *Die Zukunft der Versöhnung: Eschatologie und Emanzipation in der Aufklärung bei Hegel und in der Hegelschen Schule.* Göttingen: Vandenhoek & Ruprecht, 1971.

Corngold, Stanley. "Error in Paul de Man." *Critical Inquiry* 8, no. 3 (1982): 489–507.

———. "Heidegger's *Being and Time:* Implications for Poetics." In *The Fate of the Self: German Writers and French Theory,* 197–218. New York: Columbia University Press, 1986.

Courtine, Jean-François. "La préconcept de la phénoménologie et de la problématique de la vérité dans *Sein und Zeit.*" In Volpi et al., *Heidegger et la phénomenologie,* 81–106.

———. "Voice of Conscience and Call of Being." In Cadava, Connor, and Nancy, *Who Comes after the Subject?* 79–93.

Culler, Jonathan. "Deconstruction and the Lyric." In Haverkamp, *Deconstruction Is/in America,* 41–51.

Danneberg, Lutz, and Friedrich Vollhardt, in cooperation with Hartmut Böhme und Jörg Schönert, eds. *Wie international ist die Literaturwissenschaft?: Methoden und Theorie Diskussion in den Literaturwissenschaften; kulturelle Besonderheiten und interkultureller Austausch am Beispiel des Interpretationsproblems (1950–1990).* Stuttgart: J. B. Metzler, 1996.

Davies, Catherine Glyn. *Conscience as Consciousness: The Idea of Self-Awareness in French Philosophical Writing from Descartes to Diderot.* Oxford: Voltaire Foundation at the Taylor Institution, 1990.

de Man, Paul. *Aesthetic Ideology.* Minneapolis: University of Minnesota Press, 1996.

———. *Allegorien des Lesens.* Frankfurt am Main: Suhrkamp, 1988.

———. *Allegories of Reading: Figural Language in Rousseau, Nietzsche, Rilke, and Proust.* New Haven: Yale University Press, 1979.

———. *Blindness and Insight: Essays in the Rhetoric of Contemporary Criticism.* Minneapolis: University of Minnesota Press, 1983.

———. "A Letter." *Critical Inquiry* 8 (1982): 509–13.

———. *The Resistance to Theory.* Minneapolis: University of Minnesota Press, 1986.

Derbolav, Josef. "Hegel und die Sprache: Ein Beitrag zur Standortbestimmung der Sprachphilosophie im Systemdenken des Deutschen Idealismus." In *Sprache, Schlüssel zur Welt: Festschrift für Leo Weisgerber,* edited by Helmut Gipper, 56–86. Düsseldorf: Pädagogischer Verlag Schwann, 1959.

Derrida, Jacques. "Geschlecht II: Heidegger's Hand." In *Deconstruction and Philosophy: The Texts of Jacques Derrida,* edited by John Sallis. Chicago: University of Chicago Press, 1987.

———. "Heidegger's Ear: Philopolemology (Geschlecht IV)." In *Reading Heidegger: Commemorations,* edited by John Sallis. Bloomington: Indiana University Press, 1993.

———. "How to Avoid Speaking: Denials." In Budick and Iser, *Languages of the Unsayable,* 3–70.

———. *Limited Inc.* Evanston, IL: Northwestern University Press, 1988.

———. *Memoires: For Paul de Man.* Translated by Cecile Lindsay, Jonathan Culler, and Eduardo Cadava. New York: Columbia University Press, 1986.

———. "White Mythology: Metaphor in the Text of Philosophy." In *Margins of Philosophy,* translated by Alan Bass. Chicago: University of Chicago Press, 1982.

de Vries, Hent. "Formal Indications," *MLN* 113, no. 3 (April 1998): 635–88.

Dumarsais, [César Chesneau]. *Des tropes, ou des différents sens.* Paris: Flammarion, 1988.

Ebeling, Hans. "Das Ereignis des Führers: Heideggers Antwort." In Bad Homburg Forum, *Heidegger: Innen- und Außenansichten,* 33–57.

Edie, James N. "Appearance and Reality: An Essay on the Philosophy of the Theatre." In Bruzina and Wilshire, *Phenomenology: Dialogues and Bridges,* 339–52.

Esfeld, Michael. *Mechanismus und Subjektivität in der Philosophie von Thomas Hobbes.* Stuttgart: Frommann-holzboog, 1995.

Fédier, François. "Trois attaques contre Heidegger." *Critique* 234 (1966): 883–904.

Fehér, Istvan M. "Heidegger's Understanding of the Atheism of Philosophy: Philosophy, Theology, and Religion in His Early Lecture Courses Up to *Being and Time.*" *American Catholic Philosophical Quarterly* 49, no. 2 (1995): 189–228.

Féral, Josette. "Performance and Theatricality: The Subject Demystified." *Modern Drama* 25 (1982): 170–81.

Figal, Gunter. *Martin Heidegger: Phänomenologie der Freiheit.* Frankfurt am Main: Athenaeum, 1988.

Findlay, J. N. *Hegel: A Re-examination.* New York: Oxford University Press, 1958.

Fink, Eugen. *Hegel: Phänomenologische Interpretationen der "Phänomenologie des Geistes."* Frankfurt am Main: Vittorio Klostermann, 1977.

Foisneau, Luc. "Le vocabulaire du pouvoir: Potentia/Potestas, Power." In Zarka, *Hobbes et son vocabulaire,* 83–102.

Fontanier, Pierre. *Les Figures du Discours.* Paris: Flammarion, 1977.

Fontenelle [Bernard le Bovier]. "Eloge de M. Leibnitz." In *Oeuvres de Fontenelle,* 8:450–505. Paris: Jean-François Bastien, 1790.

Friedmann, Jonas. "Die Lehre vom Gewissen in den Systemen des ethischen Idealismus, historisch-kritisch dargestellt." Ph.D. diss., Universität Bern, 1904.

Freud, Sigmund. *Civilization and its Discontents*. Translated by James Strachey. New York: Norton, 1977.

Fulda, Hans Friedrich, and Dieter Henrich, eds. *Materialen zu Hegels "Phänomenologie des Geistes."* Frankfurt am Main: Suhrkamp, 1973.

Funke, Gerhard. "Gutes Gewissen, falsches Bewußtsein." *Zeitschrift für Philosophische Forschung* 25 (1971): 226–51.

Fuss, Peter. "Conscience." *Ethics* 74, no. 2 (1964): 111–20.

Fynsk, Christopher. *Heidegger: Thought and Historicity*. Ithaca, NY: Cornell University Press, 1986.

———. *Language and Relation: . . . that there is language*. Stanford, CA: Stanford University Press, 1996.

Gadamer, Hans-Georg. "Der Denker Martin Heidegger." In *Die Frage Martin Heideggers: Beiträge zu einem Kolloquium mit Heidegger aus Anlaß seines 80. Geburtstages; Sitzungsberichte der Heidelberger Akademie der Wissenschaften, philosophisch-historische Reihe*, no. 4 (1969): 62–68.

———. "Hegel—Vollendung der Abendländischen Metaphysik?" In *Hegel, Hölderlin, Heidegger*, edited by Helmut Gehrig, 11–23. Karlsruhe: Badenia, 1971.

———. "Martin Heidegger und die Marburger Theologie." In Pöggeler, *Heidegger: Perspektiven*, 169–79.

———. "Mensch und Sprache." In *Wahrheit und Methode*, vol. 2, 146–54.

———. "Rhetorik, Hermeneutik und Ideologiekritik." In *Wahrheit und Methode*, vol. 2, 232–50.

———. *Rhetorik und Hermeneutik: Als öffentlicher Vortrag der Jungius-Gesellschaft der Wissenschaften, gehalten am 22.6.1976 in Hamburg*. Göttingen: Vandenhoeck & Ruprecht, 1976.

———. "Über leere und erfüllte Zeit." In *Die Frage Martin Heideggers: Beiträge zu einem Kolloquium mit Heidegger aus Anlaß seines 80. Geburtstages; Sitzungsberichte der Heidelberger Akademie der Wissenschaften, philosophisch-historische Reihe*, no. 4 (1969): 17–35.

———. *Wahrheit und Methode: Grundzüge einer philosophischen Hermeneutik*. 2 vols. Tübingen: Mohr, 1990.

Garniron, Pierre. "Hobbes dans les leçons d'histoire de la philosophie de Hegel." In Zarka, *Thomas Hobbes*, 391–412.

Garver, Newton. Preface to *Speech and Phenomena, and Other Essays on Husserl's Theory of Signs*, by Jacques Derrida. Evanston, IL: Northwestern University Press, 1973.

Gasché, Rodolphe. "Joining the Text: From Heidegger to Derrida." In *The Yale Critics: Deconstruction in America*, edited by Jonathan Arac, Wlad Godzich, and Wallace Martin, 156–75. Minneapolis: University of Minnesota Press, 1983.

———. *The Wild Card of Reading: On Paul de Man*. Cambridge, MA: Harvard University Press, 1998.

Gethmann, Carl Friedrich. "Heideggers Wahrheitskonzeption in seiner Marburger Vorlesungen: Zur Vorgeschichte von *Sein und Zeit* (§4)." In Bad Homburg Forum, *Heidegger: Innen- und Außenansichten*, 101–30.

Giusti, Miguel. "Bemerkungen zu Hegels Begriff der Handlung." *Hegel-Studien* 22 (1987): 51–71.

Goyard-Fabre, Simone. "Loi civile et obéissance dans l'Etat-Léviathan." In Zarka, *Thomas Hobbes*, 289–304.

Granger, G. G. *Essai d'une philosophie du style.* Paris: Éditions Odile Jacob, 1968.

Grassi, Ernesto. *The Primordial Metaphor.* Binghamton: Medieval & Renaissance Texts & Studies in collaboration with the Italian Academy, 1994.

———. "The Rehabilitation of Rhetorical Humanism." *Diogenes* 142 (Summer 1988): 136–156.

———. *Rhetoric as Philosophy: The Humanist Tradition.* University Park: Pennsylvania State University Press, 1980.

———. *Macht des Bildes: Ohnmacht der Rationalen Sprache; Zur Rettung des Rhetorischen.* Cologne: M. DuMont Schauberg, 1970.

Greene, Robert A. "Synderesis, the Spark of Conscience, in the English Renaissance." *Journal of the History of Ideas* 52, no. 2 (April–June 1991): 195–219.

Greisch, Jean. "Identité et différence dans la pensée de Martin Heidegger." *Revues des Sciences Philosophiques et Théologiques* 57 (1973): 71–111.

———. "Mise en abîme et objeu: Ontologie et textualité." In *Le texte comme objeu philosophique,* edited by Faculté de philosophie, Institut Catholique de Paris, 251–77. Paris: Beauchesne, 1987.

———. "Les mots et les roses: La métaphore chez Martin Heidegger." *Revues des Sciences Philosophiques et Théologiques* 57 (1973): 433–55.

———. *Ontologie et temporalité: Introduction à l'ontologie.* Paris: Association André Robert, Cours Polycopies, 1985.

Griffiths, A. Phillips, ed. *Contemporary French Philosophy.* Cambridge: Cambridge University Press, 1987.

Guzzoni, Alfredo. "Das Loch: Eine Ausführung über Sein und Seiendes." *Philosophisches Jahrbuch* 75 (1967): 95–106.

Haar, Michel. *Heidegger and the Essence of Man.* Translated by William McNeill. Albany: SUNY Press, 1993.

———. "Stimmung et pensée." In Volpi et al., *Heidegger et la phénomenologie,* 265–83.

Habermas, Jürgen. *Strukturwandel der Öffentlichkeit: Untersuchungen zu einer Kategorie der bürgerlichen Gesellschaft.* Neuwied, Germany: Luchterhand, 1962.

Halliburton, David. *Poetic Thinking: An Approach to Heidegger.* Chicago: University of Chicago Press, 1981.

Hamacher, Werner. "Unlesbarkeit." In de Man, *Allegorien des Lesens,* 7–26.

Harman, Graham. *Tool-Being: Heidegger and the Metaphysics of Objects.* Frankfurt am Main: Suhrkamp, 1988; Chicago: Open Court Press, 2002.

Harries, Karsten. "Fundamental Ontology and the Search for Man's Place." In Murray, *Heidegger and Modern Philosophy,* 65–79.

———. "Heidegger as a Political Thinker." In Murray, *Heidegger and Modern Philosophy,* 304–28.

———. "Herkunft als Zukunft." In *Annäherungen an Martin Heidegger,* edited by Hermann Schäfer. Frankfurt am Main: Campus, 1996.

Harris, H. S. *Hegel: Phenomenology and System.* Indianapolis: Hackett, 1995.

Hartman, Geoffrey. "Looking Back on Paul de Man." In Waters and Godzich, *Reading de Man Reading,* 3–24.

Haverkamp, Anselm, ed. *Deconstruction Is/in America.* New York: New York University Press, 1995.

———. *Die Paradoxe Metapher.* Frankfurt am Main: Suhrkamp, 1998.

Hegel, Georg Wilhelm Friedrich. *Elements of the Philosophy of Right.* Edited by Allen Wood and translated by H. B. Nisbet. Cambridge: Cambridge University Press, 1991. Translation of *Grundlinien der Philosophie des Rechts* (Frankfurt am Main: Suhrkamp, 1993).

———. *Hegel's Phenomenology of Spirit.* Translated by A. V. Miller. Oxford: Oxford University Press, 1977. Translation of *Phenomenologie des Geistes* (Frankfurt am Main: Suhrkamp, 1993).

———. *Hegel's Philosophy of Mind, Being Part Three of the "Encyclopaedia of the Philosophical Sciences" (1830), together with the "Zusätze" in Boumann's Text (1845).* Translated by William Wallace and A. V. Miller. Oxford: Clarendon Press, 1971. Translation of *Die Philosophie des Geistes, Enzyklopädie der philosophischen Wissenschaften im Grundrisse (1830), Dritter Teil* (Frankfurt am Main: Suhrkamp, 1986).

Heidegger, Martin. *The Basic Problems of Phenomenology.* Translated by Albert Hofstadter. Bloomington: Indiana University Press, 1982. Originally published as *Die Grundprobleme der Phänomenologie* (Frankfurt am Main: Vittorio Klostermann, 1927).

———. *Being and Time.* Translated by Joan Stambaugh. Albany: SUNY Press, 1997. Translation of *Sein und Zeit* (Tübingen: Niemeyer, 1993).

———. *The Concept of Time.* Bilingual edition. Translated by William McNeill. Oxford: Blackwell, 1992.

———. *Hegel's "Phenomenology of Spirit."* Translated by Parvis Emad and Kenneth Maly. Bloomington: Indiana University Press, 1988. Originally published as *Hegels Phänomenologie des Geistes* (Frankfurt am Main: Klostermann, 1980).

———. *Heidegger: Off the Beaten Track.* Edited and translated by Julian Young and Kenneth Haynes. Cambridge: Cambridge University Press, 2002. Originally published as *Holzwege* (Frankfurt am Main: Klostermann, 1977).

———. *Introduction to Metaphysics.* Translated by Gregory Fried and Richard Polt. New Haven, CT: Yale University Press, 2000. Originally published as *Einführung in die Metaphysik* (Tübingen: Max Niemeyer, 1953).

———. Preface to *Heidegger: Through Phenomenology to Thought,* xvii–xxiii. The Hague: Martinus Nijhoff, 1967.

———. *The Principle of Reason.* Translated by Reginald Lilly. Bloomington: Indiana University Press, 1991. Originally published as *Der Satz vom Grund* (Pfullingen: Günther Neske, 1953).

———. *What Is Called Thinking?* Translated by J. Glenn Gray. New York: Harper and Row, 1968. Originally published as *Was heißt Denken?* (Tübingen: Max Niemeyer, 1954).

SELECTED BIBLIOGRAPHY

Heintel, Erich. "Der Begriff des Menschen und der 'spekulative Satz.'" *Hegel-Studien* 1 (1961): 201–27.

Heintel, Guido. "Moralisches Gewissen und substantielle Sittlichkeit in Hegels Geschichtsphilosophie." In *Geschichte und System: Festschrift für Erich Heintel zum 60. Geburtstag,* edited by Hans-Dieter Klein and Erhard Oeser, 128–43. Munich: R. Oldenbourg, 1972.

Hertz, Neil. "Lurid Figures." In Bender and Wellbery, *Ends of Rhetoric,* 100–24.

Hirsch, Emanuel. "Die Beisetzung der Romantiker in Hegels Phänomenologie." In Fulda and Henrich, *Materialen zu "Phänomenologie,"* 245–75.

Hobbes, Thomas. "A Discourse of Laws." In *Three Discourses,* 105–19.

———. "A Discourse of Rome." In *Three Discourses,* 71–102.

———. *The English Works of Thomas Hobbes of Malmesbury.* 11 vols. Edited by Sir William Molesworth. London: Bohn, 1839.

———. *Three Discourses.* Edited by Noel B. Reynolds and Arlene W. Saxonhouse. Chicago: University of Chicago Press, 1995.

Hofstadter, Albert. "Art: Death and Transfiguration; A Study in Hegel's Theory of Romanticism." *Review of National Literatures* 1, no. 2 (1970): 149–64.

Hollenbach, J. M. *Sein und Gewissen: Über den Ursprung der Gewissensregung. Eine Begegnung zwischen M. Heidegger und thomistischer Philosophie.* Baden-Baden: Bruno Grimm, 1954.

Holz, Hans Heinz. *Herr und Knecht bei Leibniz und Hegel: Zur Interpretation der Klassengesellschaft.* Neuwied, Germany: Luchterhand, 1968.

Horn, Joachim Christian. *Monade und Begriff: Der Weg von Leibniz zu Hegel.* Hamburg: Felix Meiner, 1982.

Houlgate, Stephen. *Freedom, Truth, and History: An Introduction to Hegel's Philosophy.* London: Routledge, 1991.

———. *Hegel, Nietzsche, and the Criticism of Metaphysics.* Cambridge: Cambridge University Press, 1986.

Hoy, David Couzens. "History, Historicity, and Historiography in *Being and Time.*" In Murray, *Heidegger and Modern Philosophy,* 329–53.

Hugo, Victor. "La conscience." In *La Légende des Siècles,* 25–26. Paris: Pléiade, 1950.

Hülsmann, Heinz. "Der Spekulative oder dialektische Satz." *Salzburger Jahrbuch für Philosophie* 10/11 (1966/67): 65–80.

Hyde, Michael J. "The Call of Conscience: Heidegger and the Question of Rhetoric." *Philosophy and Rhetoric* 27, no. 4 (1994): 374–96.

Hyppolite, Jean. *Genesis and Structure of Hegel's "Phenomenology of Spirit."* Translated by Samuel Cherniak and John Heckman. Evanston, IL: Northwestern University Press, 1974.

Ijsseling, Samuel. "Das Ende der Philosophie als Anfang des Denkens." In Volpi et al., *Heidegger et la phénoménologie,* 285–300.

———. *Rhetorik und Philosophie: Eine historisch-systematische Einführung.* Edited by Birgit Nehren. Translated by Michael Astroh. Stuttgart: Frommann-holzboog, 1988.

Iser, Wolfgang. "The Play of the Text." In Budick and Iser, *Languages of the Unsayable,* 325–39.

Jackson, Shannon. *Professing Performance: Theatre in the Academy from Philology to Performativity.* Cambridge: Cambridge University Press, 2004.

Jamme, Christoph. "'Allegory of Disjunction': Zur dekonstruktivistischen Lektüre Hegels und Hölderlins in Amerika." *Hegel-Studien* 23 (1988): 181–204.

Jarczyk, Gwendoline. "Texte et hors-texte." In *Le texte comme objet philosophique*, edited by the Faculté de philosophie, Institut catholique de Paris, 173–82. Paris: Beauchesne, 1987.

Jaspers, Karl. *Notizen zu Martin Heidegger.* Edited by Hans Saner. Munich: R. Piper, 1978.

———. *Von der Wahrheit.* Munich: R. Piper, 1947.

Jaume, Lucien. "La théorie de la 'personne fictive' dans le *Léviathan* de Hobbes." *Revue française de science politique* 33, no. 6 (1983): 1009–35.

———. "Le vocabulaire de la représentation politique de Hobbes à Kant." In Zarka, *Hobbes et son vocabulaire*, 231–57.

Johnston, David. *The Rhetoric of Leviathan: Thomas Hobbes and the Politics of Cultural Transformation.* Princeton, NJ: Princeton University Press, 1986.

Jung, Erich. *Entzweiung und Versöhnung in Hegels Phänomenologie des Geistes.* Edited by Hermann Röckel. Leipzig: Felix Meiner, 1940.

Jurist, Elliot L. "Recognition and Self-Knowledge." *Hegel-Studien* 21 (1986): 143–50.

Kaan, André. "Le mal et son pardon." In *Hegel-Tage Royaumont 1964: Beiträge zur Deutung der Phänomenologie des Geistes* [*Hegel-Studien, Beiheft 3*], edited by Hans-Georg Gadamer, 187–94. Bonn: Bouvier, 1966.

Kaegi, Dominic. "Die Religion in den Grenzen der blossen Existenz. Heidegger, religionsphilosophische Vorlesungen von 1920/21." *Internationale Zeitschrift für Philosophie*, no. 1 (1996): 133–49.

Kahl-Furthmann, G. *Das Problem des Nicht: Kritisch-Historische und Systematische Untersuchungen.* Meisenheim, Germany: Anton Hain, 1968.

Kahn, Victoria. *Rhetoric, Prudence, and Skepticism in the Renaissance.* Ithaca, NY: Cornell University Press, 1985.

Kainz, Howard P. *Hegel's "Phenomenology," Part II: The Evolution of Ethical and Religious Consciousness to the Absolute Standpoint.* Athens: Ohio University Press, 1983.

Kant, Immanuel. *Critique of Judgment.* Translated by Werner S. Pluhar. Indianapolis: Hackett Publishing Company, 1987.

———. *Critique of Practical Reason.* Translated by Lewis White Beck. New York: Macmillan, 1993.

Kettering, Emil. "Fundamentalontologie und Fundamentalaletheiologie." In Bad Homburg Forum, *Heidegger: Innen- und Außenansichten*, 201–14.

Kirby, Kathleen. *Indifferent Boundaries: Spatial Conceptions of Human Subjectivity.* New York: Guilford Press, 1996.

Kisiel, Theodore. *The Genesis of Heidegger's "Being and Time."* Berkeley: University of California Press, 1993.

———. "The Genetic Difference in Reading *Being and Time*." *American Catholic Philosophical Quarterly* 49, no. 2 (1995): 171–87.

Kittsteiner, Heinz D. *Die Entstehung des modernen Gewissens*. Frankfurt am Main: Suhrkamp, 1991.

———. "Vom Nutzen und Nachteil des Vergessens für die Geschichte." In Smith and Emrich, *Vom Nutzen des Vergessens*, 133–74.

Kockelmans, Joseph J. "Heidegger on Metaphor and Metaphysics." *Tijdschrift voor Filosofie* 47 (1985): 415–50.

———. *Heidegger's "Being and Time": The Analytic of Dasein as Fundamental Ontology*. Washington, D.C.: Center for Advanced Research in Phenomenology and University Press of America, 1989.

Kodalle, Klaus-M. "Sprache und Bewußtsein bei Thomas Hobbes." *Zeitschrift für philosophische Forschung* 25 (1971): 345–71.

Kolb, David. *The Critique of Pure Modernity: Hegel, Heidegger and After*. Chicago: University of Chicago Press, 1986.

Koselleck, Reinhart. *Kritik und Krise*. Frankfurt am Main: Suhrkamp, 1997.

Krell, David Farrell. *Intimations of Mortality: Time, Truth, and Finitude in Heidegger's Thinking of Being*. University Park: Pennsylvania State University Press, 1986.

Krook, Dorothea. "Thomas Hobbes's Doctrine of Meaning and Truth." *Philosophy* 31, no. 116 (January 1956): 3–23.

Kurz, Gerhard. *Metapher, Allegorie, Symbol*. Göttingen: Vandenhoeck & Ruprecht, 1997.

Lagerspetz, Eerik. "Hobbes's Logic of Law." In Airaksinen and Bertman, *Hobbes: War among Nations*, 142–53.

Lakoff, George, and Mark Johnson. *Metaphors We Live By*. Chicago: University of Chicago Press, 2003.

Langston, Douglas C. *Conscience and Other Virtues*. University Park: Pennsylvania State University Press, 2001.

Lauer, Quentin, S. J. *A Reading of Hegel's "Phenomenology of Spirit."* New York: Fordham University Press, 1993.

Lausberg, Heinrich. *Handbuch der literarischen Rhetorik: Eine Grundlegung der Literaturwissenschaft*. Stuttgart: Franz Steiner Verlag, 1990.

Lessay, Franck. "Le vocabulaire de la personne." In Zarka, *Hobbes et son vocabulaire*, 155–86.

Levinas, Emmanuel. *Beyond the Verse: Talmudic Readings and Lectures*. Translated by Gary D. Mole. Bloomington: Indiana University Press, 1994.

———. *Time and the Other*. Translated by Richard A. Cohen. Pittsburgh: Duquesne University Press, 1987.

Liebrucks, Bruno. *Die zweite Revolution der Denkungsart. Hegel: Phänomenologie des Geistes*. Vol. 5 of *Sprache und Bewußtsein*. Frankfurt am Main: Akademische Verlagsgesellschaft, 1964.

———. *Einleitung: Spannweite des Problems, von den undialektischen Gebilden zur dialektischen Bewegung*. Vol. 1 of *Sprache und Bewußtsein*. Frankfurt am Main: Akademische Verlagsgesellschaft, 1964.

Lingis, Alphonso. "Authentic Time." In *Crosscurrents in Phenomenology*, edited by Ronald Bruzina and Bruce Wilshire, 276–96. The Hague: Martinus Nijhoff, 1978.

Löwith, Karl. "Die Natur des Menschen und die Welt der Natur." In *Die Frage Martin Heideggers: Beiträge zu einem Kolloquium mit Heidegger aus Anlaß seines 80. Geburtstages; Sitzungsberichte der Heidelberger Akademie der Wissenschaften, philosophisch-historische Reihe*, no. 4 (1969): 36–49.

———. *Heidegger—Denker in dürftiger Zeit: Zur Stellung der Philosophie im 20. Jahrhundert*, Stuttgart: J. B. Metzlersche Verlagsbuchhandlung, 1984.

———. "Phänomenologische Ontologie und protestantische Theologie." In Pöggeler, *Heidegger: Perspektiven*, 54–77.

Ludwig, Bernd. "Scientia civilis more geometrico—Die philosophische Methode als architektonisches Prinzip in Hobbes' *Leviathan*." *Hobbes Studies* 8 (1995): 46–87.

Luhmann, Niklas. "Die Gewissensfreiheit und das Gewissen." *Archiv des Öffentlichen Rechts* 90, no. 3 (1965): 257–86.

———. *Soziale Systeme*. Frankfurt am Main: Suhrkamp, 1987.

Lyons, John. *Exemplum: The Rhetoric of Example in Early Modern France and Italy*. Princeton, NJ: Princeton University Press, 1989.

Machamer, Peter, and Spyros Sakellariadis. "The Unity of Hobbes's Philosophy." In Airaksinen and Bertman, *Hobbes: War among Nations*, 15–34.

Malherbe, Michel. "Hobbes et la doctrine de l'accident." *Hobbes Studies* 1 (1988): 45–62.

———. *Thomas Hobbes, ou l'oeuvre de la raison: Bibliothèque d'histoire de la philosophie*. Paris: J. Vrin, 1984.

Marías, Julián. "Philosophic Truth and the Metaphoric System." In *Interpretation: The Poetry of Meaning*, edited by Stanley Romaine Hopper and David L. Miller, 103–23. New York: Harcourt, Brace, 1967.

Martel, James. "Strong Sovereign, Weak Messiah: Thomas Hobbes on Scriptural Interpretation, Rhetoric, and the Holy Spirit." *Theory and Event*, 7.4. Baltimore: Johns Hopkins University Press, 2004.

Martin, R. M. "On the Semantics of Hobbes." *Philosophy and Phenomenological Research* 14 (1953): 205–11.

Martineau, Emmanuel. "La Modernité de *Sein und Zeit*." *Revue philosophique de Louvain* 78 (1980): 22–70.

Martinet, Marie-Madeleine. "La notion de perspective et les métaphores de l'espace." In Zarka, *Hobbes et son vocabulaire*, 125–38.

Mathie, William. "Reason and Rhetoric in Hobbes's *Leviathan*." *Interpretation* 14 (May–September 1986): 281–98.

Matros, Norbert. "Das Selbst in seiner Funktion als Gewissen." *Salzburger Jahrbuch für Philosophie* 10/11 (1967): 169–214.

McCumber, John. *The Company of Words: Hegel, Language, and Systematic Philosophy*. Evanston, IL: Northwestern University Press, 1993.

———. *Metaphysics and Oppression: Heidegger's Challenge to Western Philosophy*. Bloomington: Indiana University Press, 1999.

———. *Poetic Interaction: Language, Freedom, Reason*. Chicago: University of Chicago Press, 1989.

McNeill, William. *The Glance of the Eye: Heidegger, Aristotle, and the Ends of Theory*. Albany: SUNY Press, 1999.

————. "On the Concreteness of Heidegger's Thinking." *Philosophy Today* 36 (1992): 83–94.

Melville, Herman. *Moby-Dick, or The Whale*. New York: Penguin, 1992.

Merker, Barbara. "Konversion statt Reflexion: Eine Grundfigur der Philosophie Martin Heidegger." In Bad Homburg Forum, *Heidegger: Innen- und Außenansichten*, 215–43. Frankfurt am Main: Suhrkamp, 1989.

Miller, J. Hillis. "The Disputed Ground: Deconstruction and Literary Studies." In Haverkamp, *Deconstruction Is/in America*, 79–86.

————. *Tropes, Parables, Performatives: Essays on Twentieth-Century Literature*. New York: Harvester Wheatsheaf, 1990.

Minogue, Kenneth. "From Precision to Peace: Hobbes and Political Language." *Hobbes Studies* 3 (1990): 75–88.

Mintz, Samuel. "Leviathan as Metaphor." *Hobbes Studies* 1 (1988): 3–9.

Mörchen, Hermann. "Heideggers Satz: "'Sein' heißt 'An-wesen.'" In Bad Homburg Forum, *Heidegger: Innen- und Außenansichten*, 176–200.

Moreau, Pierre-François. "L'interprétation de l'Ecriture." In Zarka, *Thomas Hobbes*, 361–79.

Motzkin, Gabriel. "Die Bedeutsamkeit des Vergessens bei Heidegger." In Smith and Emrich, *Vom Nutzen des Vergessens*, 175–90.

————. "Heidegger's Transcendent Nothing." In Budick and Iser, *Languages of the Unsayable*, 95–116.

Murphy, Mark C. "Hobbes on Tacit Covenants." *Hobbes Studies* 7 (1994): 69–94.

Murray, Michael, ed. *Heidegger and Modern Philosophy: Critical Essays*. New Haven, CT: Yale University Press, 1978.

Naas, Michael. *Turning: From Persuasion to Philosophy; A Reading of Homer's Iliad*. Atlantic Highlands, NJ: Humanities Press, 1995.

Nagy, Gregory. "The Crisis of Performance." In Bender and Wellbery, *Ends of Rhetoric*, 43–59.

Nancy, Jean-Luc. *Hegel: The Restlessness of the Negative*. Minneapolis: University of Minnesota Press, 2002.

Nerney, Gayne. "Homo Notans: Marks, Signs, and Imagination in Hobbes's Conception of Human Nature." *Hobbes Studies* 4 (1991): 53–75.

Osier, Jean Pierre. "L'hermeneutique de Spinoza et de Hobbes." *Studia Spinozana* 3 (1987): 319–45.

Ott, Hugo. "Martin Heidegger's Catholic Origins." *American Catholic Philosophical Quarterly* 49, no. 2 (1995): 137–56.

Ottmann, Henning. *Individuum und Gemeinschaft bei Hegel*. Vol. 1, *Hegel im Spiegel der Interpretationen*. Berlin: Walter de Gruyter, 1977.

Parker, Andrew, and Eve Kosofsky Sedgwick, *Performativity and Performance*. New York: Routledge, 1995.

Parker, Patricia. "Metaphor and Catachresis." In Bender and Wellbery, *Ends of Rhetoric*, 60–73.

Parry, Geraint. "Performative Utterances and Obligation in Hobbes." *Philosophical Quarterly* 17 (1967): 246–52.

Pécharman, Martine. "La logique de Hobbes et la 'tradition aristotélienne.'" *Hobbes Studies* 8 (1995): 105–24.

————. "Le discours mental selon Hobbes." *Archives de Philosophie* 55 (1992): 553–73.

————. "Le vocabulaire de l'être dans la philosophie première: *Ens, esse, essentia.*" In Zarka, *Hobbes et son vocabulaire,* 31–59.

Peperzak, Adriaan. "Einige Thesen zur Heidegger-Kritik von Emmanuel Levinas." In *Heidegger und die praktische Philosophie,* edited by Annemarie Gethmann-Siefert and Otto Pöggeler, 373–89. Frankfurt am Main: Suhrkamp, 1988.

Pepper, Thomas. "Fleisch und das Vergessen des Blicks." In Smith and Emrich, *Vom Nutzen des Vergessens,* 191–232.

Pepperell, Keith C. "Religious Conscience and Civic Conscience in Thomas Hobbes' Civic Philosophy." *Educational Theory* 39 (Winter 1989): 17–25.

Perkins, Robert L. "Hegel and Kierkegaard: Two Critics of Romantic Irony." *Review of National Literatures* 1, no. 2 (1970): 232–54.

Phelan, Peggy, and Jill Lane, eds. *The Ends of Performance.* New York: New York University Press, 1998.

Pöggeler, Otto. "Being as Appropriation." In Murray, *Heidegger and Modern Philosophy,* 84–115.

————. *Hegels Idee einer Phänomenologie des Geistes.* Freiburg: Karl Alber, 1973.

————. "Die Komposition der Phänomenologie des Geistes." In Fulda and Henrich, *Materialen zu "Phänomenologie,"* 329–90.

————. "Literaturberichte und Kritik: Heidegger und Hegel." *Hegel-Studien* 25 (1990): 139–60.

Pöggeler, Otto, ed. *Heidegger: Perspektiven zur Deutung seines Werks.* Weinheim, Germany: Beltz Athenäum, 1994.

Prange, Klaus. "Heidegger und die sprachanalytische Philosophie." *Philosophisches Jahrbuch* 79 (1972): 39–56.

Puntel, L. Bruno. *Darstellung, Methode und Struktur: Untersuchungen zur Einheit der Systematischen Philosophie G. W. F. Hegels; Hegel-Studien, Beiheft 10.* Bonn: Bouvier, 1973.

Pye, Christopher. "The Sovereign, the Theater, and the Kingdome of Darknesse: Hobbes and the Spectacle of Power." *Representations* 8 (1984): 85–106.

Rameil, Udo. "Sittliches Sein und Subjektivität: Zur Genese des Begriffs der Sittlichkeit in Hegels Rechtsphilosophie." *Hegel-Studien* 16 (1981): 123–63.

Rapaport, Herman. *Heidegger and Derrida: Reflections on Time and Language.* Lincoln: University of Nebraska Press, 1989.

Rayner, Jeremy. "Hobbes and the Rhetoricians." *Hobbes Studies* 4 (1991): 76–91.

Readings, Bill. "The Deconstruction of Politics." In Waters and Godzich, *Reading de Man Reading,* 223–43.

Reisinger, Peter. "Reflexion und Ichbegriff." *Hegel-Studien* 6 (1971): 231–65.

Reuter, Albert. "Dialektik und Gewissen: Studien zu Hegel." Ph.D. diss., Albert-Ludwigs-Universität Freiburg, 1977.

Richardson, William J. "Heidegger's Fall." *American Catholic Philosophical Quarterly* 49, no. 2 (1995): 229–53.

————. *Heidegger: Through Phenomenology to Thought.* The Hague: Martinus Nijhoff, 1967.

Ricoeur, Paul. *Du texte à l'action: Essais d'hermeneutique II*. Paris: Éditions du Seuil, 1986.

Riley, Denise. *The Words of Selves: Identification, Solidarity, Irony*. Stanford, CA: Stanford University Press, 2000.

Robinet, André. "Pensée et langage chez Hobbes: Physique de la parole et *translatio*." *Revue internationale de Philosophie* 129 (1979): 452–83.

Rockmore, Tom. "Die geschichtliche Kehre, oder Otts Verdienst im Fall Heideggers." In *Annäherungen an Martin Heidegger*, edited by Hermann Schäfer. Frankfurt am Main: Campus, 1996.

Rosen, Stanley. "Hegel und der Eleatische Fremde." In *Hegel und die antike Dialektik*, edited by Manfred Riedel, 153–168. Frankfurt am Main: Suhrkamp, 1990.

Rösinger, Margery. *Die Einheit von Ethik und Ontologie bei Hegel*. Frankfurt am Main: Peter Lang, 1980.

Rosteck, Thomas, ed. *At the Intersection: Cultural Studies and Rhetorical Studies*. New York: Guilford Press, 1999.

Rotenstreich, Nathan. "Faces of the Social Contract." *Revue internationale de Philosophie* 129 (1979): 484–505.

Röttges, Heinz. *Der Begriff der Methode in der Philosophie Hegels*. Meisenheim, Germany: Anton Hain, 1976.

Roux, Louis. *Thomas Hobbes: Penseur entre deux mondes*. Saint-Etienne, France: Publications de l'Université de Saint-Etienne, 1981.

Rüdiger, Dietrich. "Der Beitrag der Psychologie zur Theorie des Gewissens und der Gewissensbildung." In *Jahrbuch für Psychologie, Psychotherapie und medizinische Anthropologie* 16, no. 1/2 (1968): 135–51.

Rudolph, Ross. "Hobbes et la psychologie morale: l'obligation et la vertu." In Zarka, *Thomas Hobbes*, 247–63.

Ryle, Gilbert. "Heidegger's *Sein und Zeit*." In Murray, *Heidegger and Modern Philosophy*, 53–64.

Sacksteder, William. "Hobbes: Philosophical and Rhetorical Artifice." *Philosophy and Rhetoric* 17, no. 1 (1984): 30–46.

Sallis, John. *Double Truth*. Albany: SUNY Press, 1995.

———. "Imagination and the Meaning of Being." In Volpi et al., *Heidegger et la phénomenologie*, 127–44.

Sampson, Margaret. "'Will You Hear What a Casuist He Is?' Thomas Hobbes as Director of Conscience." *History of Political Thought* 11, no. 4 (1990): 721–36.

Schaefer, Alfred. *Die Idee in Person: Hobbes' Leviathan in seiner und unserer Zeit*. Berlin: Arno Spitz, 1993.

Schalow, Frank. "The Topography of Heidegger's Concept of Conscience." *American Catholic Philosophical Quarterly* 49, no. 2 (1995): 255–73.

Schmidt, Dennis J. *The Ubiquity of the Finite: Hegel, Heidegger, and the Entitlements of Philosophy*. Cambridge, MA: MIT Press, 1988.

Schneider, Manfred. "Halkyonische Töne: Nietzsche der Sprachkunstler." *Du*, no. 6 (June 1998): 84–85.

Schöfer, Erasmus. *Die Sprache Heideggers*. Pfullingen: Günther Neske, 1962.

SELECTED BIBLIOGRAPHY

Schuhmann, Karl. "Le vocabulaire de l'espace." In Zarka, *Hobbes et son vocabulaire*, 61–82.

Schultz-Heienbrok, Isbert. "Versöhnung in Verkehrung: Zur 'Umkehrung des Bewußtseins' bei Hegel und Feuerbach." Theology diss., Kirchliche Hochschule Berlin, 1972.

Schürmann, Reiner. *Heidegger on Being and Acting: From Principles to Anarchy*. Translated by Christine-Marie Gros, in collaboration with the author. Bloomington: Indiana University Press, 1987.

Searle, John R. "How Performatives Work," *Linguistics and Philosophy* 12 (1989): 535–58.

———. *Speech Acts*. Cambridge: Cambridge University Press, 1969.

Sedgwick, Eve Kosofsky. "Shame and Performativity: Henry James's New York Edition Prefaces." In *Henry James's New York Edition: The Construction of Authorship*, edited by David McWhirter. Stanford, CA: Stanford University Press, 1995.

Sheehan, Thomas. "How (Not) to Read Heidegger." In *American Catholic Philosophical Quarterly* 49, no. 2 (1995): 275–94.

Shulman, George. "Metaphor and Modernization in the Political Thought of Thomas Hobbes." *Political Theory* 17, no. 3 (1989): 392–416.

Siep, Ludwig. "Der Kampf um Anerkennung: Zu Hegels Auseinandersetzung mit Hobbes in den Jenaer Schriften." *Hegel-Studien* 9 (1974): 155–207.

Simon, Josef. *Das Problem der Sprache bei Hegel*. Stuttgart: Kohlhammer, 1966.

Siscar, Marcos. *Jacques Derrida: Rhétorique et Philosophie*. Paris: L'Harmattan, 1998.

Skinner, Quentin. *Reason and Rhetoric in the Philosophy of Hobbes*. Cambridge: Cambridge University Press, 1996.

———. "The Study of Rhetoric as an Approach to Cultural History: The Case of Hobbes." In *Main Trends in Cultural History*, edited by Willem Melching, 17–53. Amsterdam: Rodopi, 1994.

Smith, Gary, and Hinderk M. Emrich, eds. *Vom Nutzen des Vergessens*. Berlin: Akademie, 1996.

Smith, P. Christopher. *The Hermeneutics of Original Argument: Demonstration, Dialectic, Rhetoric*. Evanston, IL: Northwestern University Press, 1998.

Solomon, Robert C. *In the Spirit of Hegel: A Study of G. W. F. Hegel's "Phenomenology of Spirit."* New York: Oxford University Press, 1983.

Spanos, William V. *Heidegger and Criticism: Retrieving the Cultural Politics of Destruction*. Minneapolis: University of Minnesota Press, 1993.

Stelzenberger, Johannes. *Das Gewissen*. Paderborn, Germany: Ferdinand Schöningh, 1961.

———. *Syneidesis, conscientia, Gewissen: Studie zum Bedeutungswandel eines moraltheologischen Begriffes*. Paderborn, Germany: Ferdinand Schöningh, 1963.

Stoker, Hendrik Gerhardus. *Das Gewissen: Erscheinungsformen und Theorien*. Bonn: Cohen, 1925.

Störmer-Caysa, Uta, ed. *Über das Gewissen: Texte zur Begründung der neuzeitlichen Subjektivität*. Weinheim, Germany: Beltz Athenäum, 1995.

Strong, Tracy B. "How to Write Scripture: Words, Authority and Politics in Thomas Hobbes." *Critical Inquiry* 20, no. 1 (1993): 128–59.

Surber, Jere Paul. "Hegel's Speculative Sentence." *Hegel-Studien* 10 (1975): 211–30.

Taminiaux, Jacques. *Dialectic and Difference: Finitude in Modern Thought.* Atlantic Highlands, NJ: Humanities Press, 1985.

———. *Le théâtre des philosophes: La tragédie, l'être, l'action.* Grenoble: Jérôme Millon, 1995.

Taylor, Charles. *Hegel.* Cambridge: Cambridge University Press, 1975.

Thomä, Dieter. *Die Zeit des Selbst und die Zeit danach: Zur Kritik der Textgeschichte Martin Heideggers, 1910–1976.* Frankfurt am Main: Suhrkamp, 1990.

———. "Was heißt 'Verantwortung des Denkens'?: Systematische Überlegungen mit Berücksichtigung Martin Heideggers." *Deutsche Zeitschrift für Philosophie* 45, no. 4 (1997): 559–72.

Tricaud, François. "Le vocabulaire de la passion." In Zarka, *Hobbes et son vocabulaire,* 139–54.

———. "Quelques éléments sur la question de l'accès aux textes dans les études Hobbiennes." *Revue internationale de Philosophie* 129 (1979): 392–414.

Tugendhat, Ernst. "Das Sein und das Nichts." In *Philosophische Aufsätze,* 36–66.

———. "Die sprachanalytische Kritik der Ontologie." In *Philosophische Aufsätze,* 21–35.

———. *Der Wahrheitsbegriff bei Husserl und Heidegger.* Berlin: de Gruyter, 1967.

———. "Heideggers Seinsfrage." In *Philosophische Aufsätze,* 108–135.

———. *Philosophische Aufsätze.* Frankfurt am Main: Suhrkamp, 1992.

Tukiainen, Arto. "The Commonwealth as a Person in Hobbes's *Leviathan.*" *Hobbes Studies* 7 (1994): 44–55.

Valadier, Paul. *Eloge de la Conscience.* Paris: Éditions du Seuil, 1994.

van Buren, John. "The Ethics of *formale Anzeige* in Heidegger." *American Catholic Philosophical Quarterly* 49, no. 2 (1995): 157–70.

Vattimo, Gianni. *The Adventure of Difference: Philosophy after Nietzsche and Heidegger.* Translated by Cyprian Blamires with the assistance of Thomas Harrison. Baltimore: Johns Hopkins University Press, 1993.

———. *The End of Modernity: Nihilism and Hermeneutics in Postmodern Culture.* Translated by Jon R. Snyder. Baltimore: Johns Hopkins University Press, 1988.

Vincenzo, Joseph P. "The Nature and Legitimacy of Hegel's Critique of the Kantian Moral Philosophy." *Hegel-Studien* 22 (1987): 73–87.

Volkmann-Schluck, K. H. "Das Problem der Sprache." In *Die Frage Martin Heideggers: Beiträge zu einem Kolloquium mit Heidegger aus Anlaß seines 80. Geburtstages; Sitzungsberichte der Heidelberger Akademie der Wissenschaften, philosophisch-historische Reihe,* no. 4 (1969): 50–61.

Vollbrecht, Peter. *Das Diskursive und das Poetische: Über den Unterschied philosophischer und poetischer Sprache am Beispiel von Hegel und Celan.* Würzburg: Königshausen und Neumann, 1988.

Volpi, Franco. "*Dasein* comme *praxis:* L'assimilation et la radicalisation heideggérienne de la philosophie pratique d'Aristote." In Volpi et al., *Heidegger et la phénoménologie,* 1–42.

Volpi, Franco, et al. *Heidegger et l'idée de la phénoménologie.* Dordrecht: Kluwer, 1988.

von Leyden, W. "Parry on Performatives and Obligation in Hobbes." *Philosophical Quarterly* 23 (July 1973): 258–59.

von Wolzogen, Christoph. "Heideggers Schweigen: Zur Rede 'Edmund Husserl zum 70. Geburtstag.'" *Internationale Zeitschrift für Philosophie*, no. 2 (1997): 288–302.

Wahl, Jean. *Le malheur de la conscience dans la philosophie de Hegel.* Paris: Les Éditions Rieder, 1929.

Warminski, Andrzej. *Readings in Interpretation: Hölderlin, Hegel, Heidegger.* Minneapolis: University of Minnesota Press, 1987.

Waters, Lindsay, and Wlad Godzich, eds. *Reading de Man Reading.* Minneapolis: University of Minnesota Press, 1989.

Watkins, J. W. N. *Hobbes's System of Ideas.* London: Hutchinson University Library, 1965.

Watson, George. "Hobbes and the Metaphysical Conceit." *Journal of the History of Ideas* 16 (1955): 558–62.

Weiler, Gershon. "Hobbes and Performatives." *Philosophy* 45 (July 1970): 210–20.

Weiß, Ulrich. *Das philosophische System von Thomas Hobbes.* Stuttgart: Frommann-holzboog, 1980.

Well, Karlheinz. *Die "schöne Seele" und ihre "sittliche Wirklichkeit": Überlegungen zum Verhältnis von Kunst und Staat bei Hegel.* Frankfurt am Main: Peter Lang, 1986.

Whelan, Frederick G. "Language and its Abuses in Hobbes' Political Philosophy," *American Political Science Review* 75, no. 1 (1981): 59–75.

Willms, Bernard. "La politique comme philosophie première: Hobbes penseur radical de la politique." In Zarka, *Thomas Hobbes*, 91–104.

———. "Leviathan and the Post-Modern." *History of European Ideas* 10, no. 5 (1989): 569–76.

Wilshire, Bruce. "Theatre as Phenomenology: The Disclosure of Historical Life." In Bruzina and Wilshire, *Phenomenology: Dialogues and Bridges*, 353–61.

Wohlfart, Günter. *Denken der Sprache: Sprache und Kunst bei Vico, Hamann, Humboldt, und Hegel.* Freiburg: Karl Alber, 1984.

Wolfers, Benedikt. *"Geschwätzige Philosophie": Thomas Hobbes' Kritik an Aristoteles.* Würzburg: Königshausen und Neumann, 1991.

Wood, David. *The Deconstruction of Time.* Evanston, IL: Northwestern University Press, 2001.

———. *Philosophy at the Limit: Problems of Modern European Thought.* London: Unwin Hyman, 1990.

Yakira, Elhanan. "Pensée et calcul chez Hobbes et Leibniz." In Zarka, *Thomas Hobbes*, 127–37.

Zarka, Yves Charles, ed. *Hobbes et son vocabulaire: Études de lexicographie philosophique.* Paris: J. Vrin, 1992.

———. *Thomas Hobbes: Philosophie première, théorie de la science et politique.* With the collaboration of Jean Bernhardt. Paris: Presses Universitaires de France, 1990.

Žižek, Slavoj. *Der erhabenste aller Hysteriker: Lacans Rückkehr zu Hegel.* Vienna: Turia & Kant, 1991.

Zumthor, Paul. "Rhétorique et poétique." In *Langue, texte, énigme*, 93–124. Paris: Éditions du Seuil, 1975.

Index

Kittsteiner, Heinz D., 112n5
knowledge, 16, 20, 28–31, 32–34, 39–42,
46, 54, 71, 72, 75–78, 104; privacy and,
16, 19, 30–32, 42, 48, 54; publicity
and, 19, 25, 27, 29, 31, 34, 40, 45, 48,
53–54, 104, 118n26
Krell, David, 81, 92

lability, 10, 17, 47, 105
Lakoff, George, 113n6
Lauer, Quentin, 66, 124n26
law: civil, 26, 27, 34–37, 42, 115n2,
120n40; evil and, 58, 65, 69, 125n34,
126n36; moral, 7; of sovereignty, 20
leviathan, 42–45
Levinas, Emmanuel, 114n23
literalness, 3–4, 6, 14, 28, 41–45, 84–85,
88–89, 96, 107–10, 111n2, 111n4,
119n26, 133n34, 135n51
love, 14, 16
Luther, Martin, 109
lying. See deception.
Lyons, John, 120n39

Martel, James, 22, 121n47
Marx, Karl, 109
McCumber, John, 76, 84, 132n20
McNeill, Will, 133–34n35, 134n37
Melville, Herman, 3
memory, 14
metaphor, 3–6, 110, 111n2, 113n6; in Augustine, 13–16; dangers of, 19–21, 24–
26, 35, 45–46, 104–5, 118n24, 118n26;
and eloquence, 22–24; and Heidegger,
84, 85, 89, 101; Hobbes's use of, 42–45,
117n13; and the invention of privacy,
29–31, 37, 45, 48, 53, 54, 104–5; and
paradiastole, 31–34; and proper usage,
38–42, 44–46, 108. See also catachresis;
figuration.
metonymy, 108–10
Mintz, Samuel, 20
misfire, 48, 78, 103, 106
moral genius, 48, 55, 65–66, 73, 106,
124n24
morality, 16

name, 16, 24–26, 42, 46, 83, 125n32; of
duty, 51, 58–59, 105; of conscience, 30–
32; order of names, 16, 19, 20, 25,

32–34, 37–42, 44, 45–46, 47, 48, 54,
105, 108, 119n26
Nancy, Jean-Luc, 75
nominalism, 20, 24, 38, 51, 105
"not-about." See "aboutness;" "not"-
statements.
"not"-statements, 89–91, 99–100, 101,
102–3, 107, 133n34, 135n50

opinion. See privacy, private opinion.
order of names. See name.

paradiastole (rhetorical redescription),
31–33, 41–42, 43, 53, 59, 120n37
Parker, Andrew, 113n10
passions, 20– 24, 31, 32, 42
performativity, performance, 8–12, 21, 22,
34, 44, 46–47, 48, 49–52, 59–65, 69, 70,
73–79, 80, 82, 113n10, 115nn1–3,
118n22, 130n8, 136n3; performance of
duty, 17, 56–57; performative difficulty,
108, 132n22; performative figures, 4, 8,
16, 48, 104–5, 113n9; performative success, 16, 49, 52, 63, 64, 65, 73, 78, 106;
performative texts, 4, 5, 16, 17, 20,
59, 74–79, 85–94, 99–103, 105–10,
113n9, 127n47, 129n58, 129n60. See also
bindingness; figuration; metaphor.
politics, 21, 25, 32
predication, 41, 77–78, 83, 105, 108
privacy, 27, 28, 29, 30, 34, 35, 36, 37, 38,
39, 40, 43, 45, 51, 53; private conscience, 16, 17, 19, 26, 27, 33, 38, 104;
private opinion, 28, 30, 31, 33, 34, 38,
40, 45, 46, 48, 53, 54, 104
proper meaning, proper usage, proper
term, 3, 12, 17, 19, 22–26, 28, 39–42, 44,
45–46, 80, 83, 85–86, 88, 101, 103, 106,
107
prosopopoeia, 109–10
publicity, 27, 28–42, 43, 45–46, 53

question of being. See being, question of.
Quintilian, 32

Racine, Jean, 109
reading, 42, 44, 49, 108–10; *Being and
Time* and, 80, 82, 88, 96, 102–3; the
heart and, 23–24, 44; *Phenomenology of
Spirit* and, 17, 49, 50, 79, 122n2

About the Author

Karen S. Feldman is a lecturer in the departments of rhetoric and German at the University of California, Berkeley.